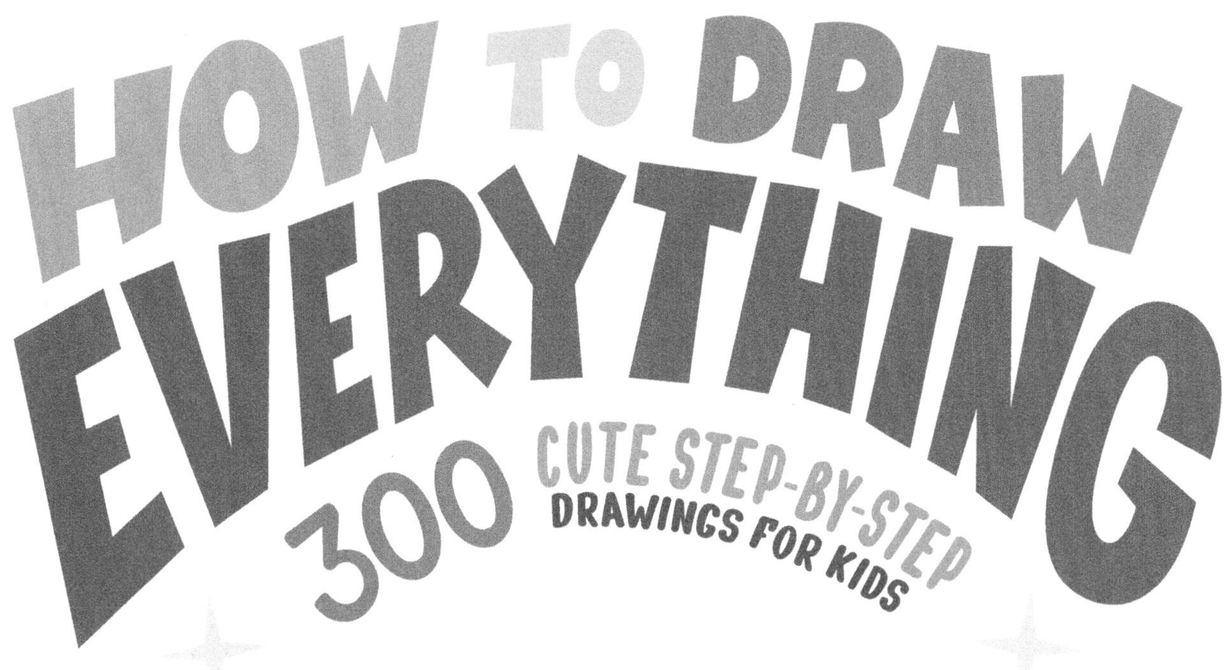

A Creative and Guided Step-by-Step Journey

Copyright © 2025 by Amelia J. Bloom
Published by Meadow & Moon Press
ISBN 978-1-7643640-03
First Edition (2025)

To my family, whose love has always made room for my biggest dreams.
To my partner, Jeff—thank you for walking beside me through them all.

Welcome, Little Artist!

Are you ready to draw, imagine, and have lots of fun?

This book will guide you step by step through 4 levels, starting with the easiest and building your confidence as you go!

You'll begin with basic shapes, then slowly add more fun details in each level.

Level 1 has more instructions to help you see how shapes become drawings. In Levels 2, 3 and 4 you'll keep practicing and growing your own style with just a few tips to help along the way.

Don't worry if it's not perfect-every artist starts with a scribble!

Grab your pencils-let's start drawing!

This book belongs to:

____

A Little Surprise Just For You!

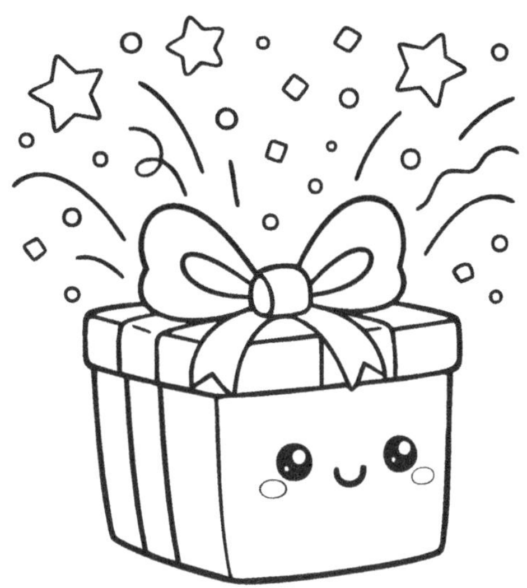

As a little thank-you for supporting my work, I've included a special bonus gift for your young artist.

You can access it by scanning the QR code at the end of the book. It's kept there so this surprise stays just for families who own How to Draw Everything for Kids 300.

I hope it brings even more fun to your child's drawing time.

Happy drawing—and thank you for being part of this creative adventure!

Amelia J. Bloom

CONTENTS

1. SIMPLE SHAPES ARE EVERYWHERE

**Did you know everything you see is made of shapes?
They're the building blocks of drawings!**

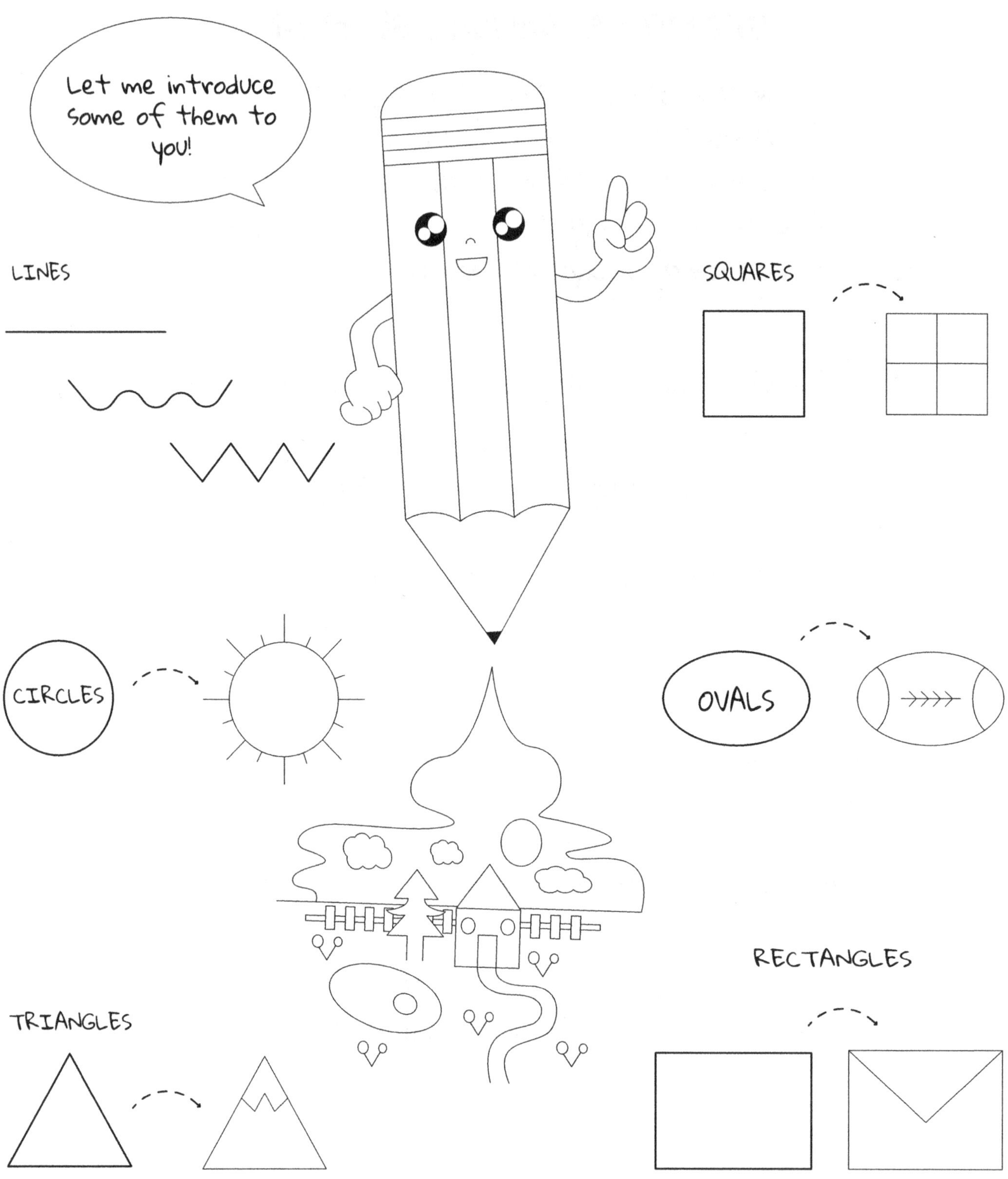

2. SAMPLE ROBOT

**LOOK AT THIS ROBOT...
CAN YOU SEE THE BASIC SHAPES ON IT?**

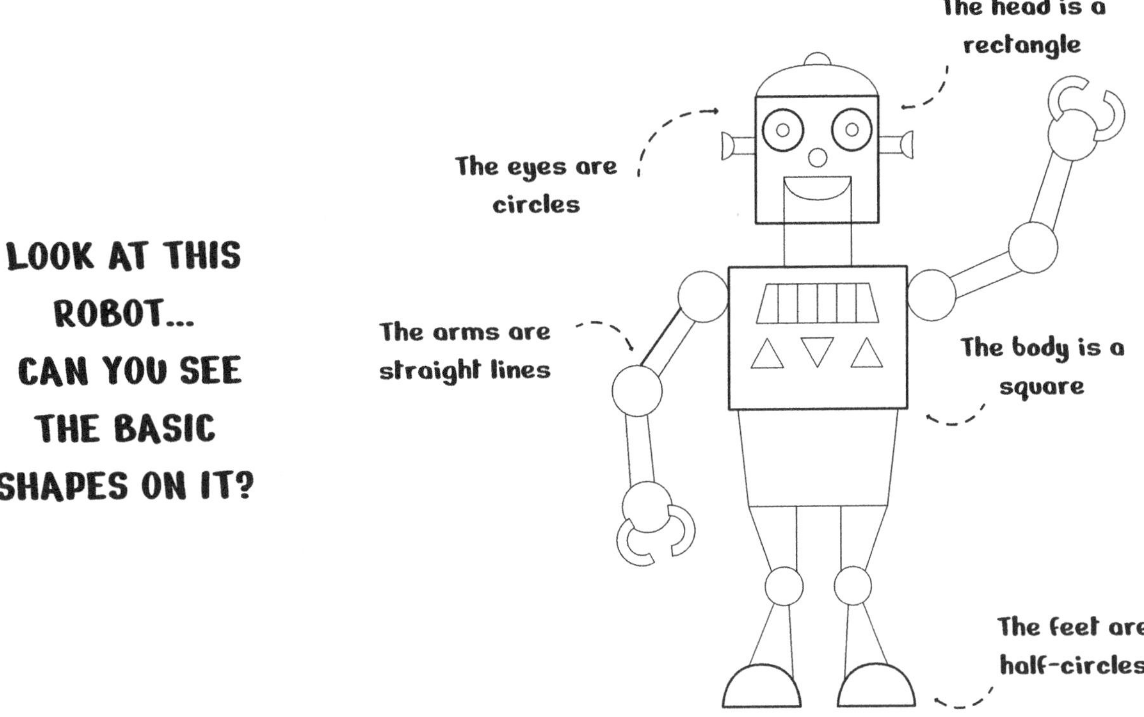

Now it's your turn! How about creating something with the basic shapes we've learned?

3. DRAWING SHAPES: CUPCAKE

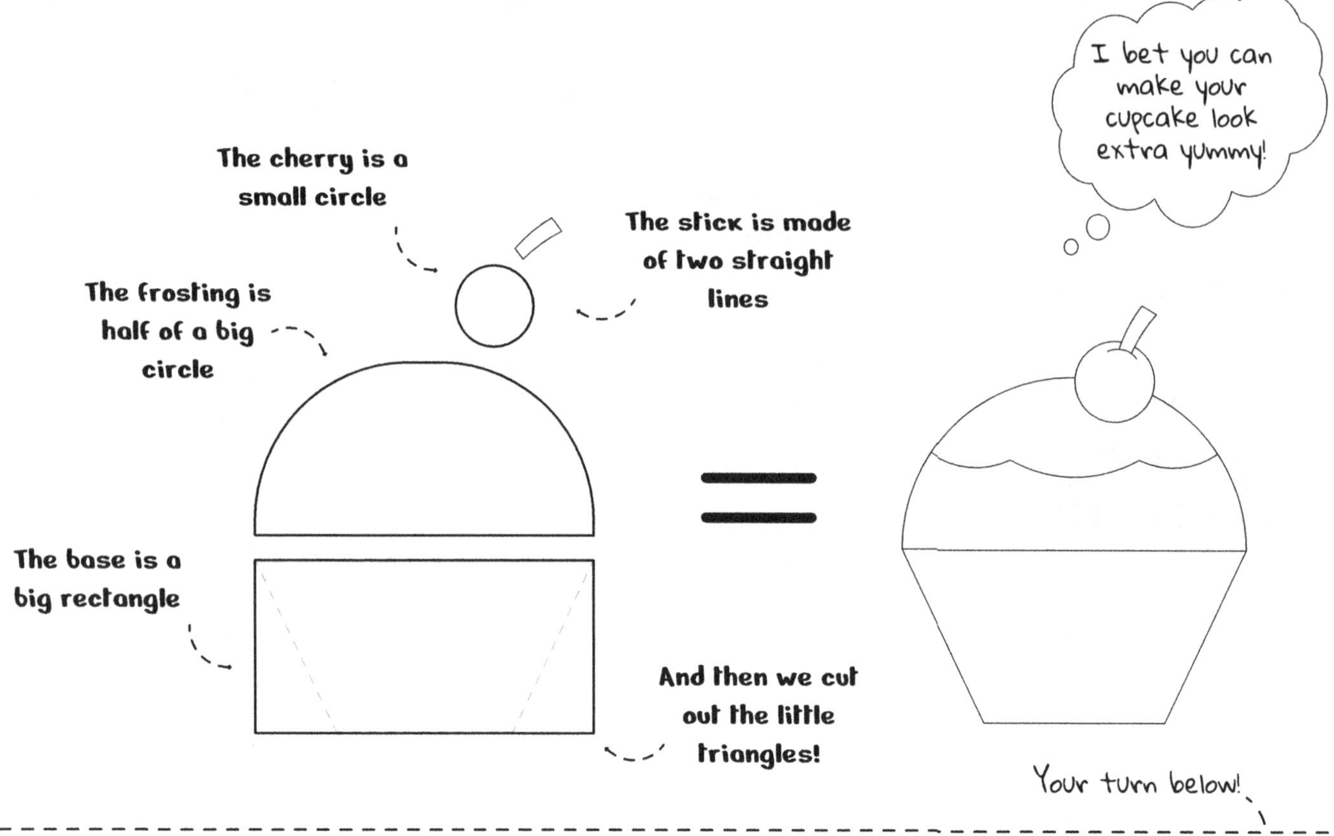

4. DRAWING SHAPES: FISH

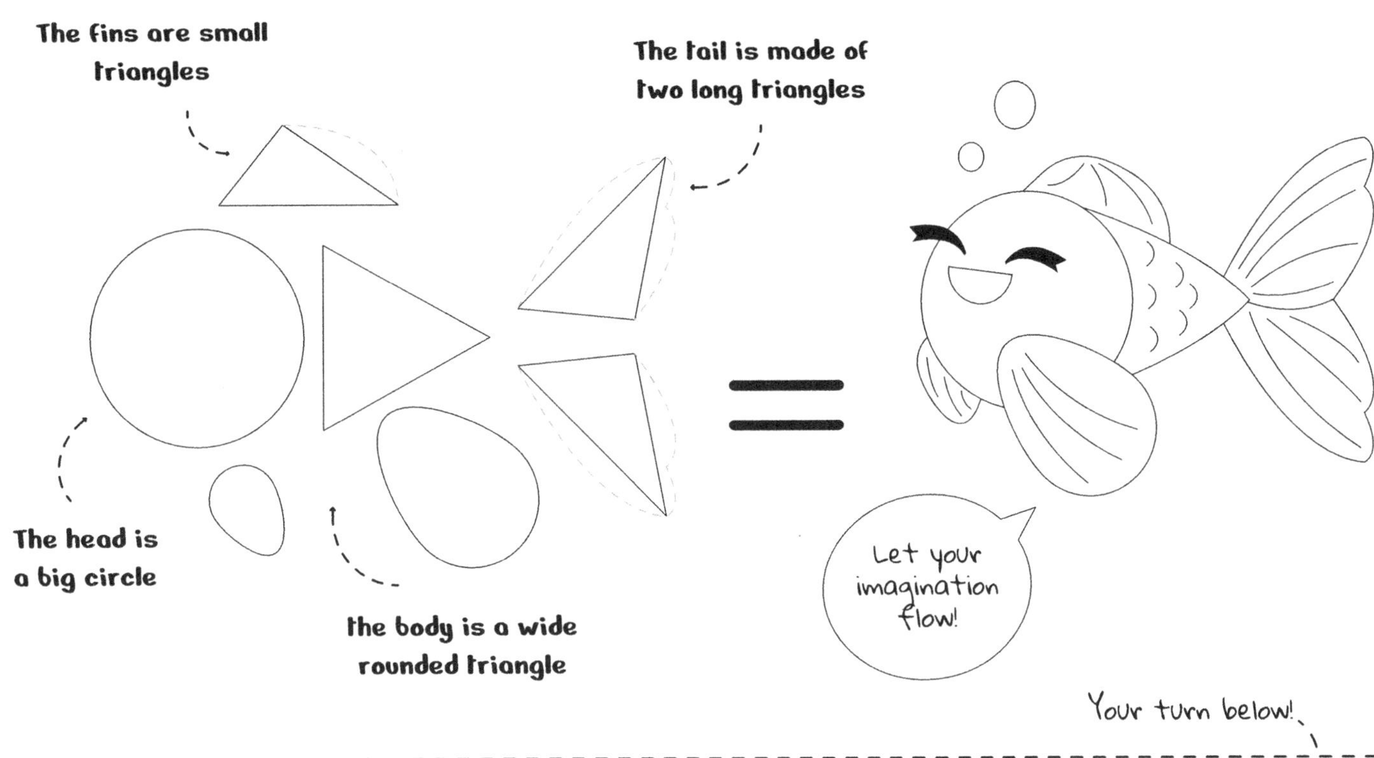

5. DRAWING SHAPES: TRAIN

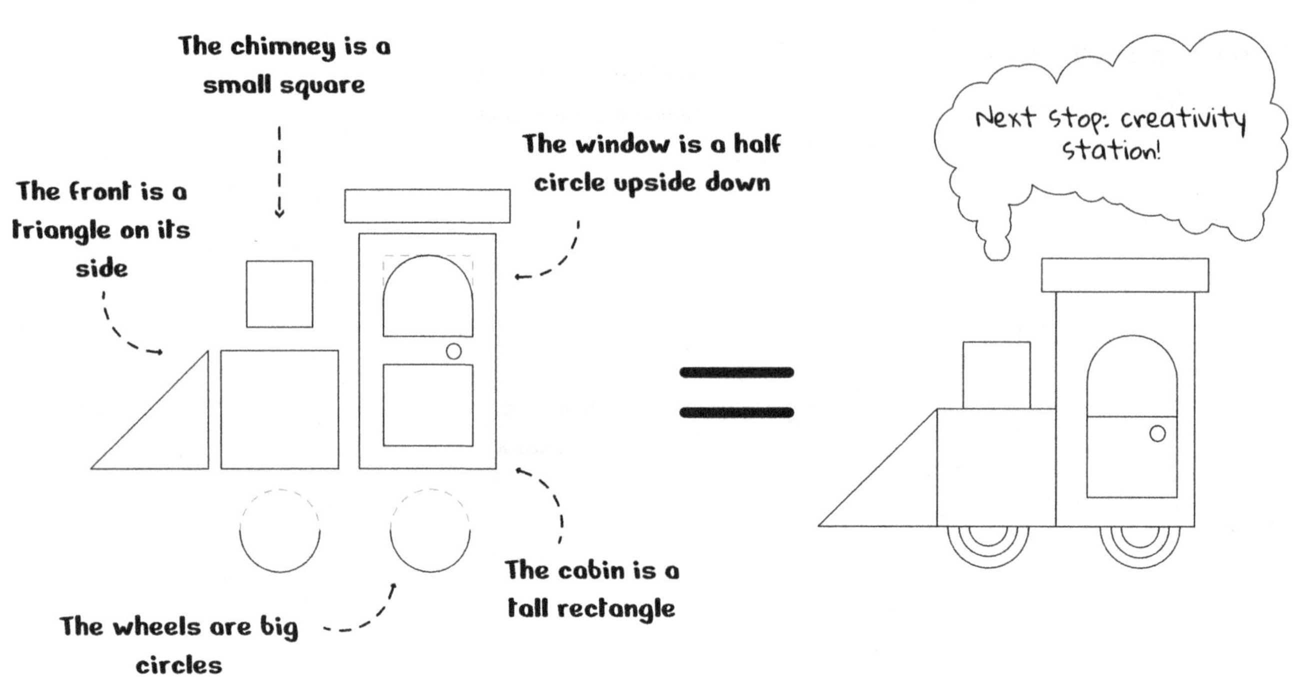

Your turn below!

FUN DRAWING CATEGORIES!

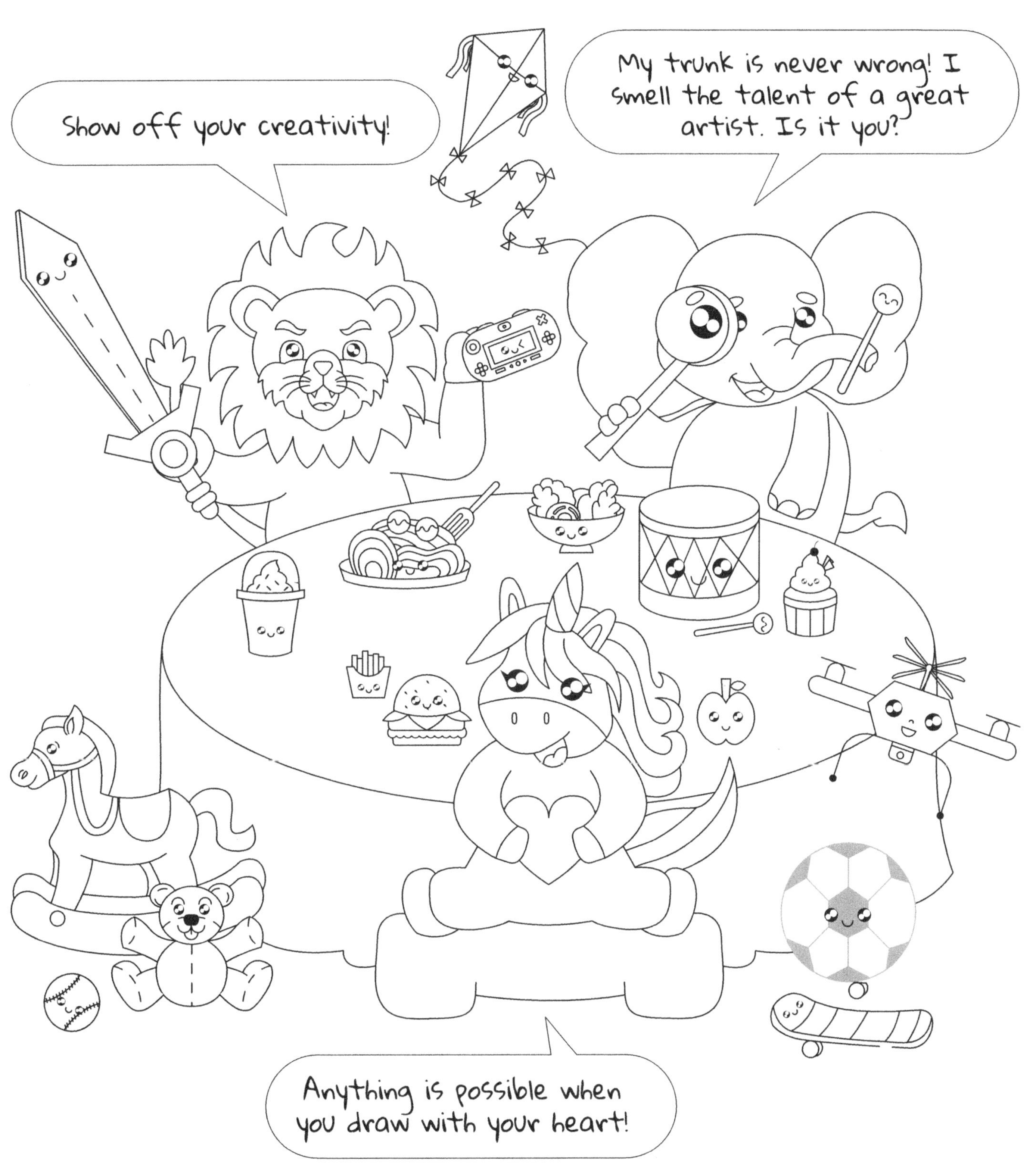

LEVEL 1:

TASTY FOOD & FUN KITCHEN STUFF

Pear...16
Pizza slice...16
Corndog...16
Strawberry...17
Lemon...17
Watermelon...17
Juice...18
Milkshake...18
Hot chocolate...18
Cup of tea...19
Yogurt...19
Water...19
Milk carton...20
Ice cream...20
Honey jar...20
Donuts...21
Croissant...21
Hamburger...21
French fries...22
Popcorn...22
Cupcake...22
Pancakes...23
Taco...23
Sandwich...23
Gingerbread...24
Hotdog...24

Lollipop...24
Bowl of cereal...25
Carrot...25
Brownie...25
Peanut butter...26
Pretzel...26
Corn...26
Cinnamon roll...27
Apple pie...27
Pumpkin...27
Popsicle...28
Animal crackers...28
Banana split...28
Candy...29
Eggplant...29
Spaghetti...29
Sushi...30
Spatula...30
Bowl...30
Cutting board...31
Cheesecake...31
Chocolate bar...31
Cheese sandwich...32
Mushroom...32
Avocado...32
Bagel...33

Macarons...33
Cotton candy...33
Salad...34
Noodles...34
Marshmallow...34
Onion...35
Chicken...35
Coconut...35
Bread...36
Eggs...36
Broccoli...36
Carrot cake...37
Cookies...37
Soup...37
Jelly...38
Spoon...38
Fork...38
Knife...39
Teapot...39
Frying pan...39
Cake...40
Orange...40
Cherry...40
Kiwi...41
Mango...41
Pineapple...41

PEAR

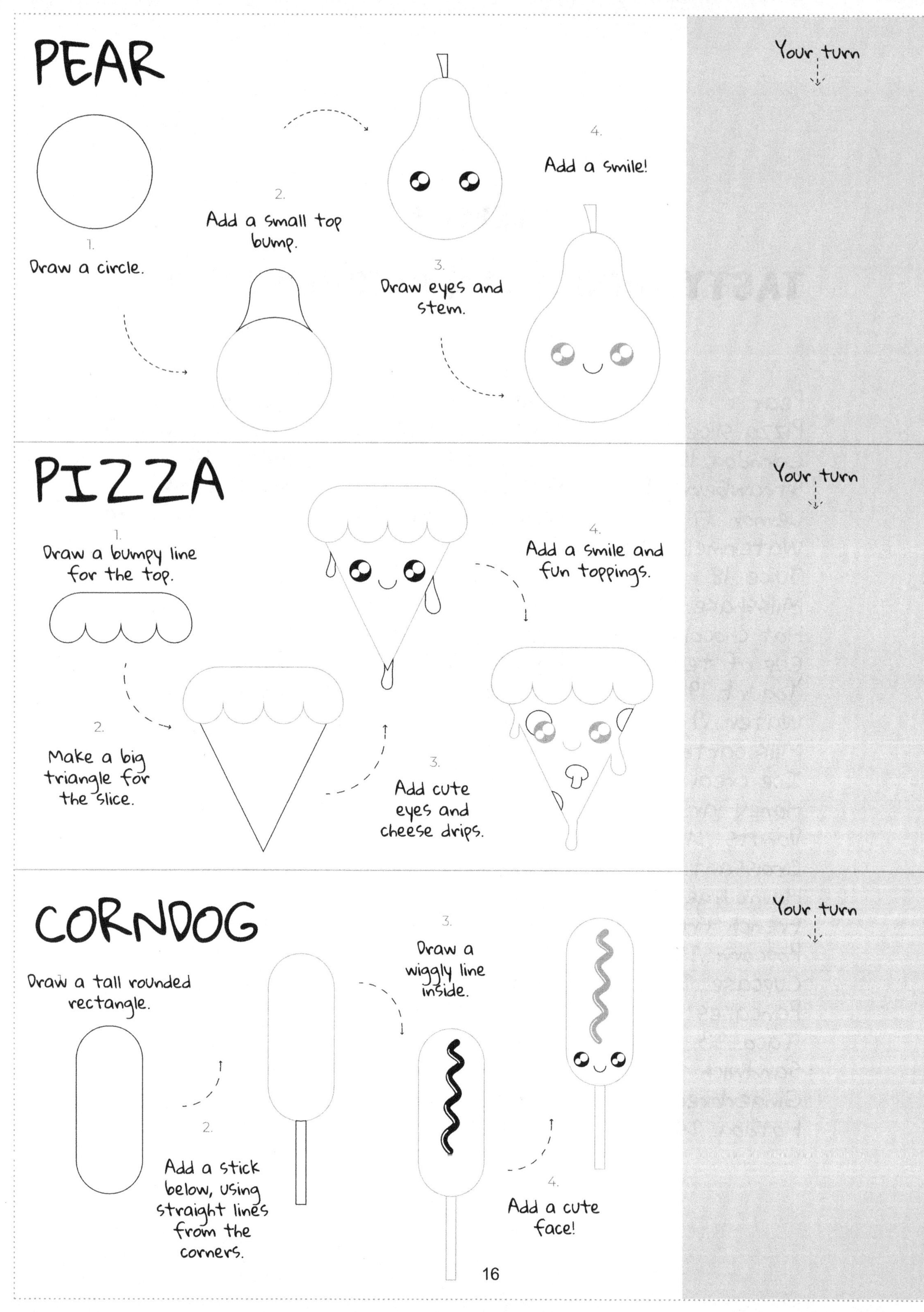

1. Draw a circle.

2. Add a small top bump.

3. Draw eyes and stem.

4. Add a smile!

PIZZA

1. Draw a bumpy line for the top.

2. Make a big triangle for the slice.

3. Add cute eyes and cheese drips.

4. Add a smile and fun toppings.

CORNDOG

Draw a tall rounded rectangle.

2. Add a stick below, using straight lines from the corners.

3. Draw a wiggly line inside.

4. Add a cute face!

STRAWBERRY

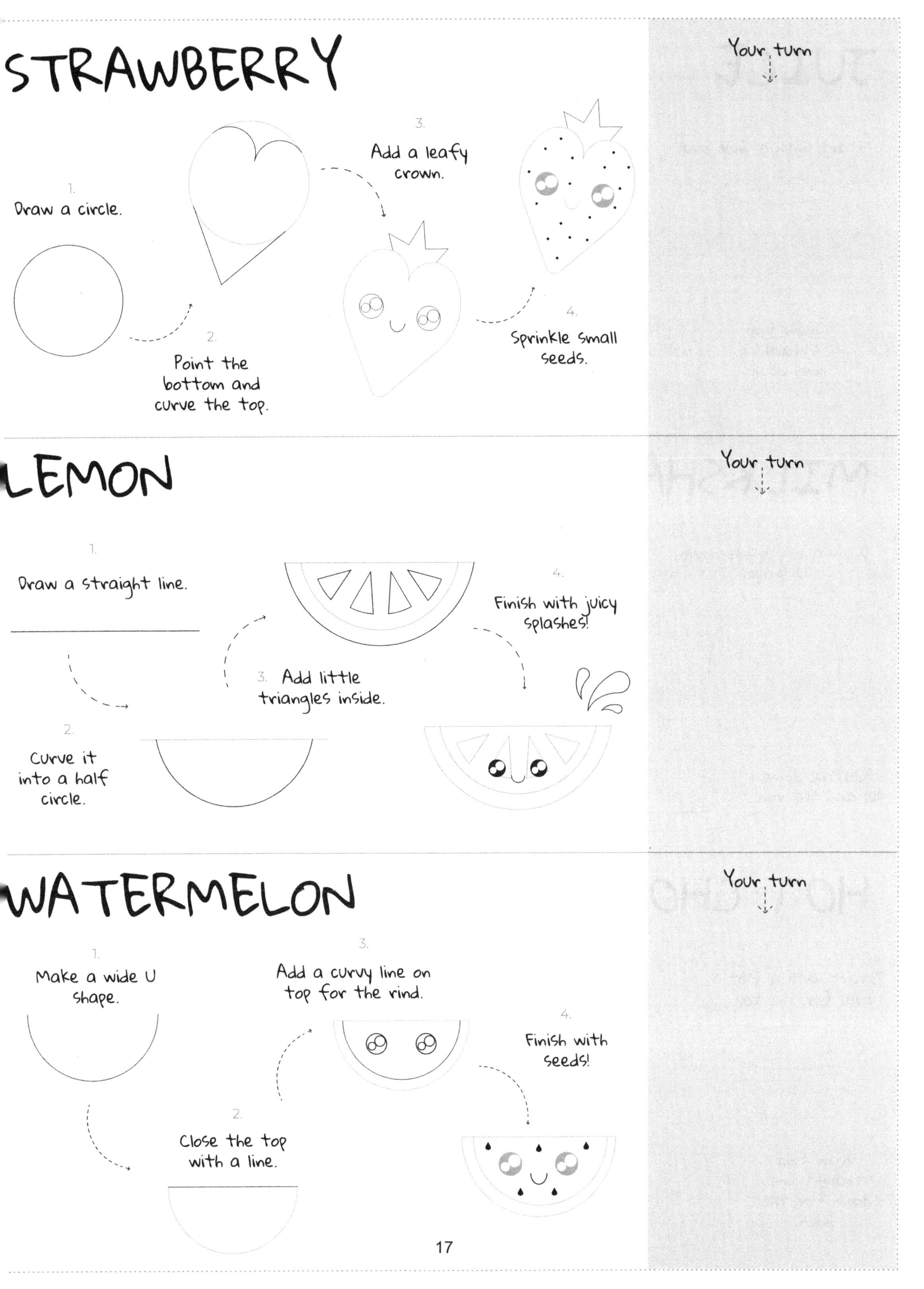

1. Draw a circle.

2. Point the bottom and curve the top.

3. Add a leafy crown.

4. Sprinkle small seeds.

LEMON

1. Draw a straight line.

2. Curve it into a half circle.

3. Add little triangles inside.

4. Finish with juicy splashes!

WATERMELON

1. Make a wide U shape.

2. Close the top with a line.

3. Add a curvy line on top for the rind.

4. Finish with seeds!

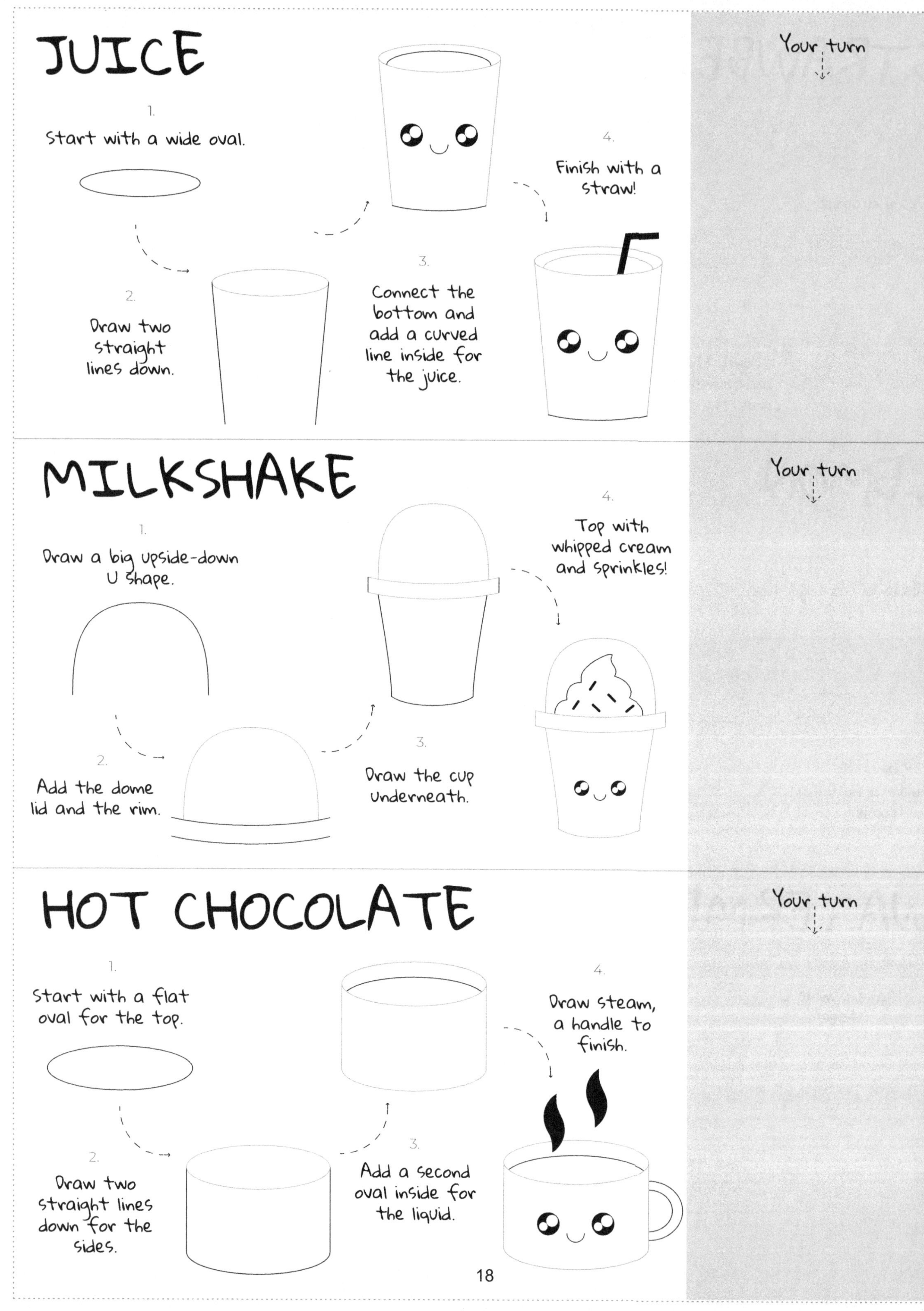

JUICE

1.
Start with a wide oval.

2.
Draw two straight lines down.

3.
Connect the bottom and add a curved line inside for the juice.

4.
Finish with a straw!

Your turn

MILKSHAKE

1.
Draw a big upside-down U shape.

2.
Add the dome lid and the rim.

3.
Draw the cup underneath.

4.
Top with whipped cream and sprinkles!

Your turn

HOT CHOCOLATE

1.
Start with a flat oval for the top.

2.
Draw two straight lines down for the sides.

3.
Add a second oval inside for the liquid.

4.
Draw steam, a handle to finish.

Your turn

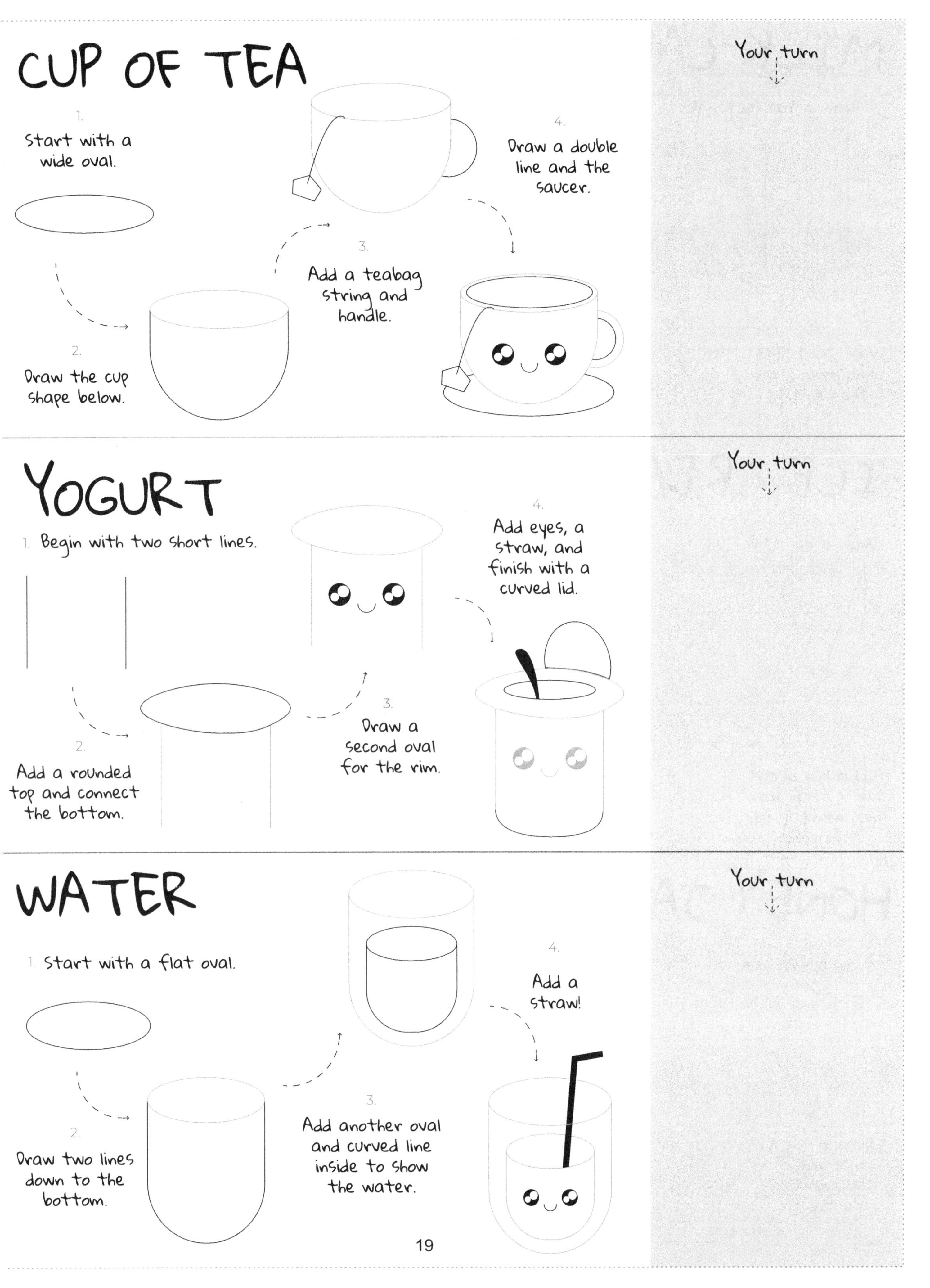

CUP OF TEA

1. Start with a wide oval.

2. Draw the cup shape below.

3. Add a teabag string and handle.

4. Draw a double line and the saucer.

YOGURT

1. Begin with two short lines.

2. Add a rounded top and connect the bottom.

3. Draw a second oval for the rim.

4. Add eyes, a straw, and finish with a curved lid.

WATER

1. Start with a flat oval.

2. Draw two lines down to the bottom.

3. Add another oval and curved line inside to show the water.

4. Add a straw!

MILK CARTON

1. Draw a tall rectangle

2. Draw short lines going down from the corners.

3. Connect the lines at the bottom to make the sides.

4. Add a straw and a smile to finish.

ICE CREAM

1. Draw a big letter V.

2. Add a line across the V, then draw lines going up for the cone.

3. Draw a wavy scoop and vertical lines on the cone.

4. Add two scoops on top, like clouds, and a smile.

HONEY JAR

1. Draw a flat oval.

2. Draw a big curve under the oval to shape the jar.

3. Add another oval inside and curved lines to show the glass jar.

4. Finish with a honey dipper dripping a bit of honey

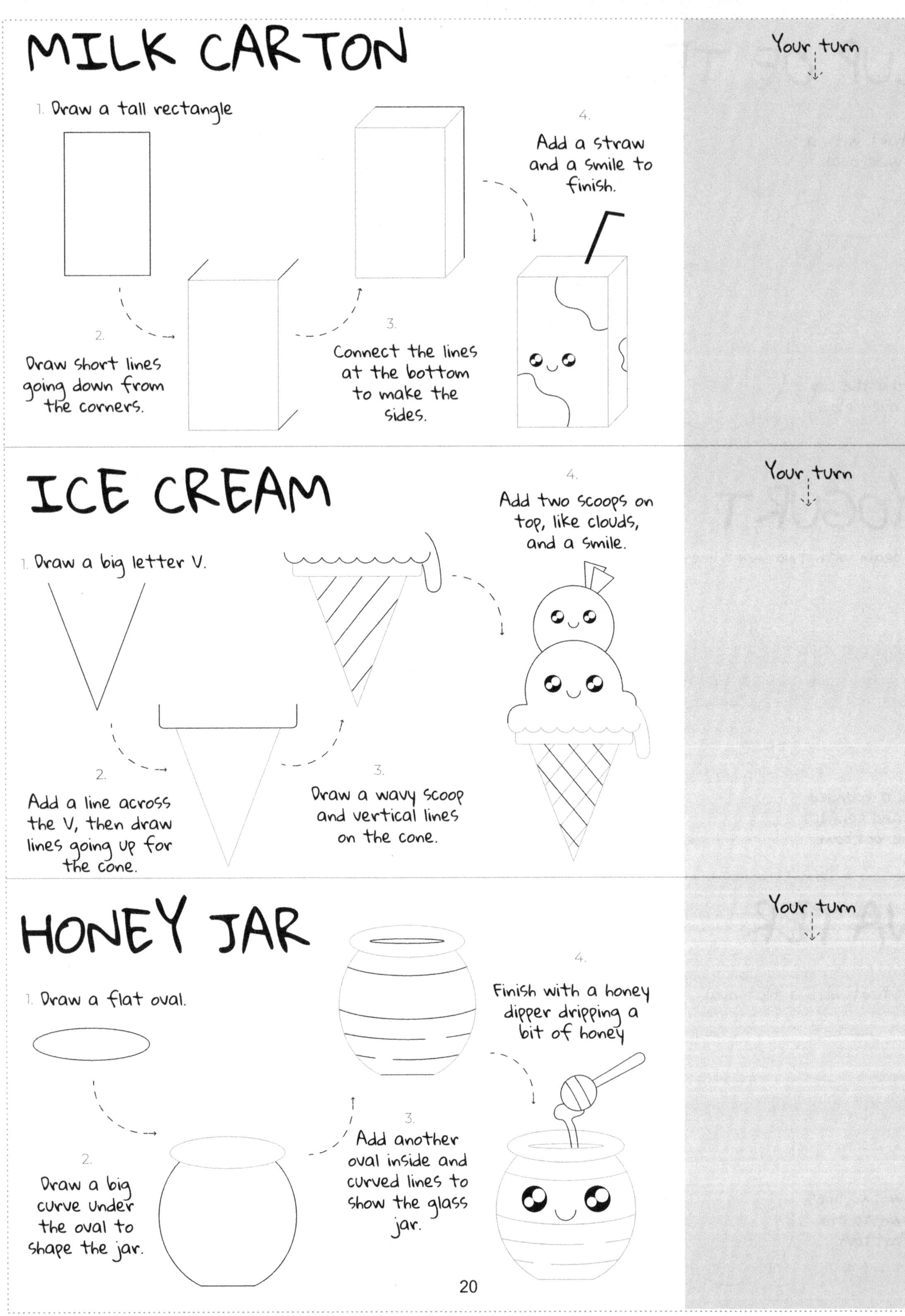

Your turn

Your turn

Your turn

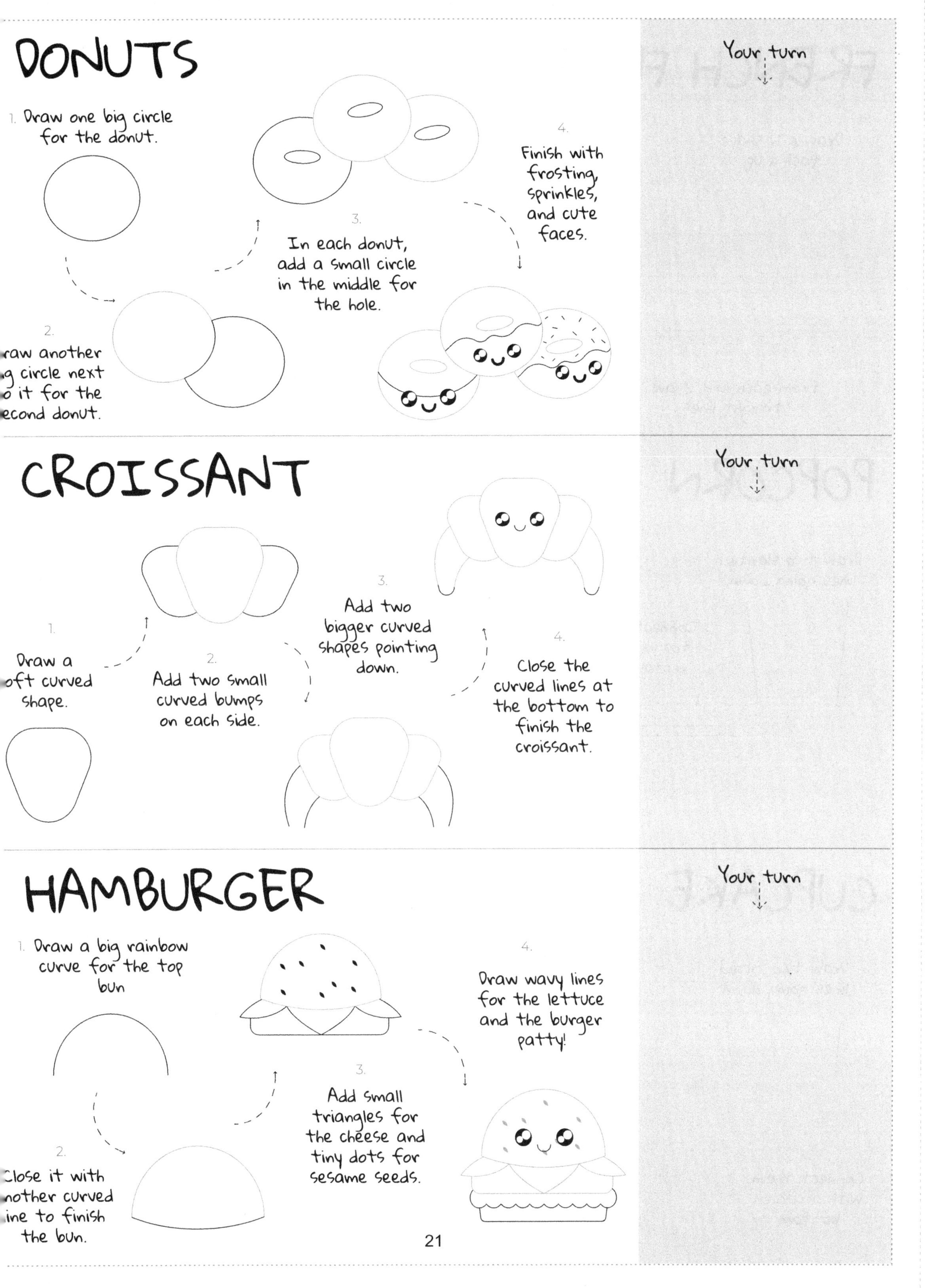

DONUTS

1. Draw one big circle for the donut.

2. Draw another big circle next to it for the second donut.

3. In each donut, add a small circle in the middle for the hole.

4. Finish with frosting, sprinkles, and cute faces.

CROISSANT

1. Draw a soft curved shape.

2. Add two small curved bumps on each side.

3. Add two bigger curved shapes pointing down.

4. Close the curved lines at the bottom to finish the croissant.

HAMBURGER

1. Draw a big rainbow curve for the top bun

2. Close it with another curved line to finish the bun.

3. Add small triangles for the cheese and tiny dots for sesame seeds.

4. Draw wavy lines for the lettuce and the burger patty!

FRENCH FRIES

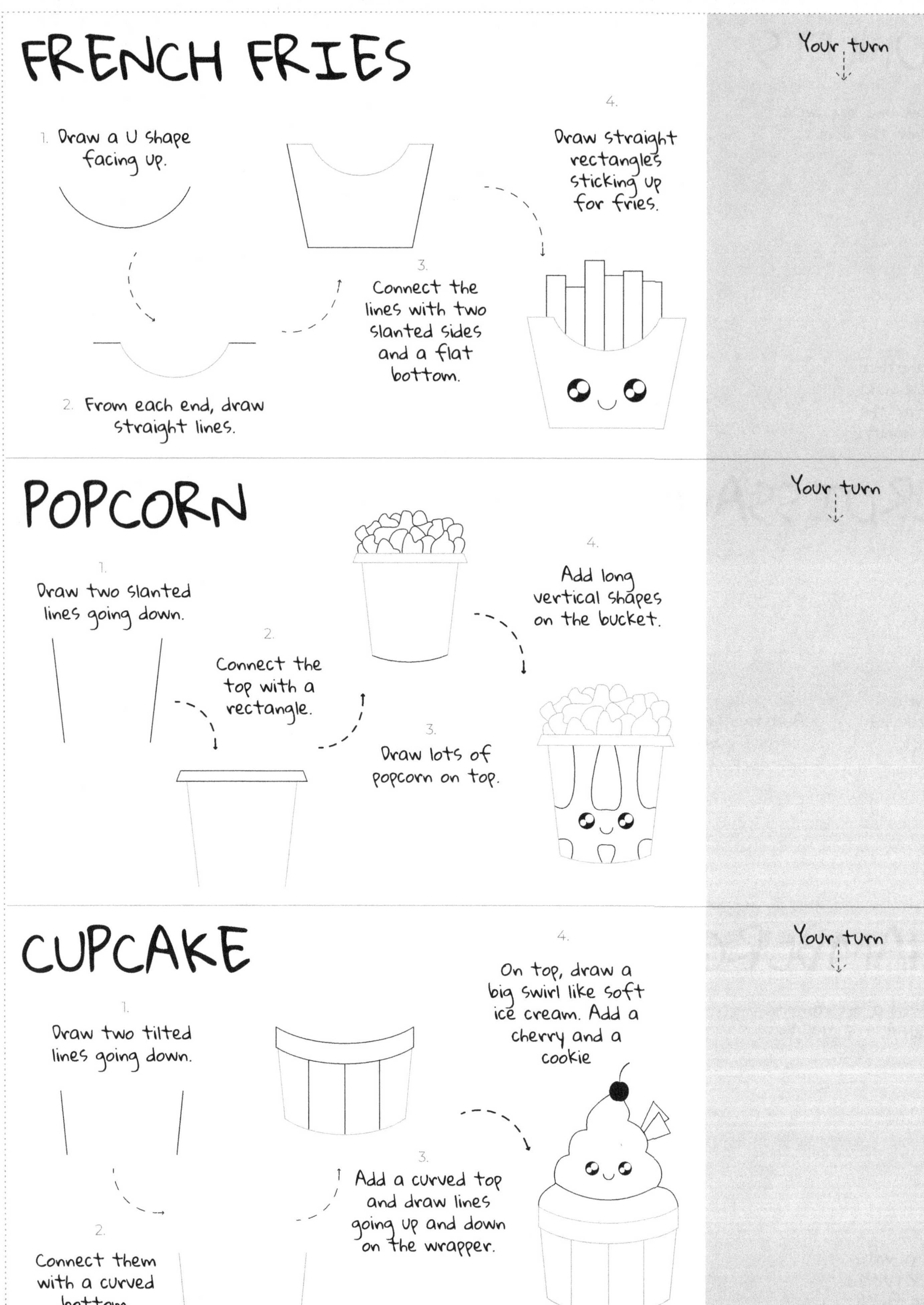

POPCORN

CUPCAKE

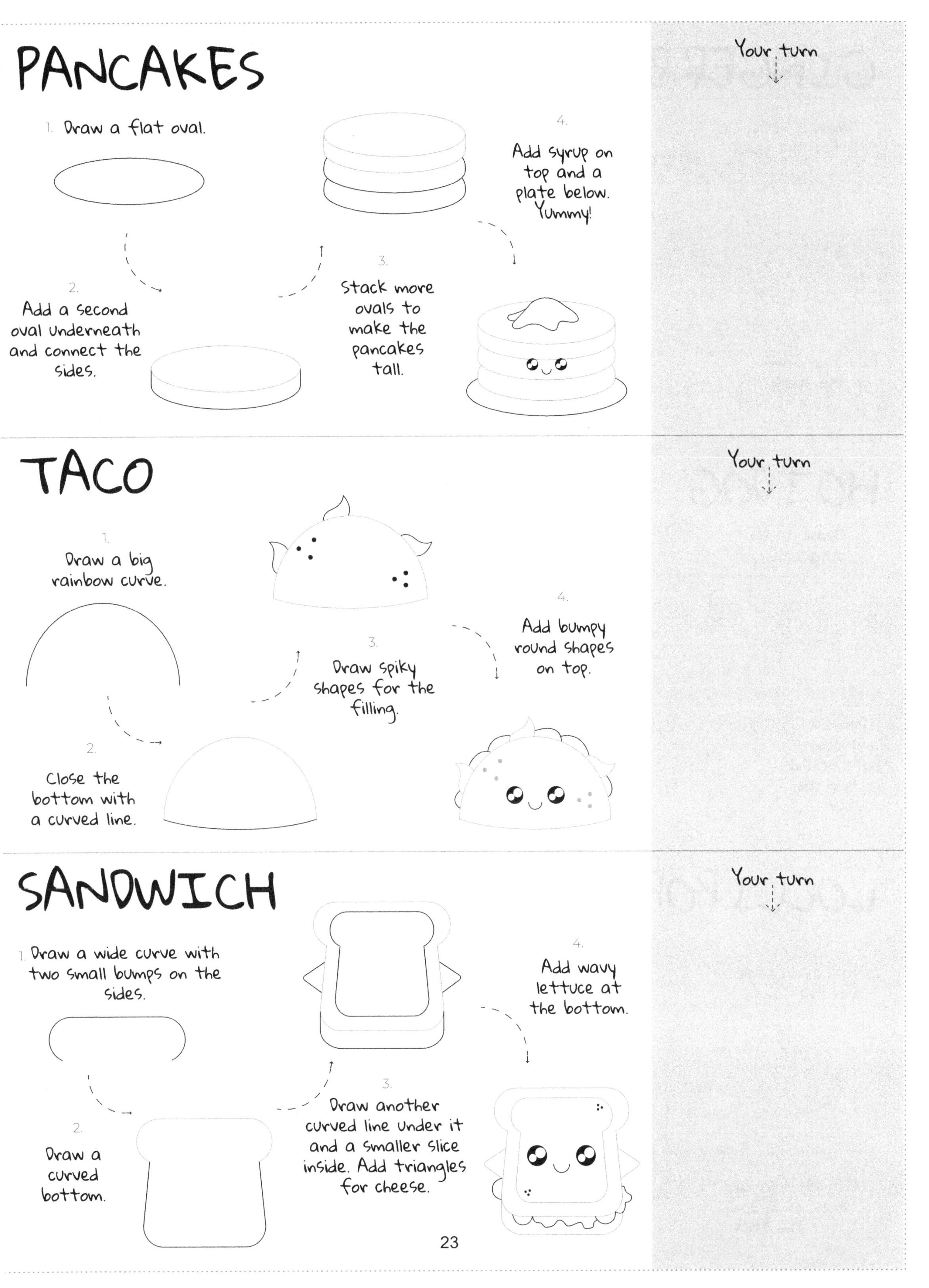

PANCAKES

TACO

SANDWICH

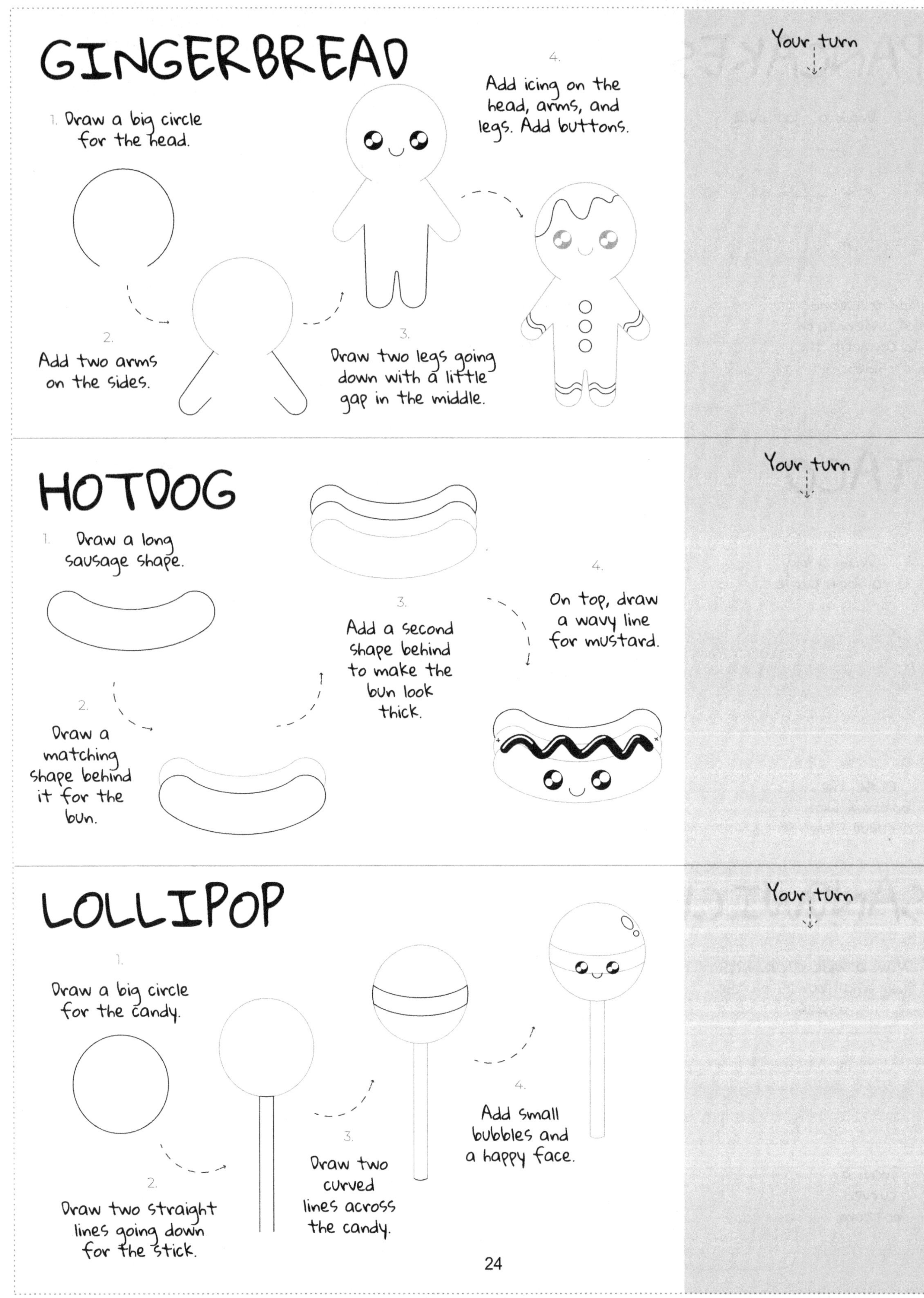

GINGERBREAD

1. Draw a big circle for the head.

2. Add two arms on the sides.

3. Draw two legs going down with a little gap in the middle.

4. Add icing on the head, arms, and legs. Add buttons.

Your turn

HOTDOG

1. Draw a long sausage shape.

2. Draw a matching shape behind it for the bun.

3. Add a second shape behind to make the bun look thick.

4. On top, draw a wavy line for mustard.

Your turn

LOLLIPOP

1. Draw a big circle for the candy.

2. Draw two straight lines going down for the stick.

3. Draw two curved lines across the candy.

4. Add small bubbles and a happy face.

Your turn

BOWL OF CEREAL

1.
Draw a wide oval for the top.

2.
Draw another oval inside for the cereal line.

3.
Draw two curved lines to make the bowl. Add a short shape for the stand.

4.
Add cereal loops, a spoon, and a happy face.

CARROT

1. Draw a slanted triangle.

2. Close the bottom with a curved line.

3.
Add short lines across. Draw a tiny bump on top!

4.
Add big leafy shapes on top.

BROWNIE

1. Draw a square or a tall rectangle.

2. Draw two short lines going back from the top corners.

3.
Connect the lines to make a cube.

4.
On top, draw a wavy line for frosting.

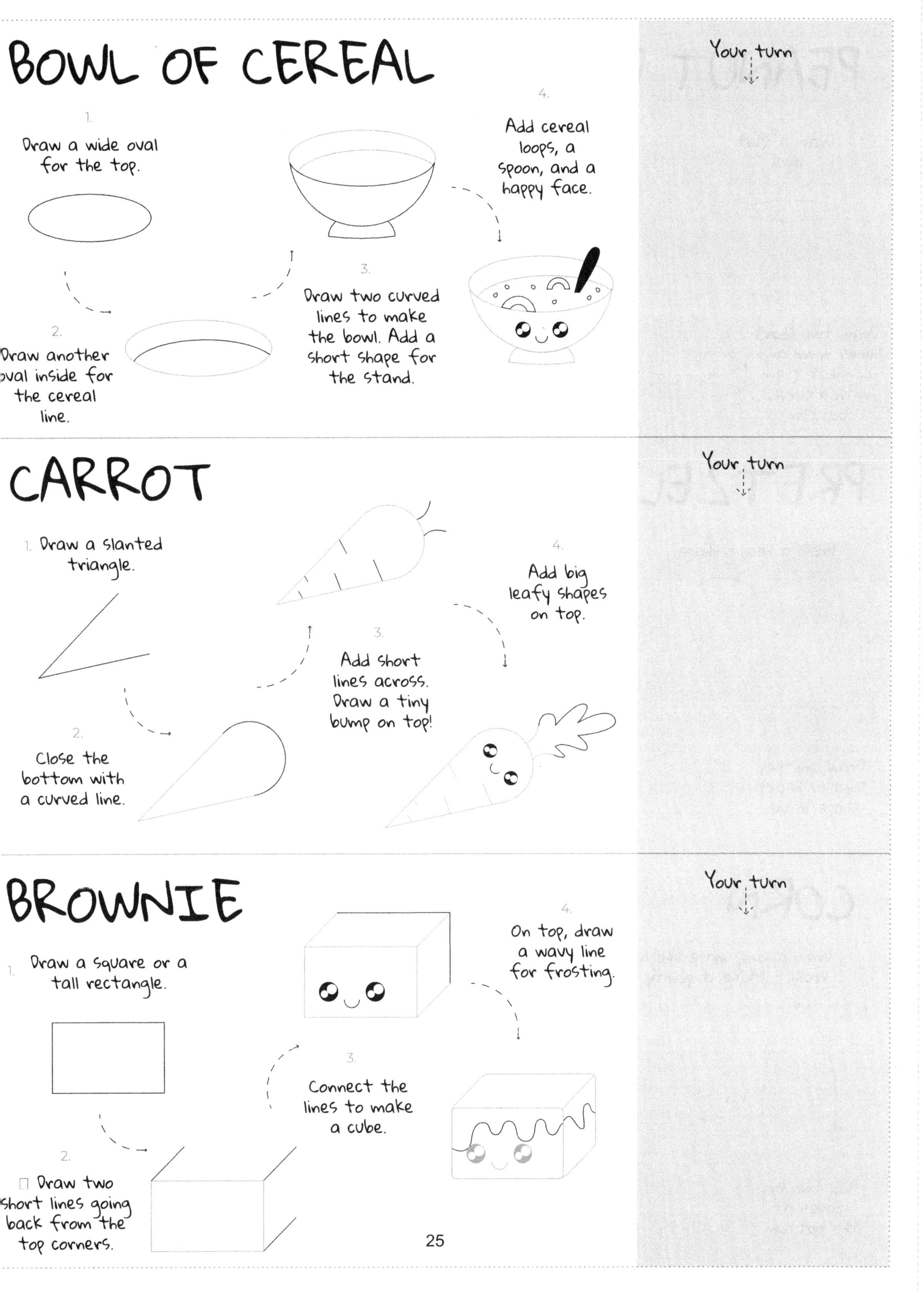

PEANUT BUTTER

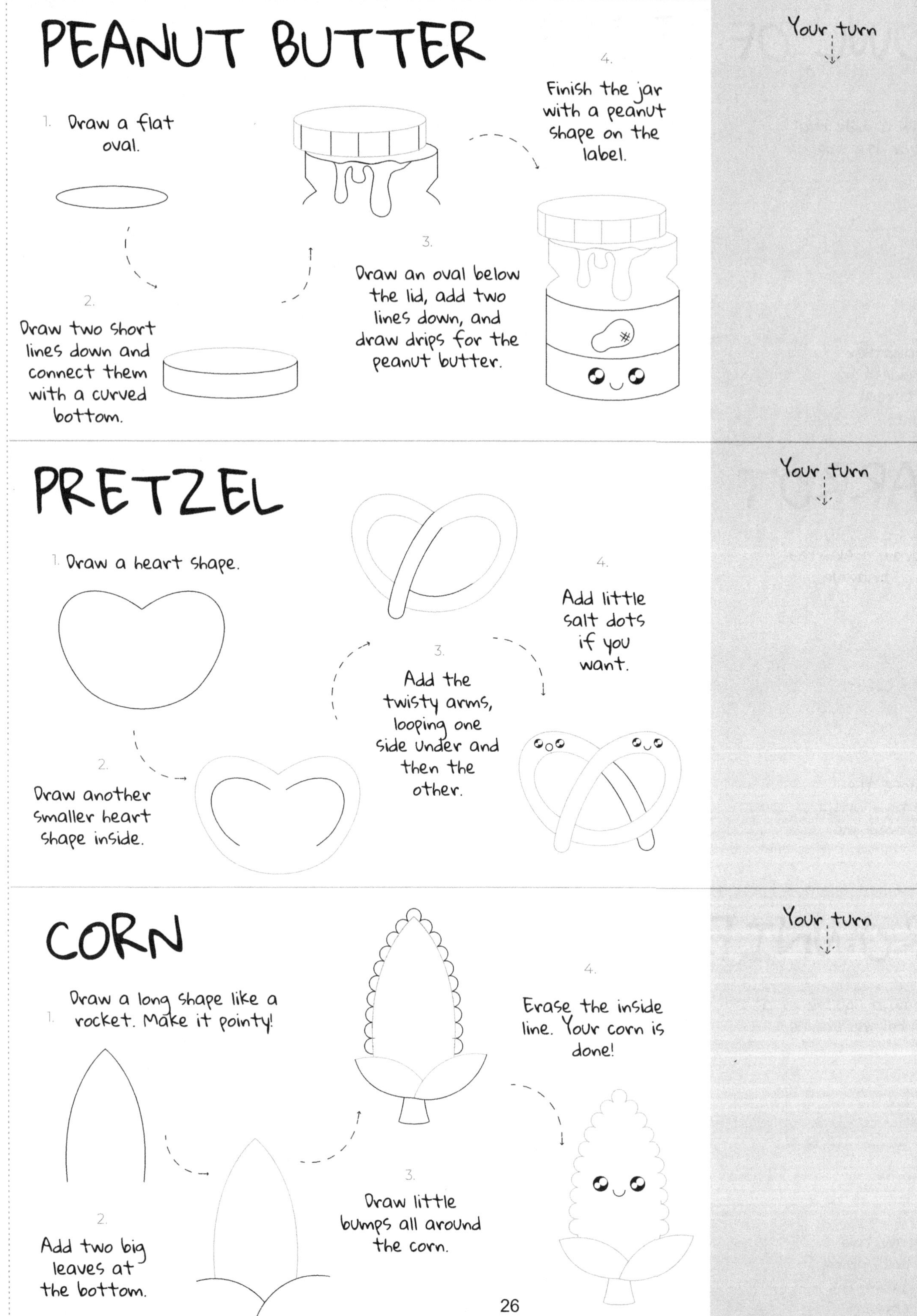

1. Draw a flat oval.

2. Draw two short lines down and connect them with a curved bottom.

3. Draw an oval below the lid, add two lines down, and draw drips for the peanut butter.

4. Finish the jar with a peanut shape on the label.

PRETZEL

1. Draw a heart shape.

2. Draw another smaller heart shape inside.

3. Add the twisty arms, looping one side under and then the other.

4. Add little salt dots if you want.

CORN

1. Draw a long shape like a rocket. Make it pointy!

2. Add two big leaves at the bottom.

3. Draw little bumps all around the corn.

4. Erase the inside line. Your corn is done!

CINNAMON ROLL

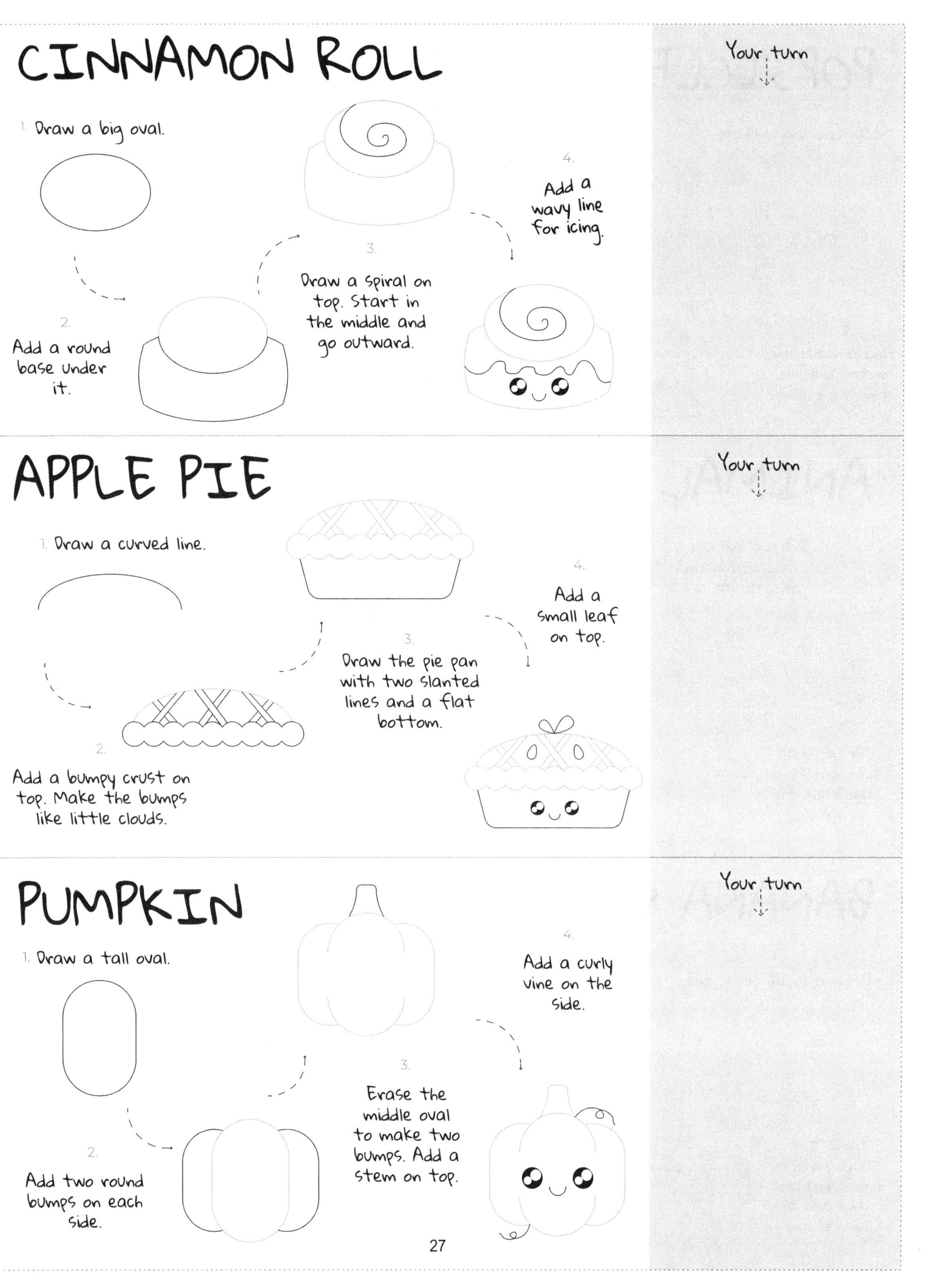

1. Draw a big oval.

2. Add a round base under it.

3. Draw a spiral on top. Start in the middle and go outward.

4. Add a wavy line for icing.

APPLE PIE

1. Draw a curved line.

2. Add a bumpy crust on top. Make the bumps like little clouds.

3. Draw the pie pan with two slanted lines and a flat bottom.

4. Add a small leaf on top.

PUMPKIN

1. Draw a tall oval.

2. Add two round bumps on each side.

3. Erase the middle oval to make two bumps. Add a stem on top.

4. Add a curly vine on the side.

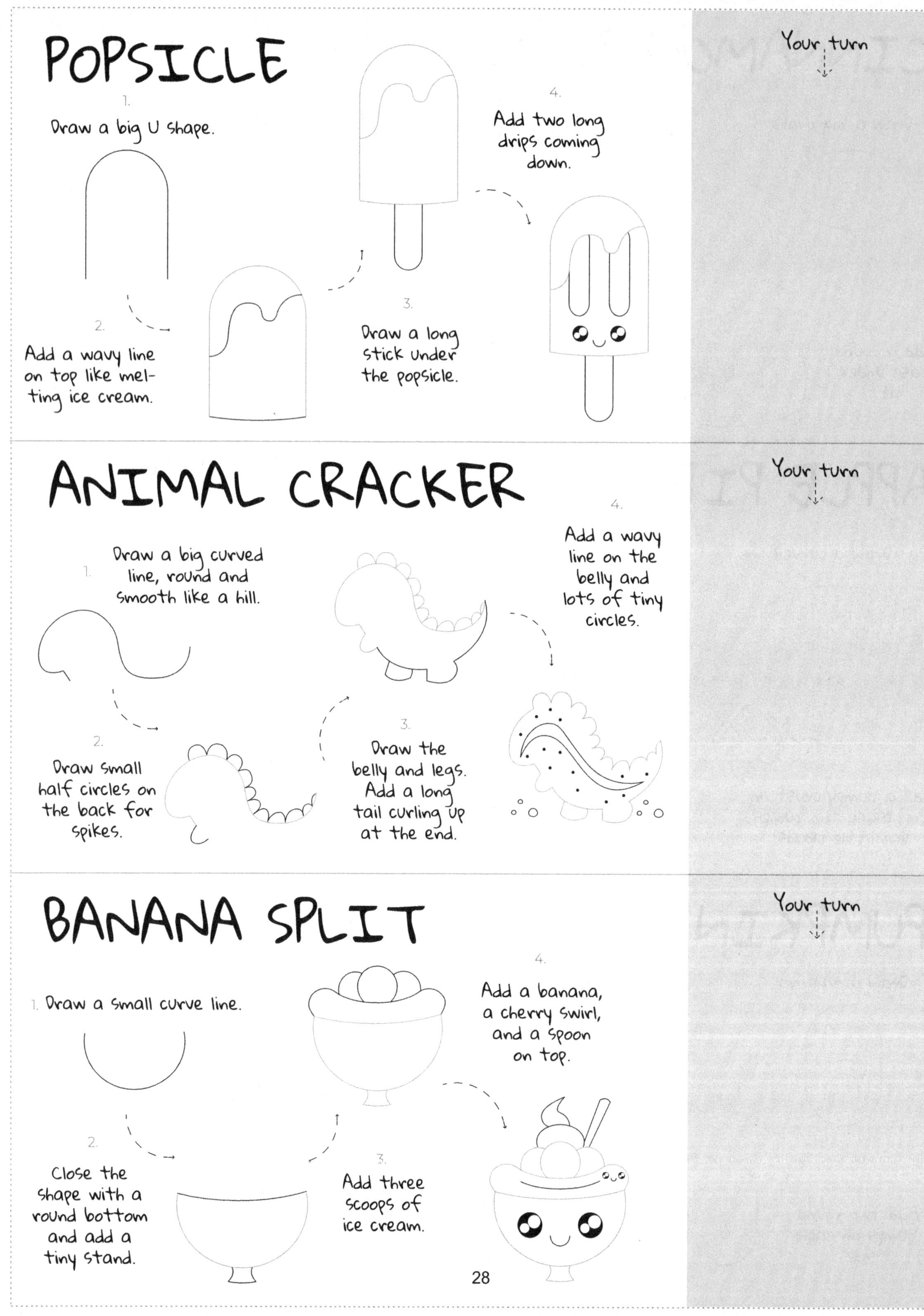

POPSICLE

1.
Draw a big U shape.

2.
Add a wavy line on top like melting ice cream.

3.
Draw a long stick under the popsicle.

4.
Add two long drips coming down.

ANIMAL CRACKER

1.
Draw a big curved line, round and smooth like a hill.

2.
Draw small half circles on the back for spikes.

3.
Draw the belly and legs. Add a long tail curling up at the end.

4.
Add a wavy line on the belly and lots of tiny circles.

BANANA SPLIT

1. Draw a small curve line.

2.
Close the shape with a round bottom and add a tiny stand.

3.
Add three scoops of ice cream.

4.
Add a banana, a cherry swirl, and a spoon on top.

28

CANDY

1. Draw a big circle.

2. Add two slanted lines on each side for the wrappers.

3. Turn the lines into wavy wrappers.

4. Add a curved stripe across the candy.

EGGPLANT

1. Draw a slanted oval.

2. Add a long curved line and connect it back to the oval.

3. Draw the leafy top.

4. Add two small ovals for eyes to make a happy eggplant.

SPAGHETTI

1. Draw a big wide oval.

2. Add two bumpy shapes on top.

3. Draw two small circles on top for meatballs.

4. Draw a third bumpy shape in the middle. Add lots of wavy lines for spaghetti. Then draw a fork.

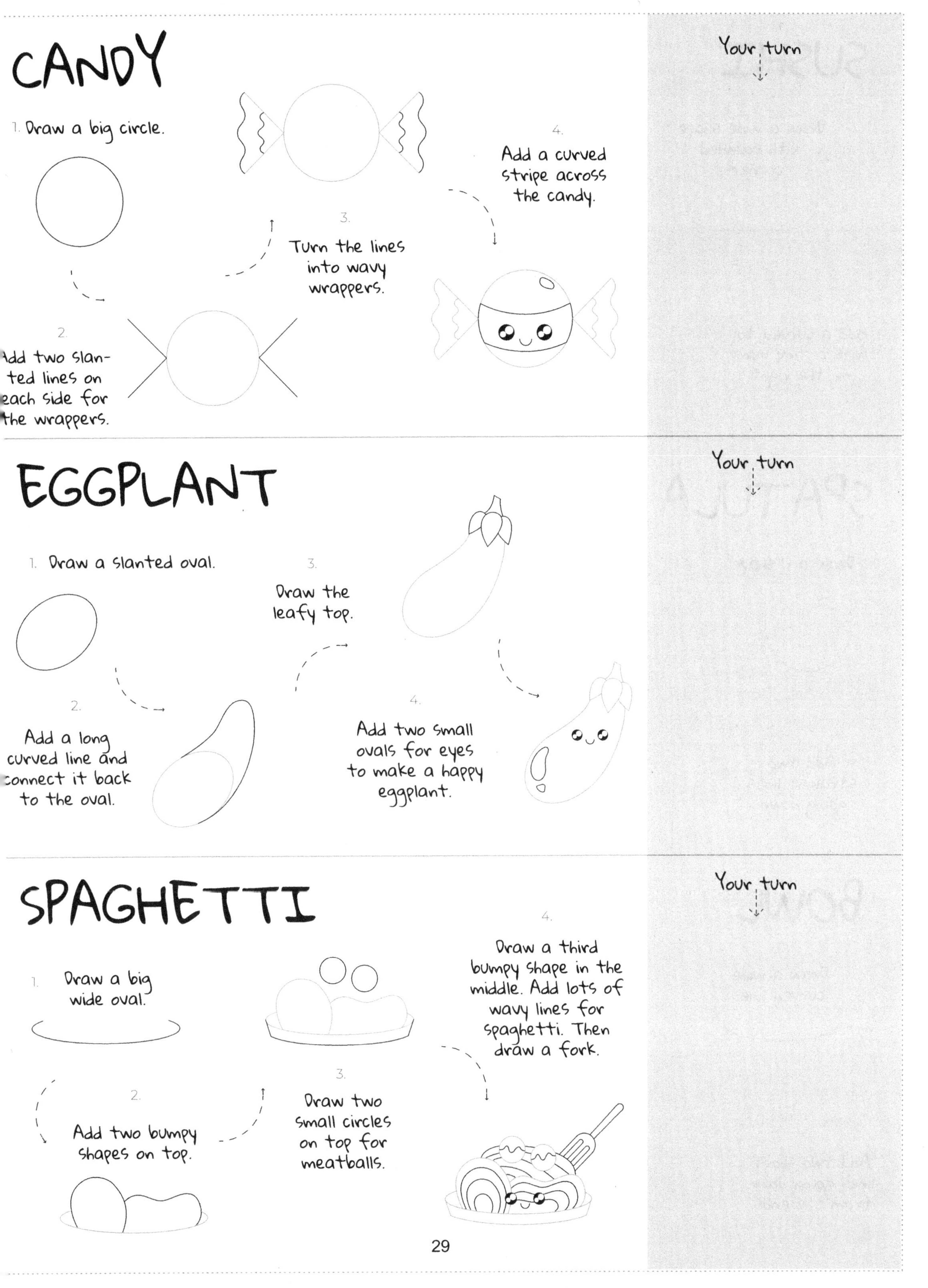

29

SUSHI

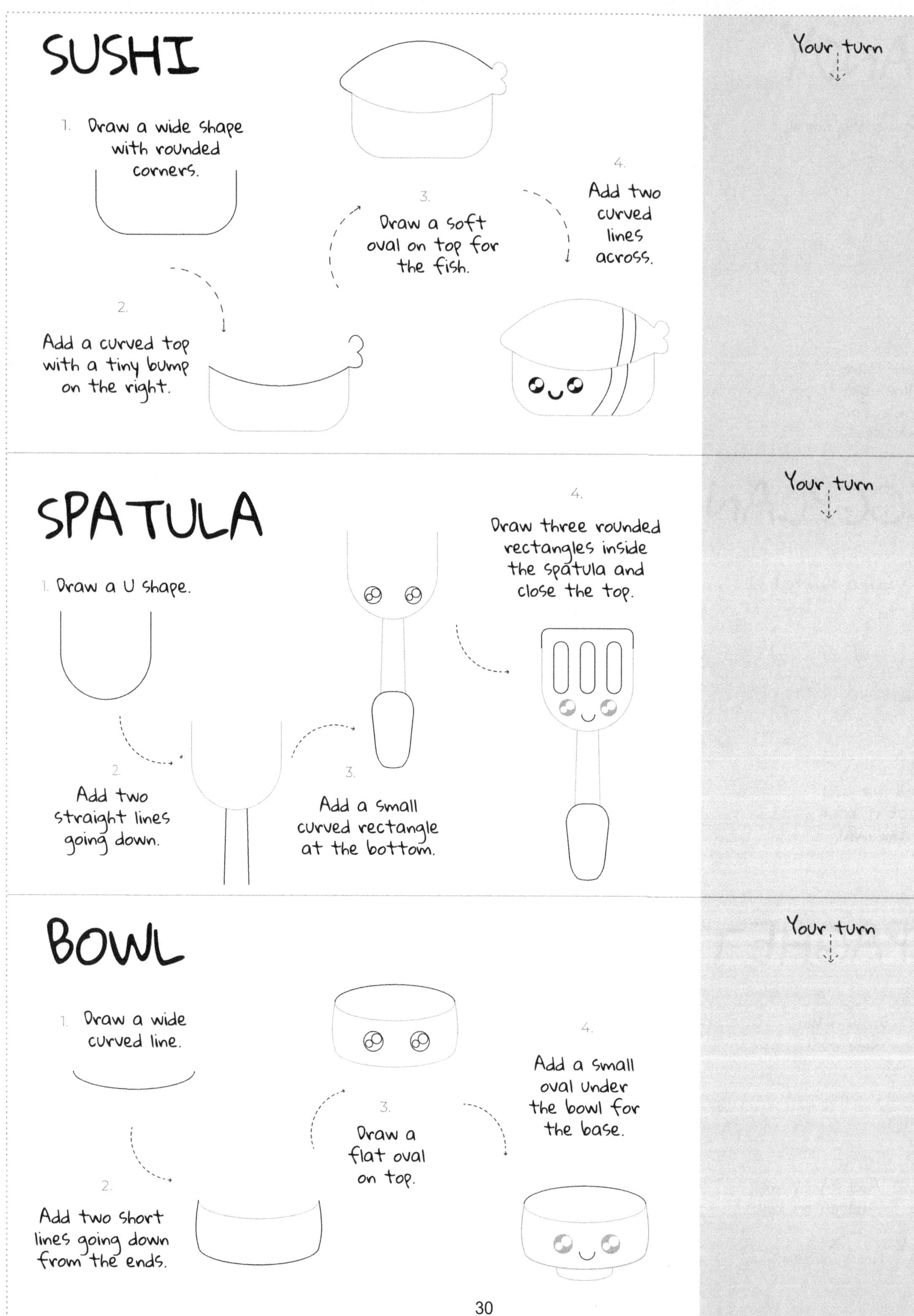

1. Draw a wide shape with rounded corners.

2. Add a curved top with a tiny bump on the right.

3. Draw a soft oval on top for the fish.

4. Add two curved lines across.

SPATULA

1. Draw a U shape.

2. Add two straight lines going down.

3. Add a small curved rectangle at the bottom.

4. Draw three rounded rectangles inside the spatula and close the top.

BOWL

1. Draw a wide curved line.

2. Add two short lines going down from the ends.

3. Draw a flat oval on top.

4. Add a small oval under the bowl for the base.

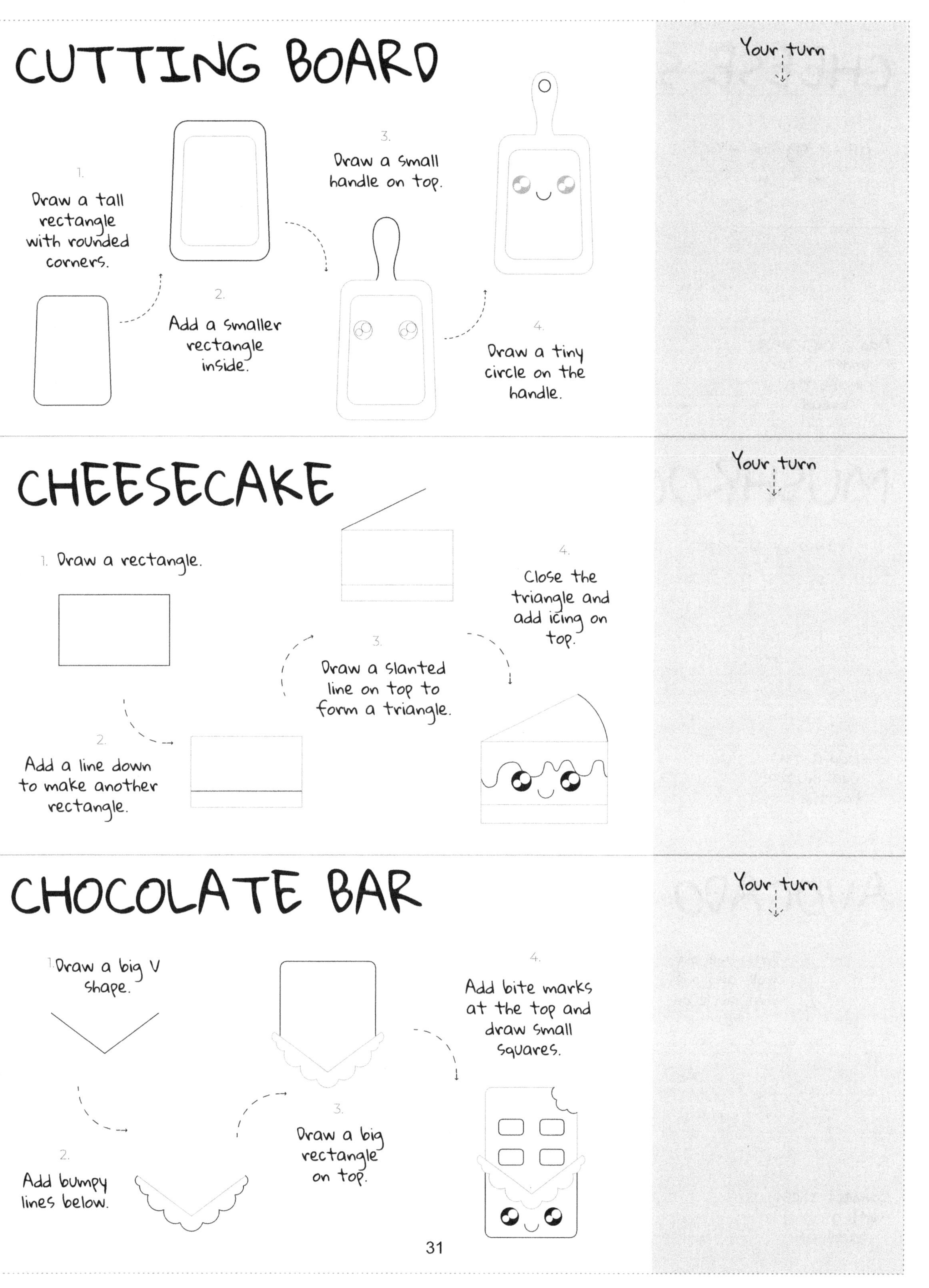

CUTTING BOARD

1.
Draw a tall rectangle with rounded corners.

2.
Add a smaller rectangle inside.

3.
Draw a small handle on top.

4.
Draw a tiny circle on the handle.

Your turn

CHEESECAKE

1. Draw a rectangle.

2.
Add a line down to make another rectangle.

3.
Draw a slanted line on top to form a triangle.

4.
Close the triangle and add icing on top.

Your turn

CHOCOLATE BAR

1. Draw a big V shape.

2.
Add bumpy lines below.

3.
Draw a big rectangle on top.

4.
Add bite marks at the top and draw small squares.

Your turn

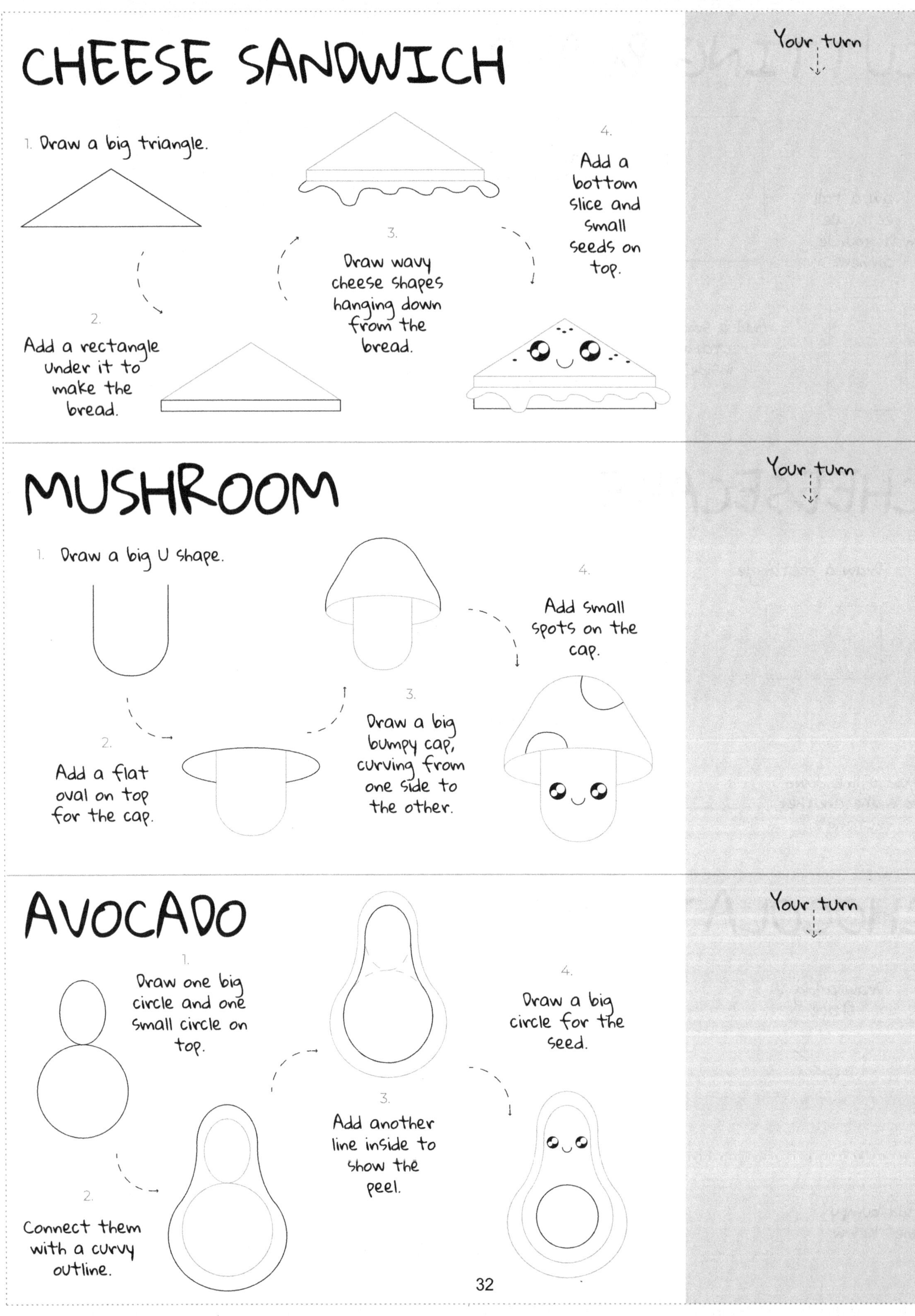

CHEESE SANDWICH

1. Draw a big triangle.

2. Add a rectangle under it to make the bread.

3. Draw wavy cheese shapes hanging down from the bread.

4. Add a bottom slice and small seeds on top.

MUSHROOM

1. Draw a big U shape.

2. Add a flat oval on top for the cap.

3. Draw a big bumpy cap, curving from one side to the other.

4. Add small spots on the cap.

AVOCADO

1. Draw one big circle and one small circle on top.

2. Connect them with a curvy outline.

3. Add another line inside to show the peel.

4. Draw a big circle for the seed.

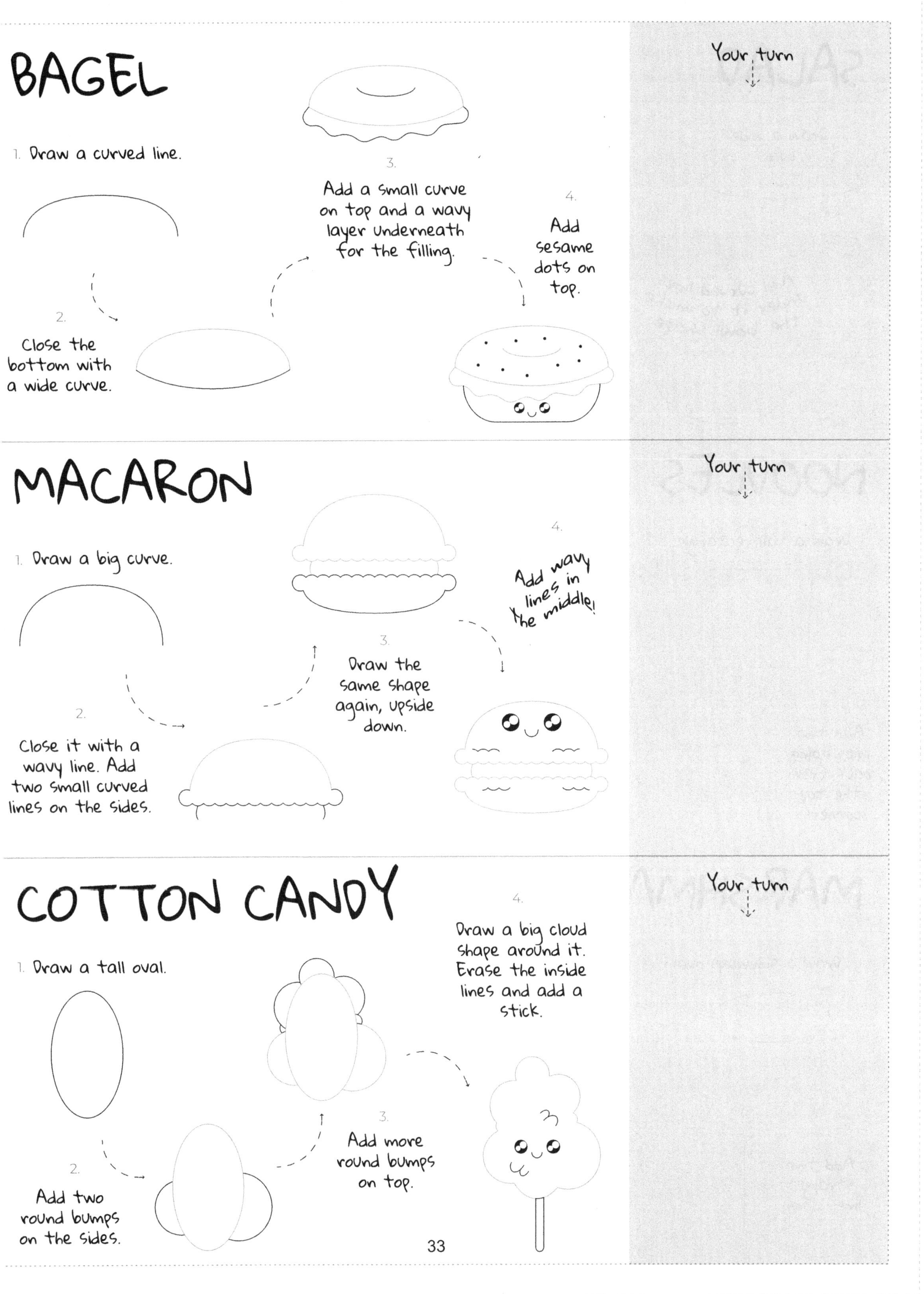

BAGEL
1. Draw a curved line.
2. Close the bottom with a wide curve.
3.
Add a small curve on top and a wavy layer underneath for the filling.
4.
Add sesame dots on top.
Your turn

MACARON
1. Draw a big curve.
2. Close it with a wavy line. Add two small curved lines on the sides.
3. Draw the same shape again, upside down.
4.
Add wavy lines in the middle!
Your turn

COTTON CANDY
1. Draw a tall oval.
2. Add two round bumps on the sides.
3. Add more round bumps on top.
4.
Draw a big cloud shape around it. Erase the inside lines and add a stick.
Your turn

33

SALAD

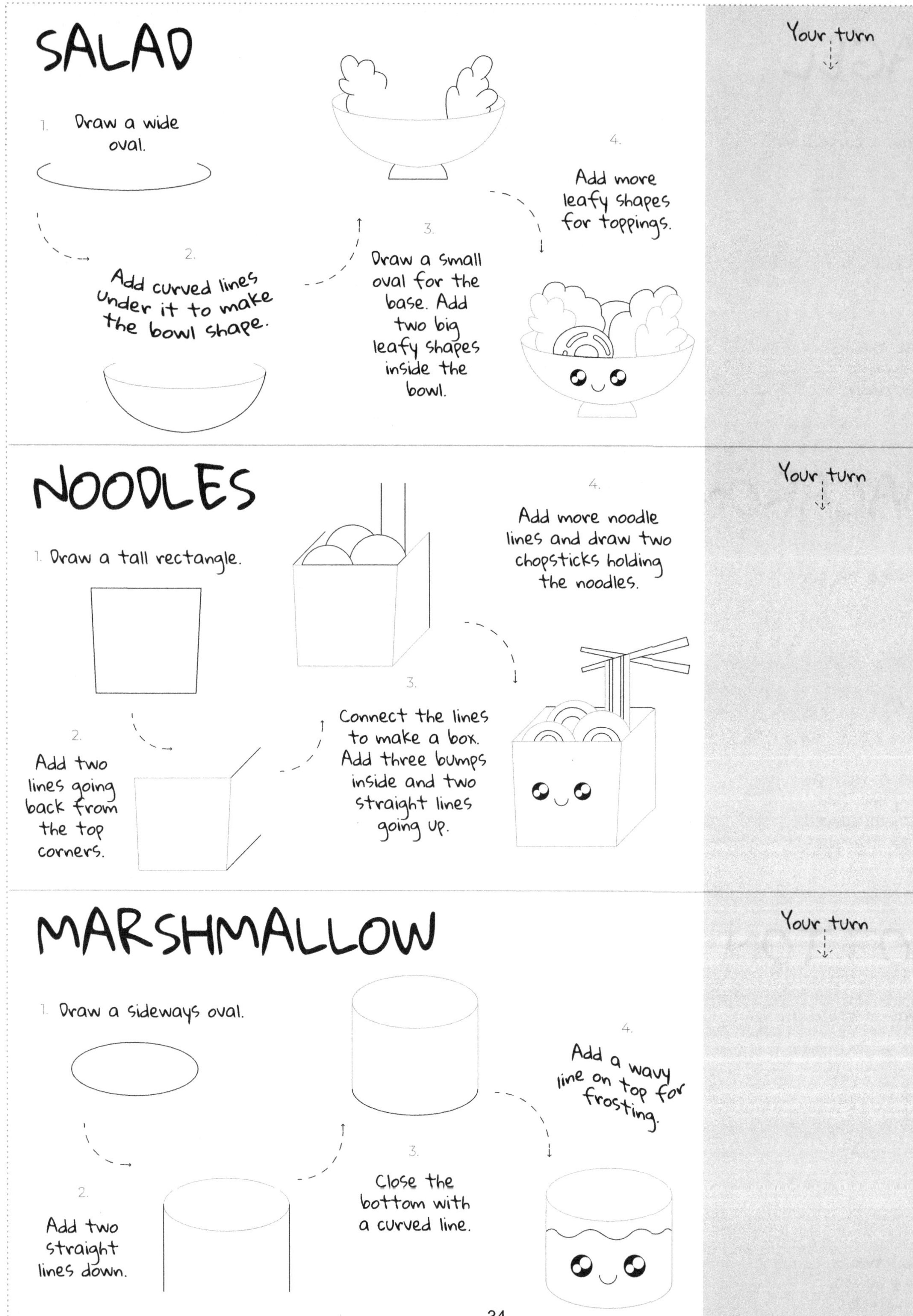

NOODLES

MARSHMALLOW

ONION

1. Draw a big circle.

2. Add two curved lines on top.

3. Draw two long leaves curving down like ribbons.

4. Add curved lines on the onion and little roots at the bottom.

Your turn

CHICKEN

1. Draw a flat half oval.

2. Add two slanted lines going down.

3. Draw three big bumps for the drumsticks. Then close the bottom.

4. Add the bones sticking out and a stripe on the bucket.

Your turn

COCONUT

1. Draw a big circle.

2. Add a curved line across, like it's cut in half.

3. Erase the top of the circle. Draw another oval inside to show the edge.

4. Add a straw and short lines for the coconut hairs.

Your turn

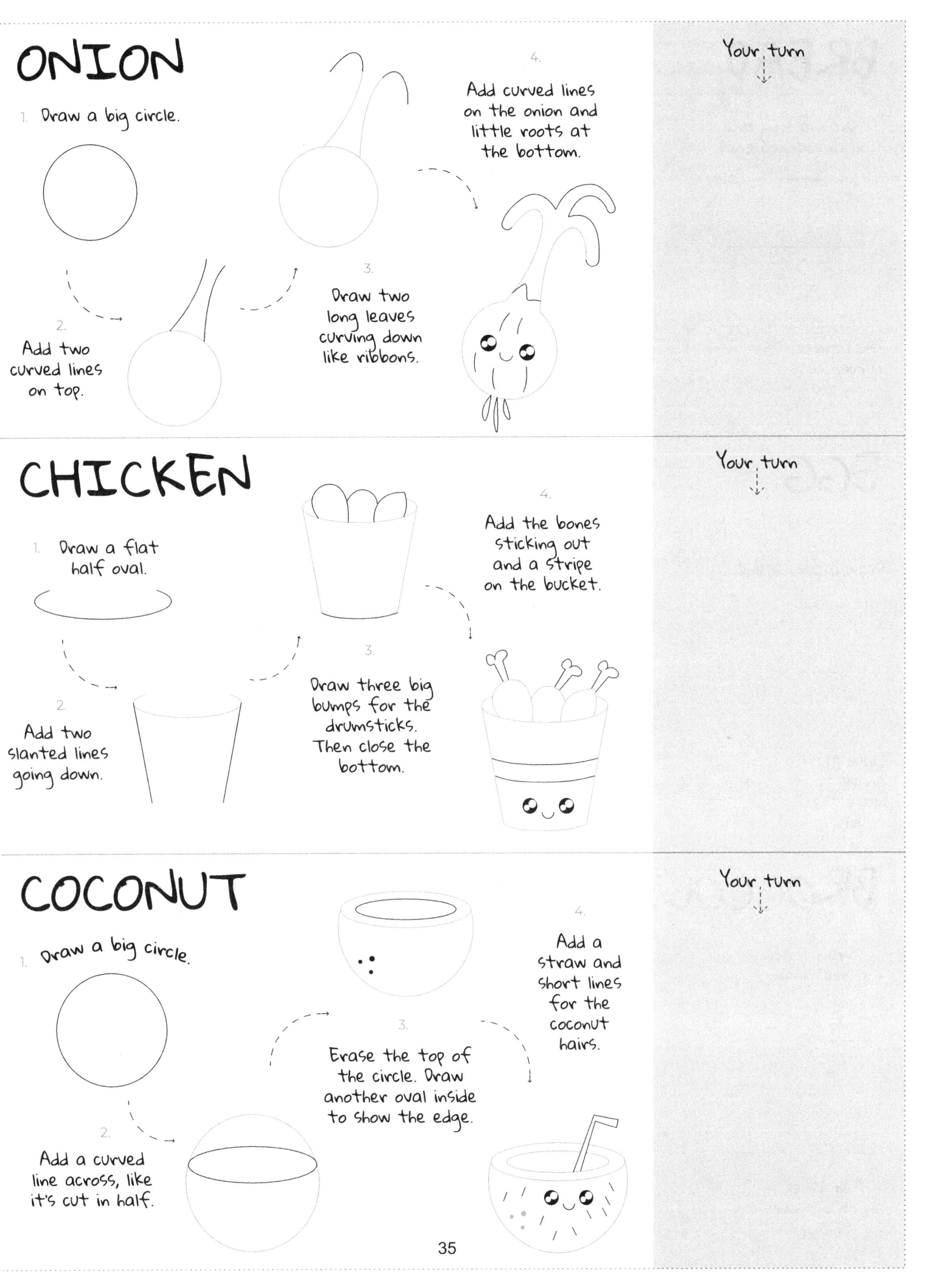

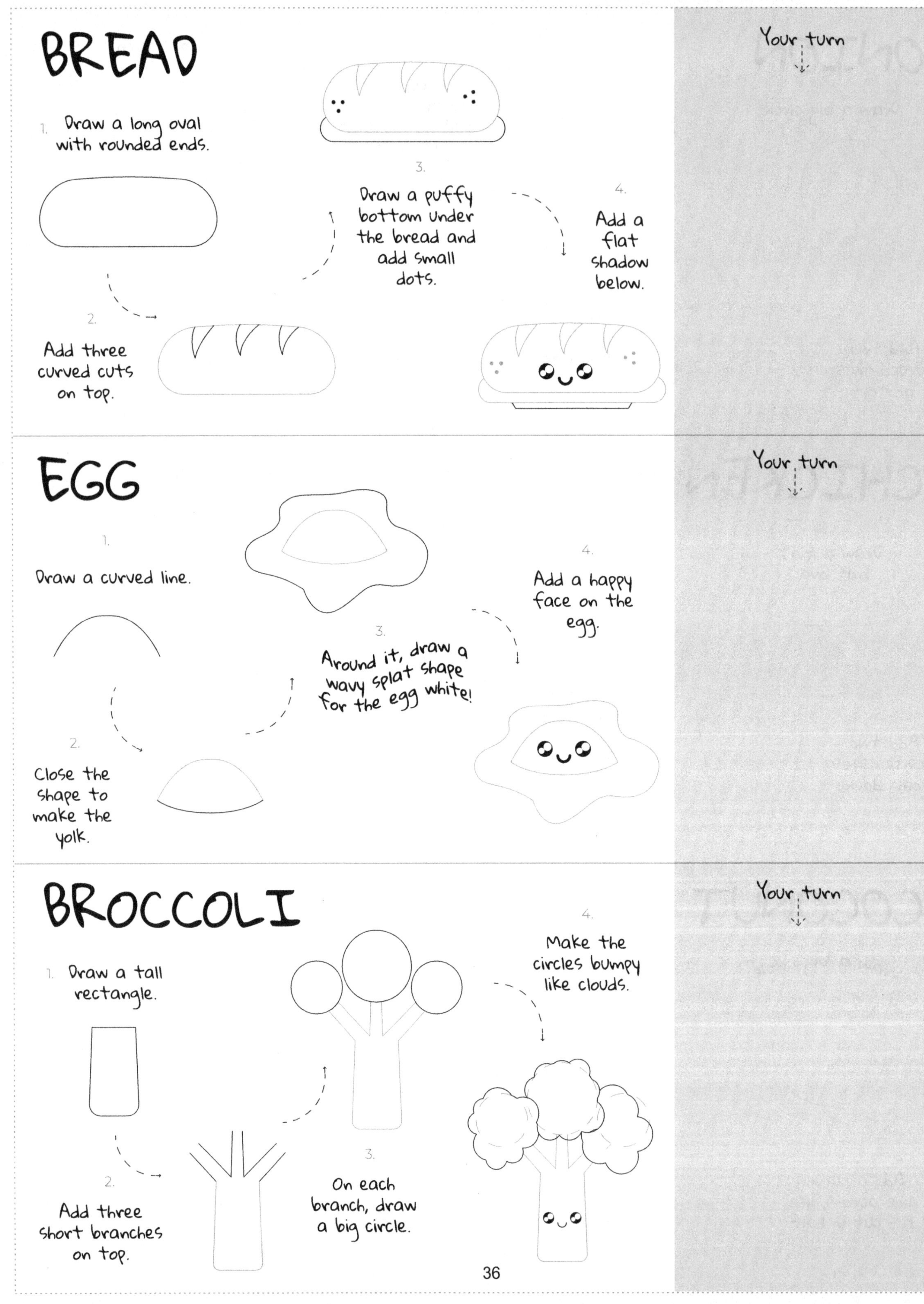

BREAD

1. Draw a long oval with rounded ends.

2. Add three curved cuts on top.

3. Draw a puffy bottom under the bread and add small dots.

4. Add a flat shadow below.

EGG

1. Draw a curved line.

2. Close the shape to make the yolk.

3. Around it, draw a wavy splat shape for the egg white!

4. Add a happy face on the egg.

BROCCOLI

1. Draw a tall rectangle.

2. Add three short branches on top.

3. On each branch, draw a big circle.

4. Make the circles bumpy like clouds.

CARROT CAKE

1. Draw a slanted rectangle.

2. Add one slanted line on top to start the triangle.

3. Add a line across the front and close the triangle.

4. Draw a wavy line for frosting and a tiny carrot on top.

COOKIE

1. Draw a circle.

2. Add a small circle touching it.

3. Erase the overlap and draw two bumps for the bite marks.

4. Add chocolate chips.

SOUP

1. Draw a wide U shape.

2. Add a curved line on top.

3. Draw an oval for the soup surface and add a spoon sticking out.

4. Add steam and little toppings.

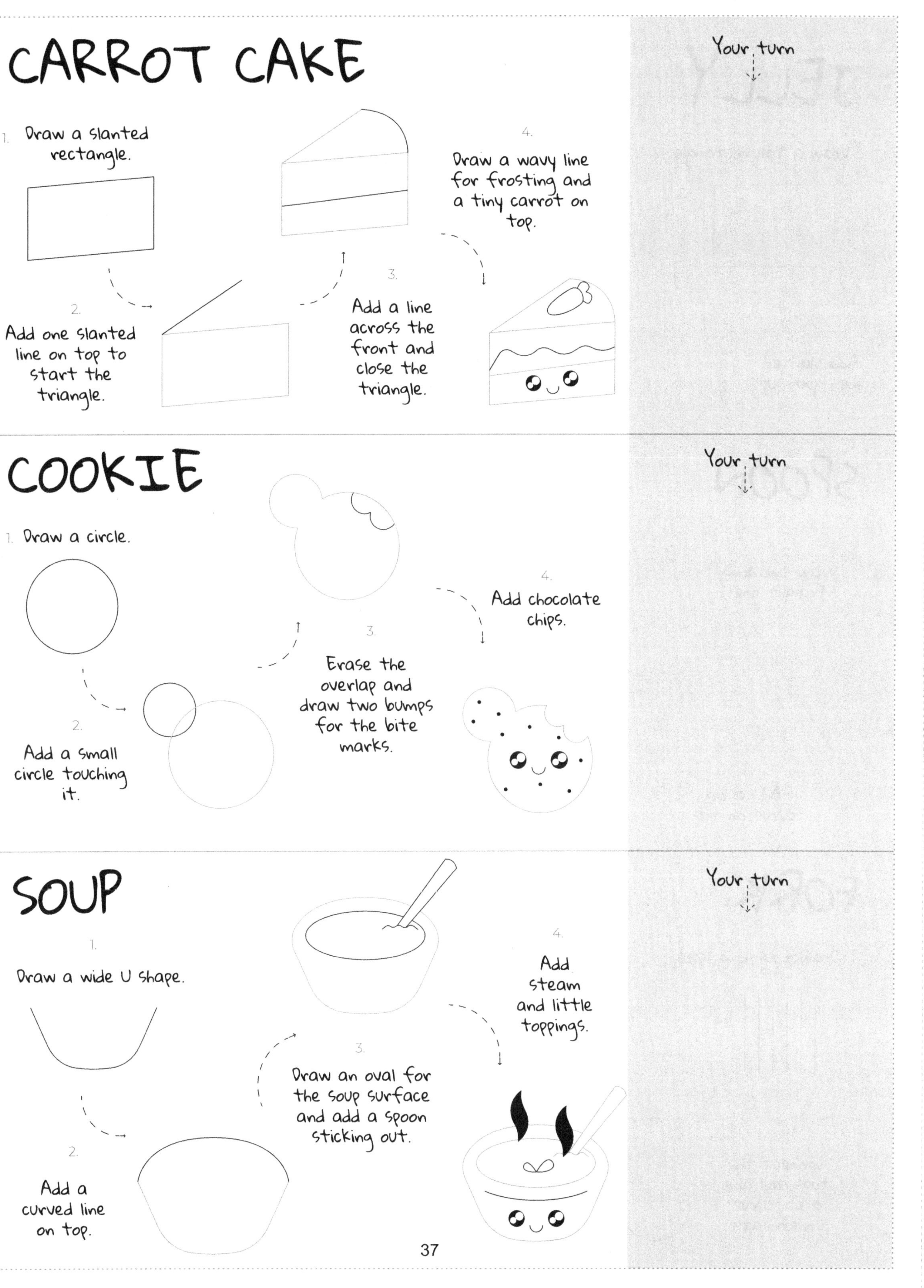

JELLY

1. Draw a tall rectangle.

2. Add slanted lines going up.

3. Add three round bumps on top and erase the rectangle line.

4. Draw wavy lines to show the jelly!

SPOON

1. Draw two long straight lines.

2. Add a big curve on top.

3. Close the top with a second curve.

4. Draw a curved line for the smile.

FORK

1. Draw four long lines.

2. Connect the tops and add a big curve underneath.

3. Draw two straight lines down.

4. Round the handle tip.

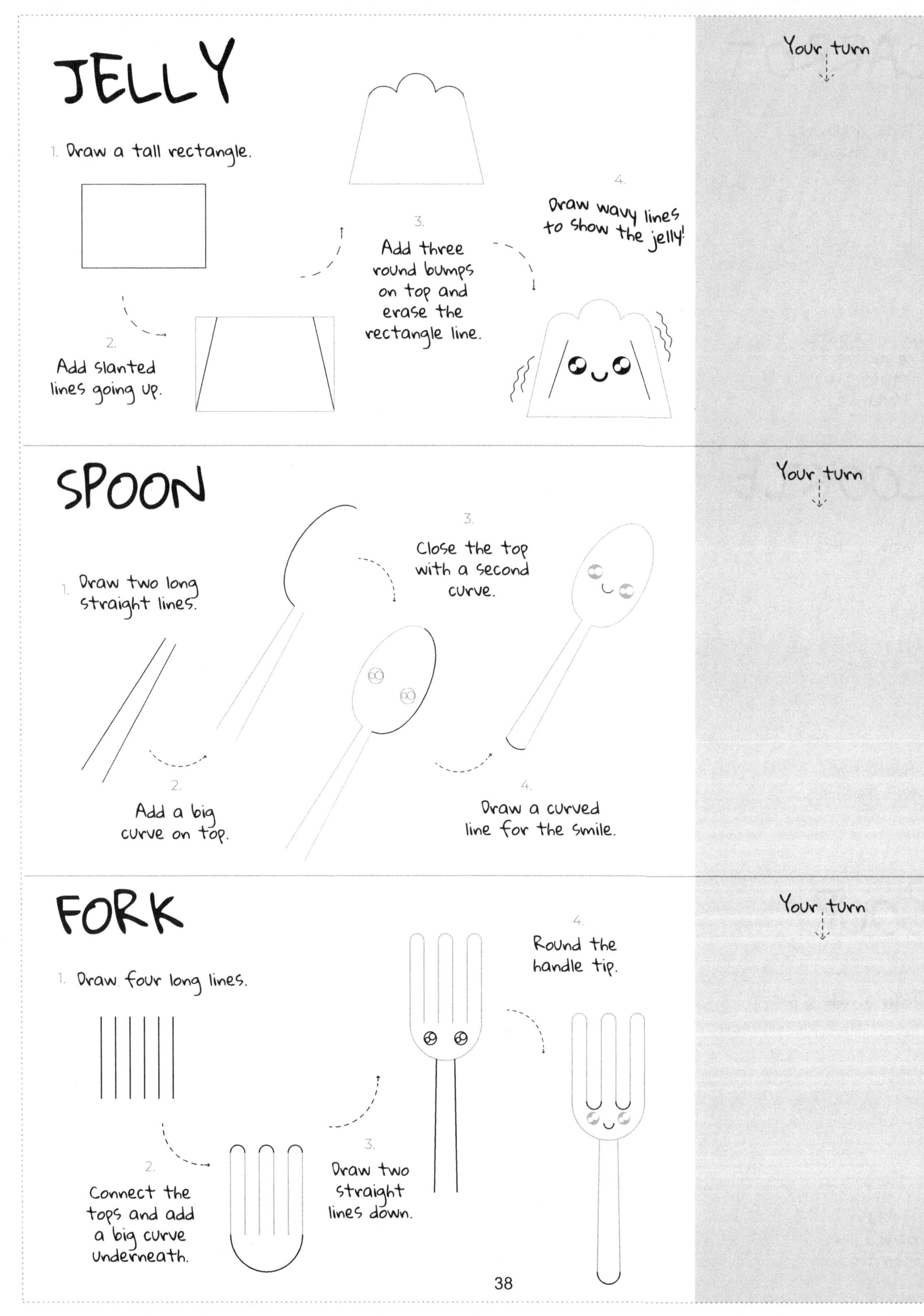

KNIFE

1. Draw a straight vertical line.

2. Add a curved top.

3. Add a thick handle on the left using straight lines.

4. Finish with a curved top.

TEAPOT

1. Draw a big arc.

2. Add a bumpy curve at the bottom.

3. Add a spout and a handle.

4. Draw a small lid on top.

FRYING PAN

1. Draw a wide oval.

2. Add a curved line below to shape the pan.

3. Draw another oval inside the pan. Add two straight lines going out for the handle.

4. Draw a small oval at the end of the handle.

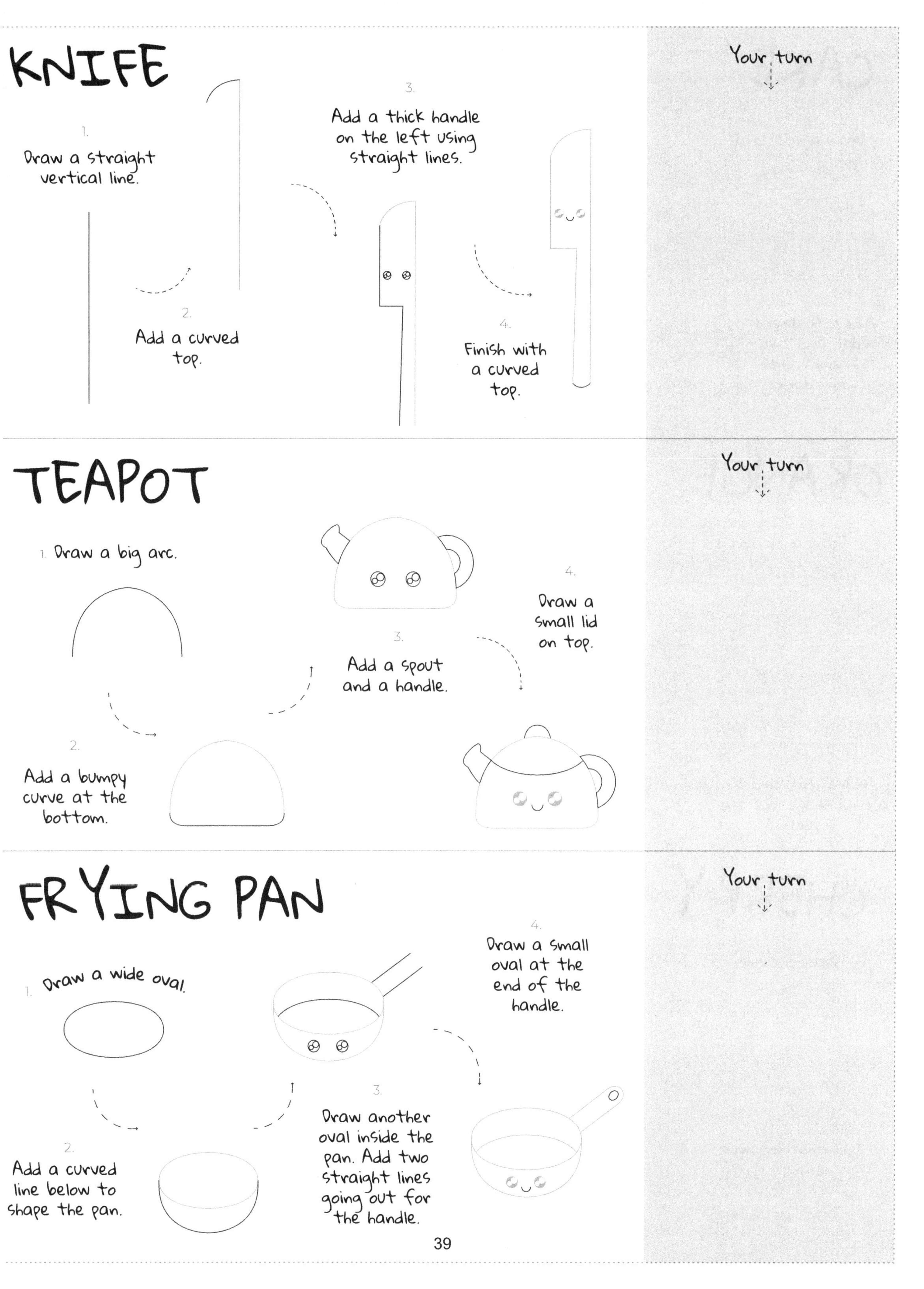

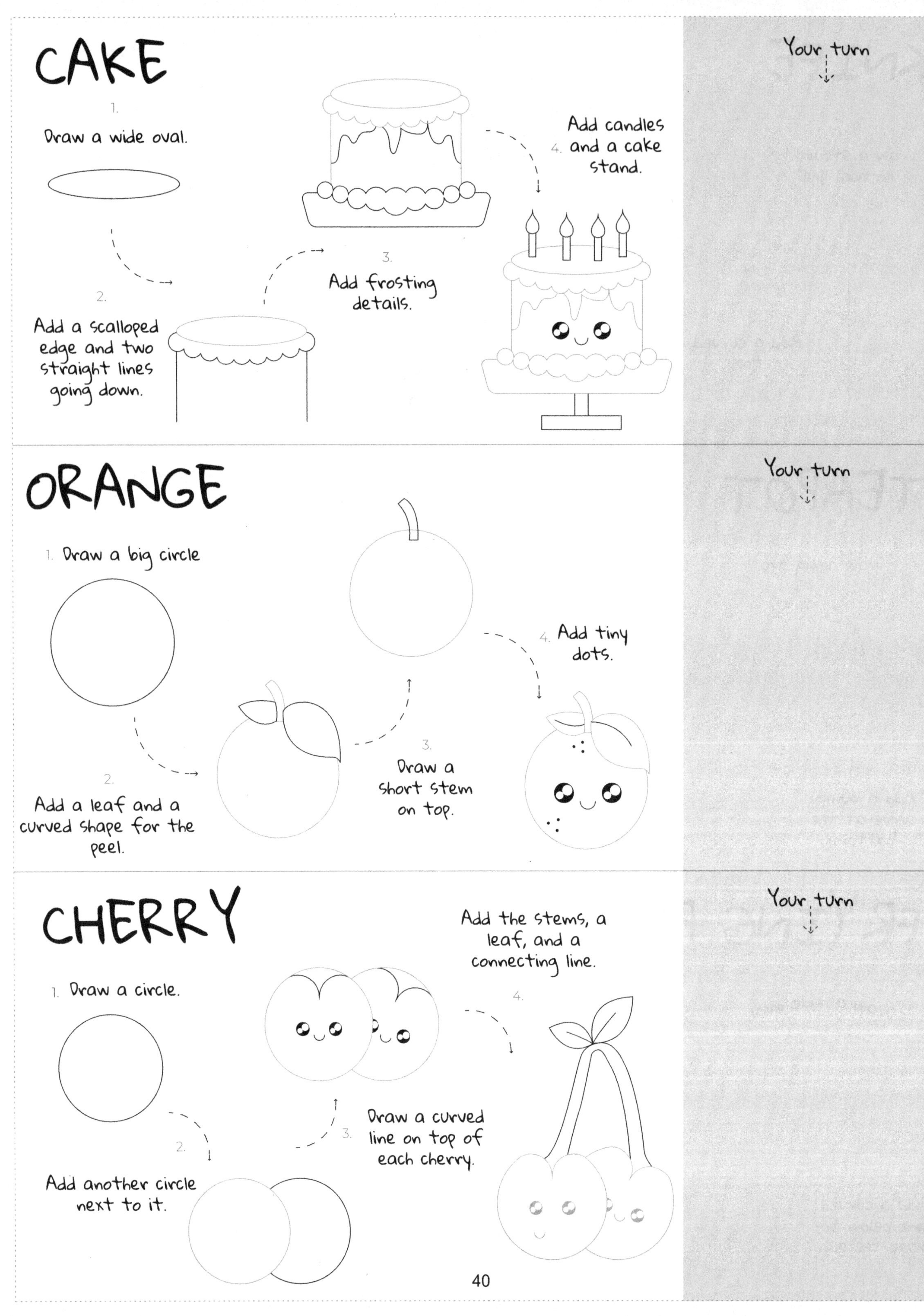

CAKE
1.
Draw a wide oval.
2.
Add a scalloped edge and two straight lines going down.
3.
Add frosting details.
4. Add candles and a cake stand.
Your turn

ORANGE
1. Draw a big circle
2. Add a leaf and a curved shape for the peel.
3. Draw a short stem on top.
4. Add tiny dots.
Your turn

CHERRY
1. Draw a circle.
2. Add another circle next to it.
3. Draw a curved line on top of each cherry.
4. Add the stems, a leaf, and a connecting line.
Your turn

KIWI

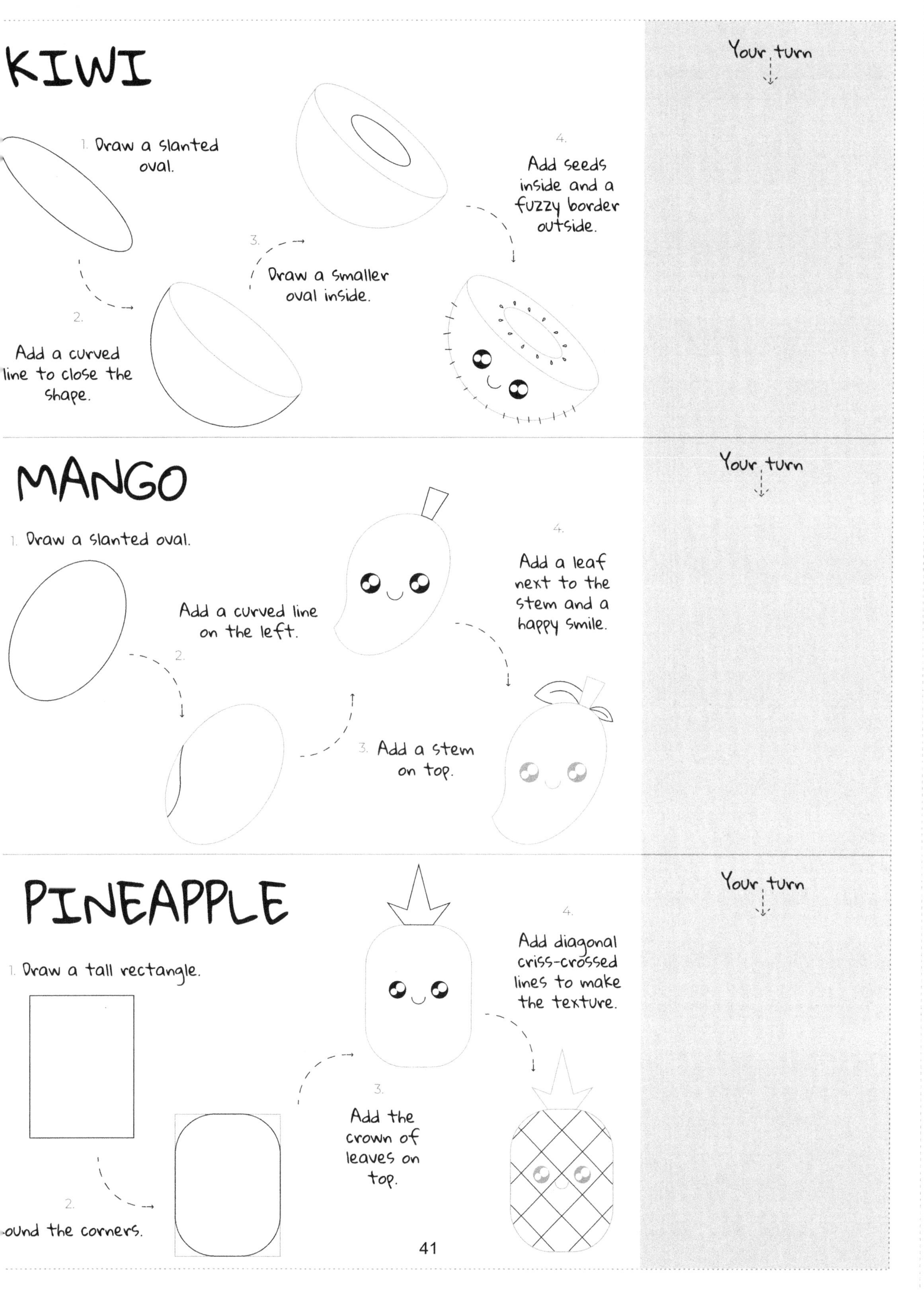

1. Draw a slanted oval.

2. Add a curved line to close the shape.

3. Draw a smaller oval inside.

4. Add seeds inside and a fuzzy border outside.

MANGO

1. Draw a slanted oval.

2. Add a curved line on the left.

3. Add a stem on top.

4. Add a leaf next to the stem and a happy smile.

PINEAPPLE

1. Draw a tall rectangle.

2. ...ound the corners.

3. Add the crown of leaves on top.

4. Add diagonal criss-crossed lines to make the texture.

41

LEVEL 2:

TOYS AND COOL STUFF

TEDDY BEAR

Start with big ovals for the head and body. Both arms, legs, and ears are the same on each side, just flip them like a mirror!

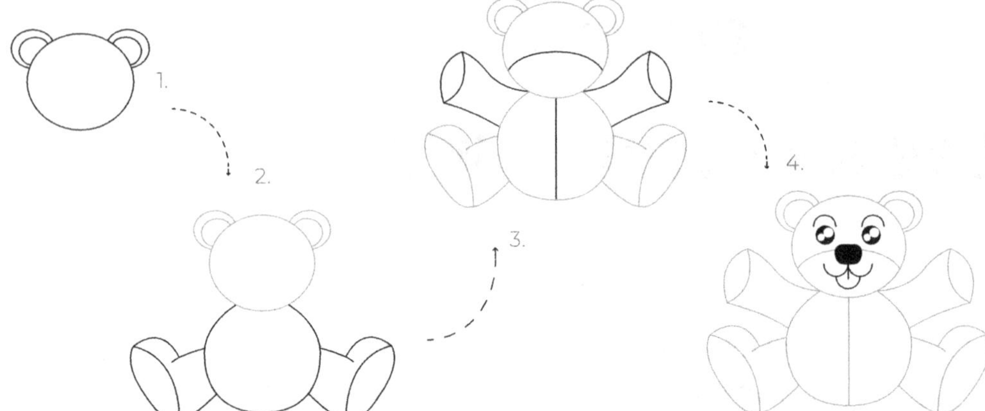

CAMPING TENT

Start with two triangles for the tent's sides. Then add the front flap, stakes, and cute details!
Tip: Keep both sides even so the tent looks balanced.

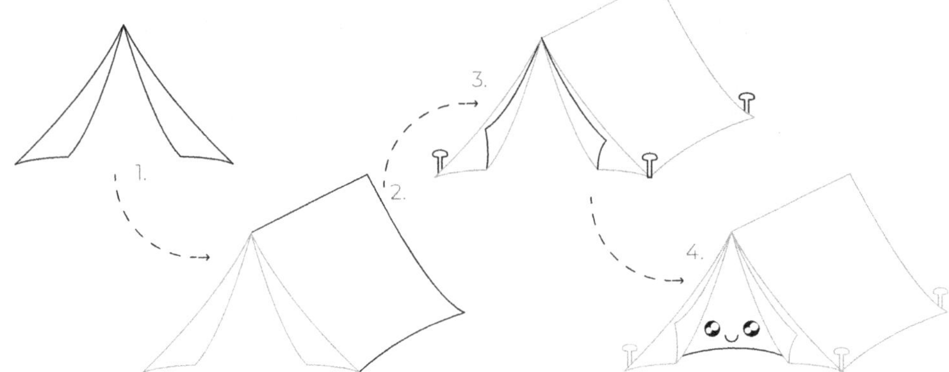

MAGIC CLOCK

Start with a big circle and curly shapes on top. Then add the tall base and clock details.
Tip: Make the top fancy so it looks truly magical!

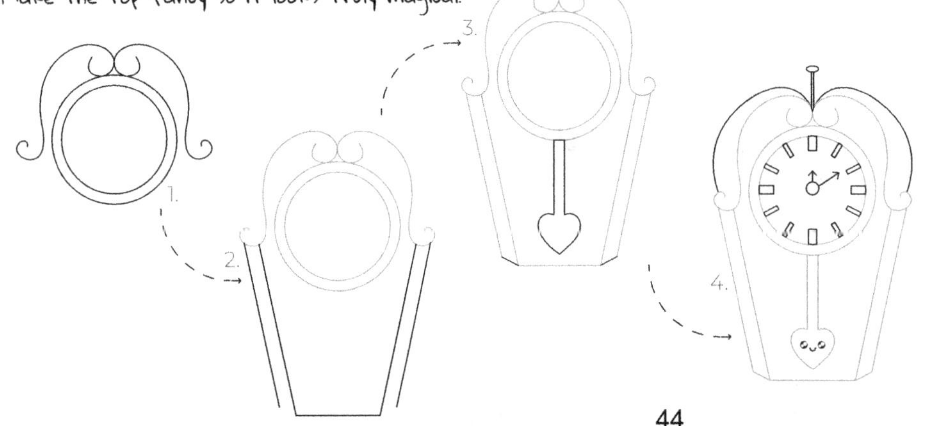

SPACESHIP

Begin with a tall oval—then add wings and fire!

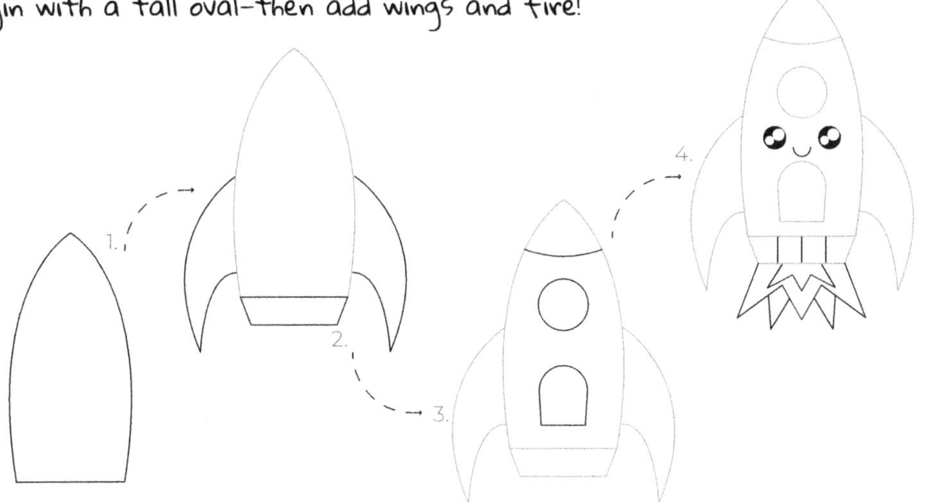

TOY AIRPLANE

Start with the main body of the plane. Then add the tail, wings, and fun details.
Tip: Keep the shapes smooth so it looks ready to fly!

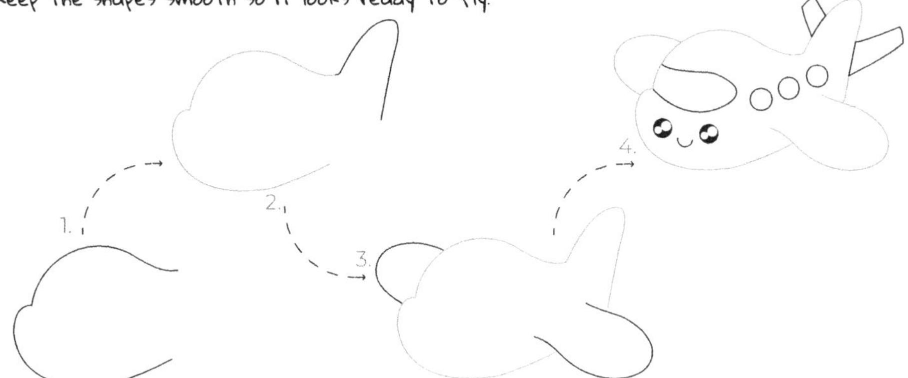

MR. POTATO

Start with the egg-shaped body and head. Then add arms, a face, and fun accessories.

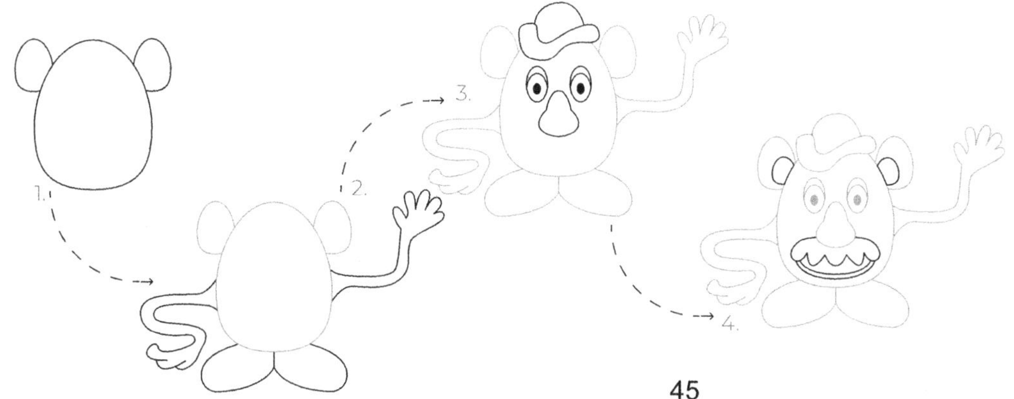

SPOOKY CAT

Start with an upside-down "U" for the spooky ground and add a gravestone at the bottom. Then draw the cat on top with triangle ears and spooky extras.

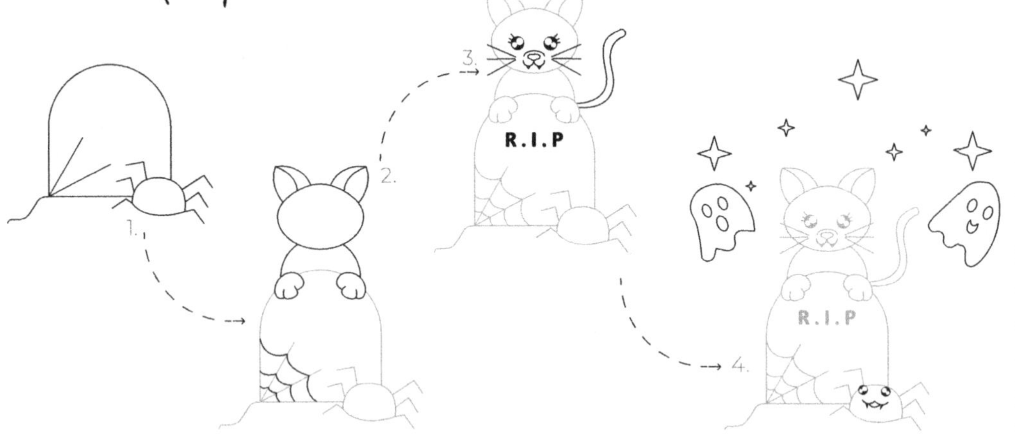

Your turn

HALLOWEEN PUMPKIN

Begin with a big oval for the pumpkin's body. Add a short stem on top, then draw curved lines to make it round and bumpy.

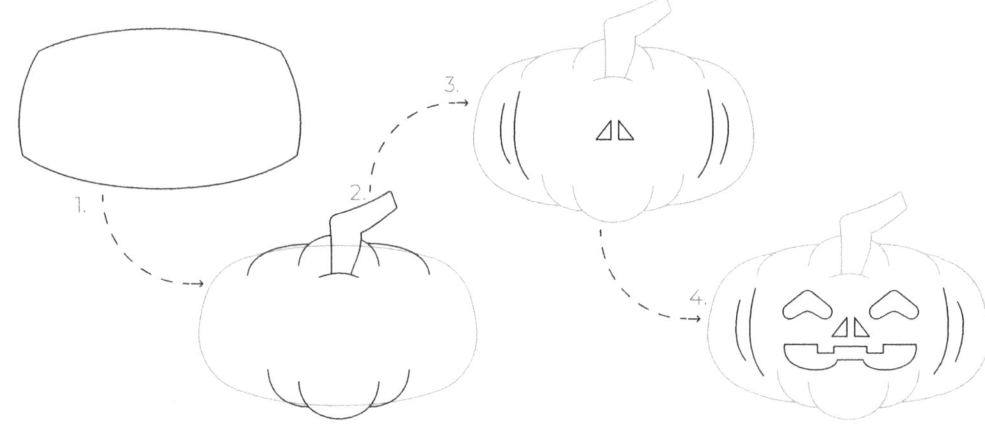

Your turn

SNOWMAN

Start with two circles stacked on top of each other!

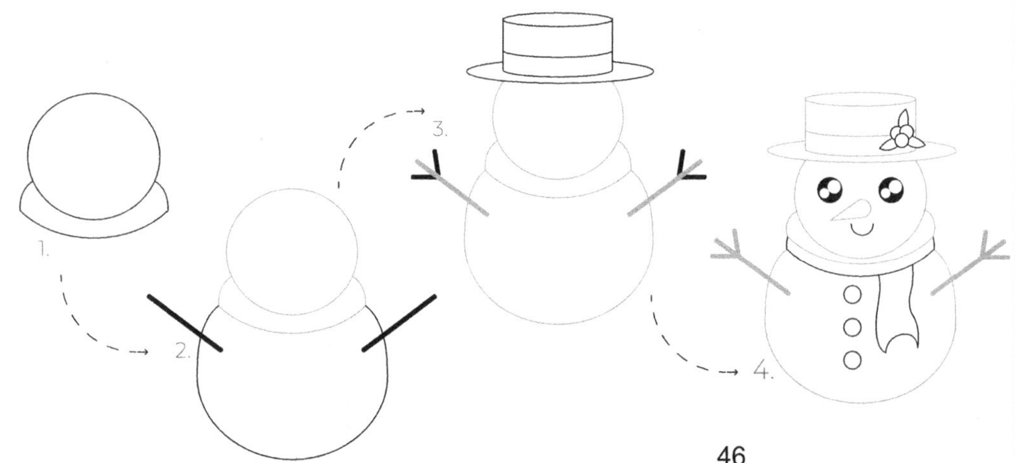

Your turn

RAINBOW

Start with a curve and two fluffy clouds!

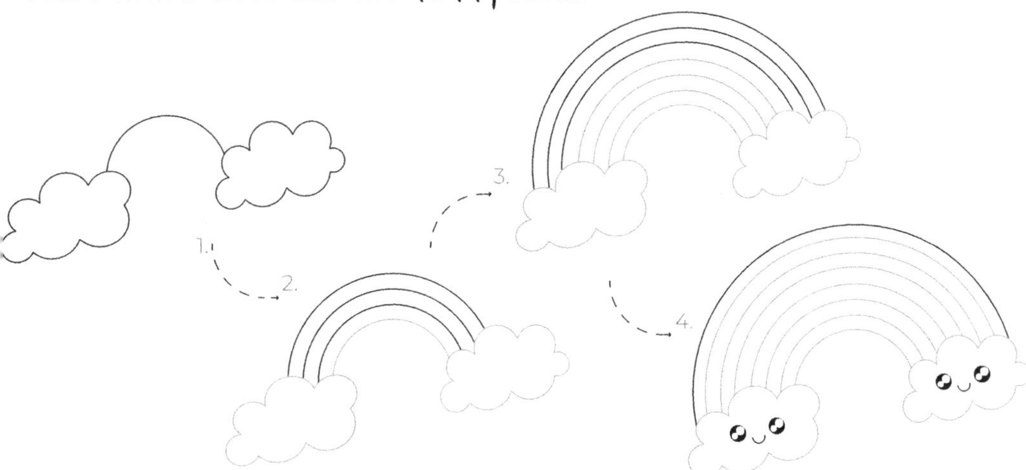

POTION BOTTLE

Begin with a round base and a tall neck!

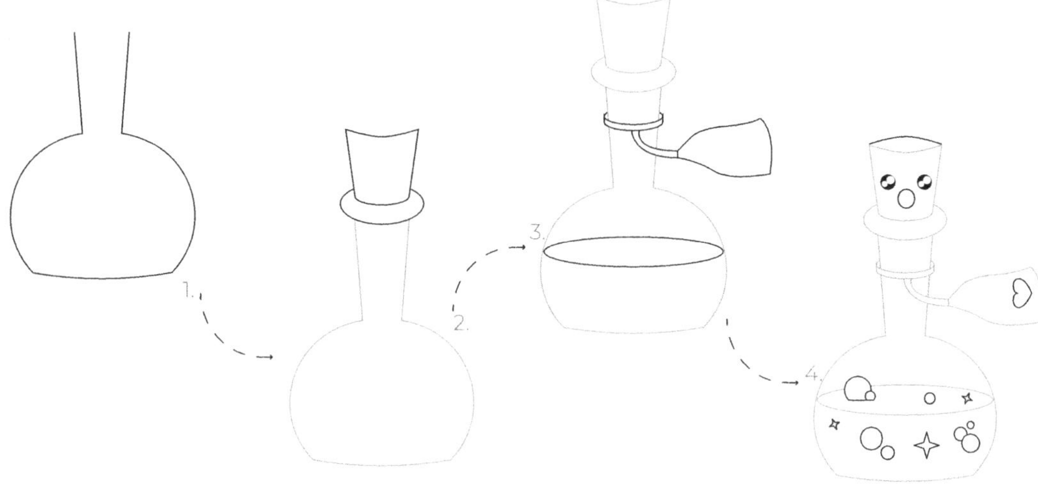

POKEBALL

Draw a big circle, then add a circle in the middle!

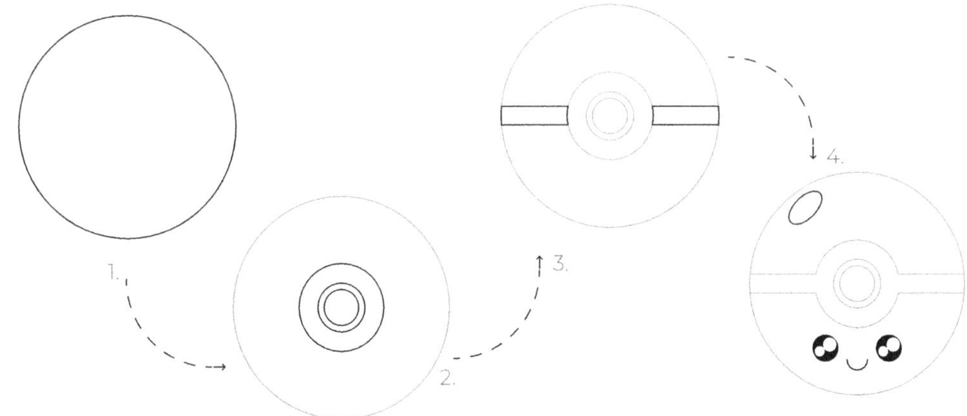

GUITAR

Start with the long neck and tuning head. Then add the round body, strings, and sound hole.
Tip: The frets and straight little strings look cool!

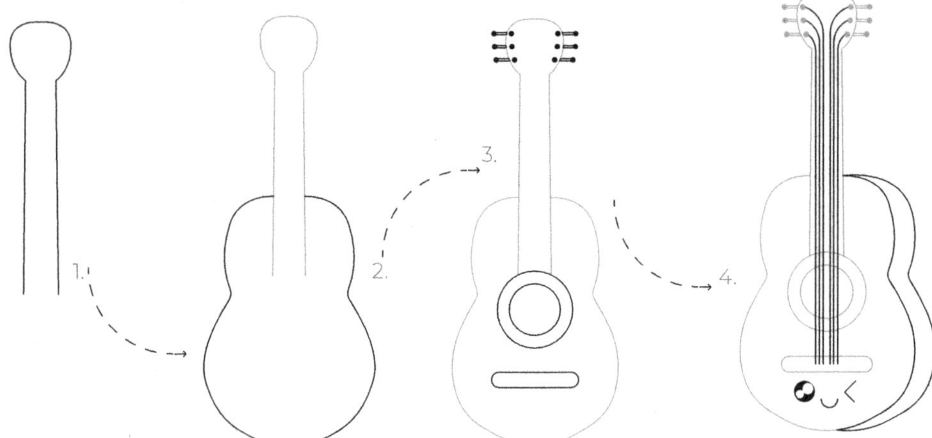

MERMAID

Start with the head, arms, and hands. Then add the body, tail, and flowing hair.

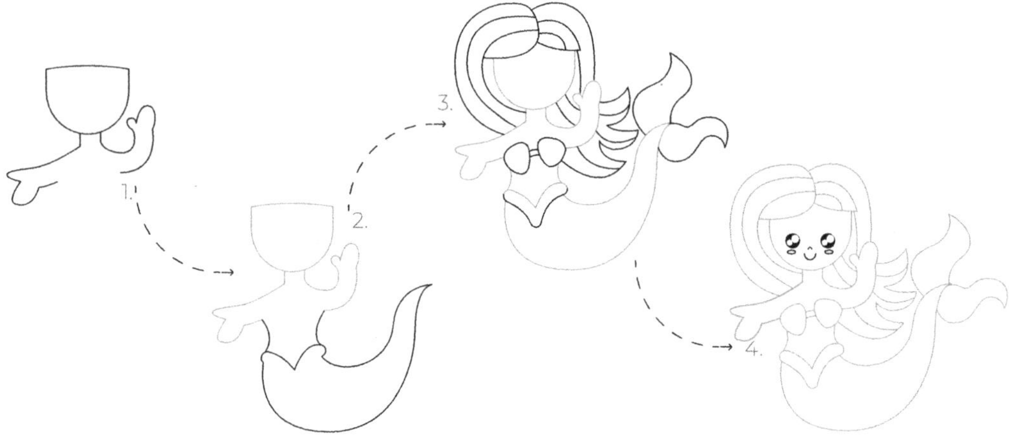

DINOSAUR

Start with the head and long curved neck. Next, draw the arched back and tail.
Tip: Make the neck extra tall for a gentle giant look!

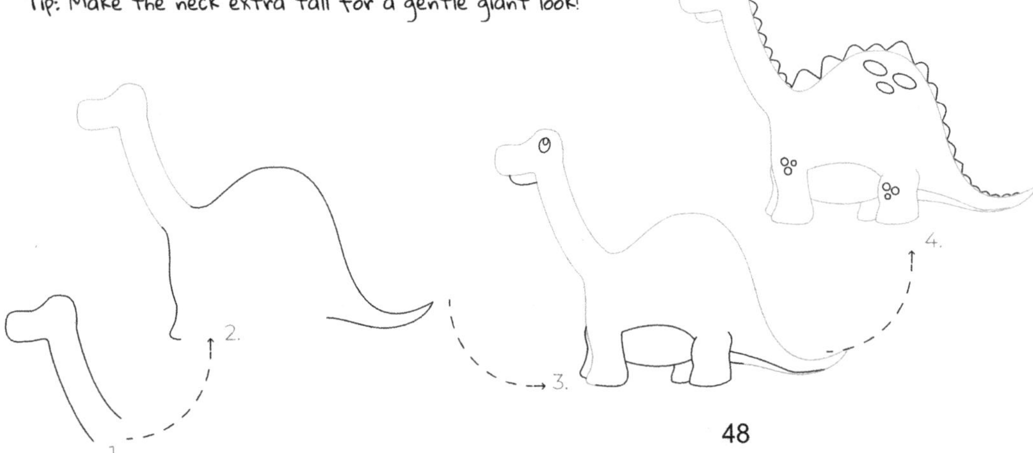

EASTER EGG

Start with a big egg shape and decorate it.

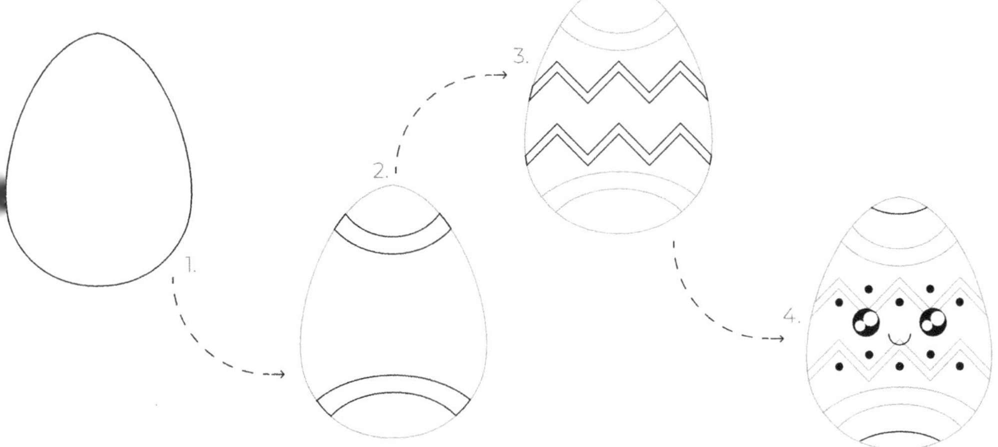

SUPERHERO

Start with the head and arms. Then add the flying cape and upper body.
Tip: Keep the arms strong and flying for a powerful pose!

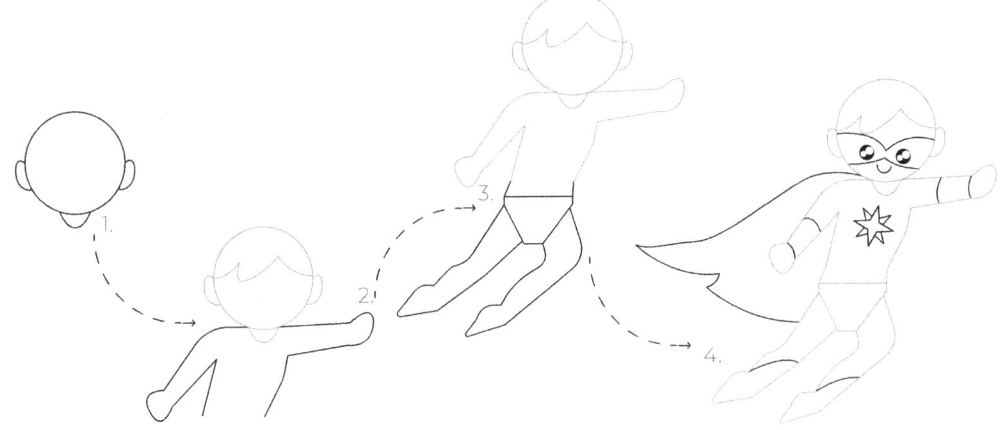

LEGO

Start with a square for the head. Then build the body, arms, and legs using rectangles.

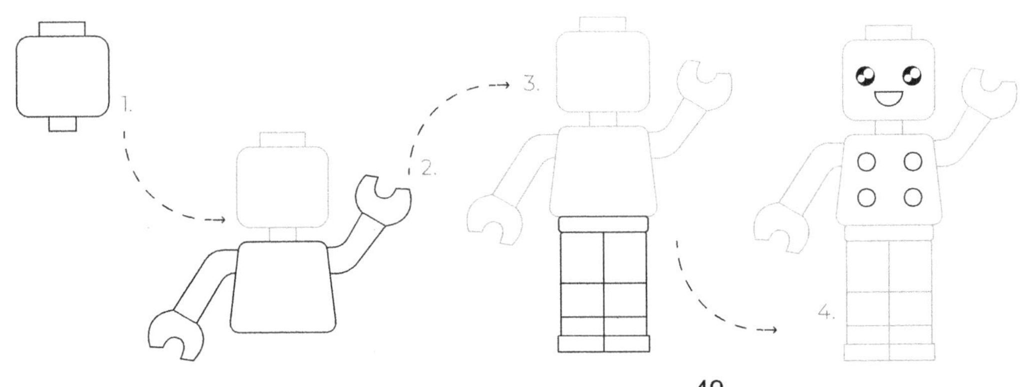

HOCKEY STICK

Start with a long, straight line and bend it at the bottom like an "L".
Then add the blade, tape, and the hockey puck.

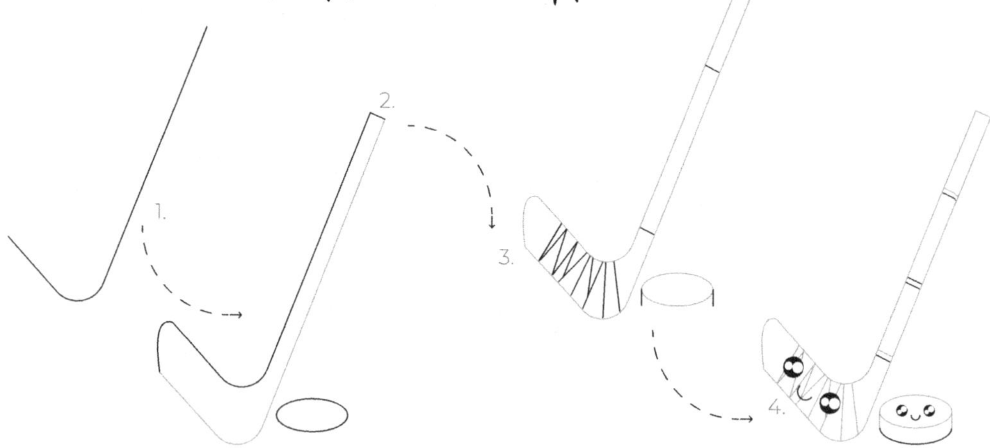

SKATEBOARD

Begin with a long curved shape for the board.

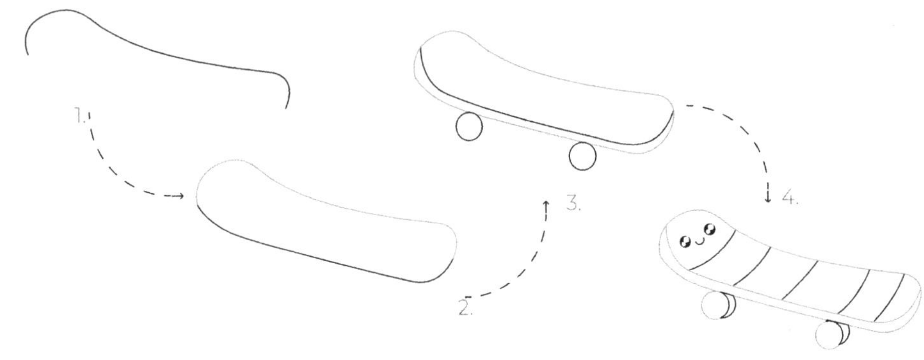

SOCCER BALL

Draw a big circle and add a shape in the middle like a soccer ball patch.
Then shade the ball with lines and more patches around it.

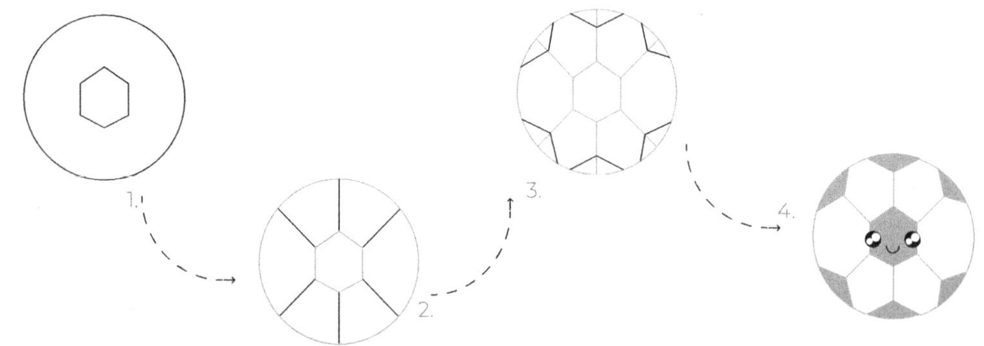

SANTA CLAUS

Start with the head, hat, and the tip of the beard. Then add the body, boots, and belt.
Tip: The big round belly of Santa looks extra jolly!

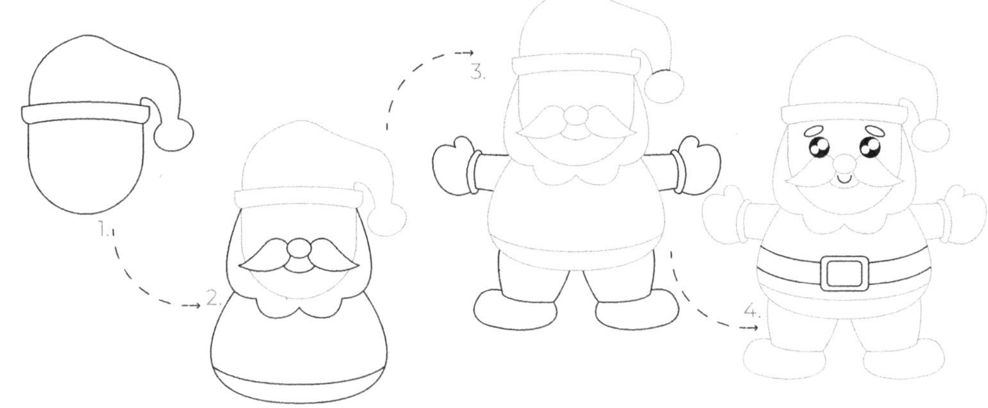

BICYCLE

Begin with three circles. Two for the wheels, one for the gears. Then connect them with straight lines to build the frame.

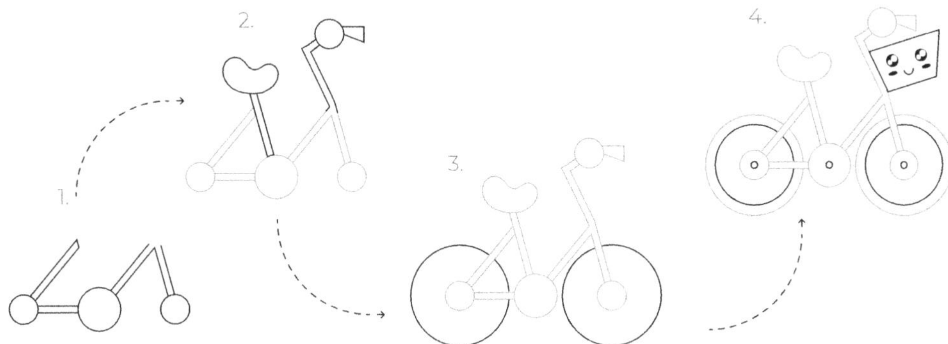

BASKETBALL HOOP

Start with a square for the backboard. Then add an oval for the hoop and a triangle for the net.

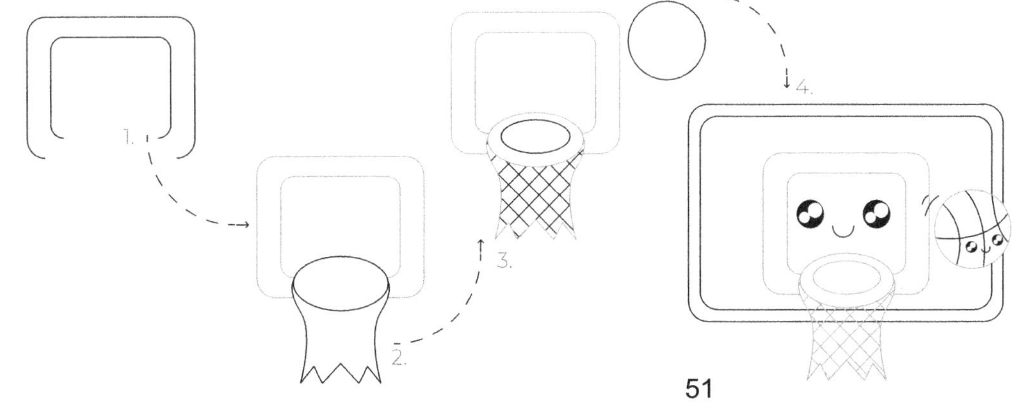

CHEERLEADER

Start with the head and two ponytails. Then add the arms, body, and skirt.
Tip: Make the pom-poms big and fluffy for extra cheer!

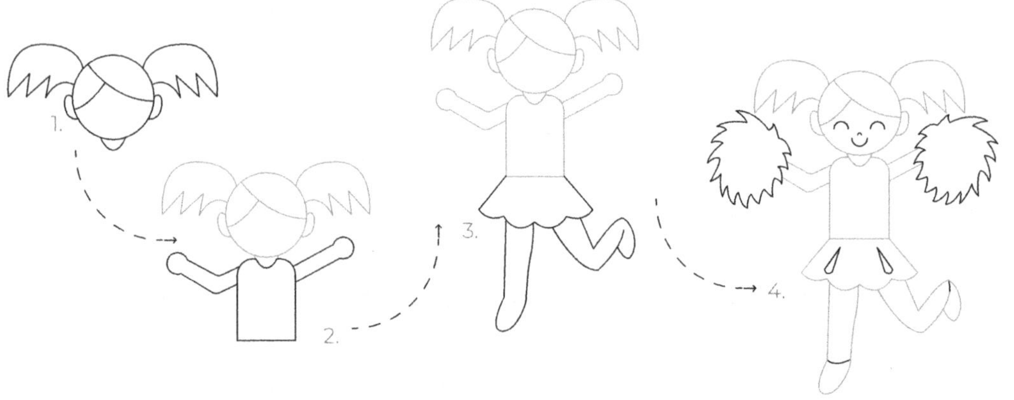

BASEBALL GLOVE

Start with a large mitten shape. Then curve the fingers and add the small stitches.
Tip: Keep the pocket deep so it can catch the ball!

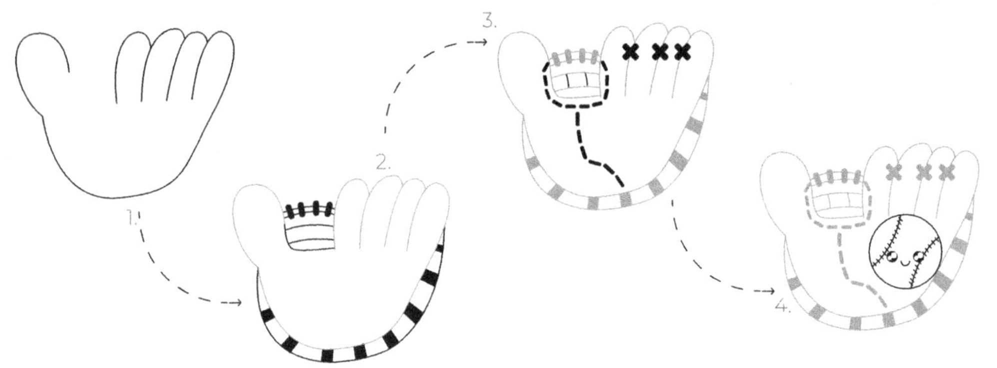

ROLLER SKATE

Start with a curved boot shape. Then add the laces and four small circles for wheels.
Tip: Add fun colors to your design to make it unique!

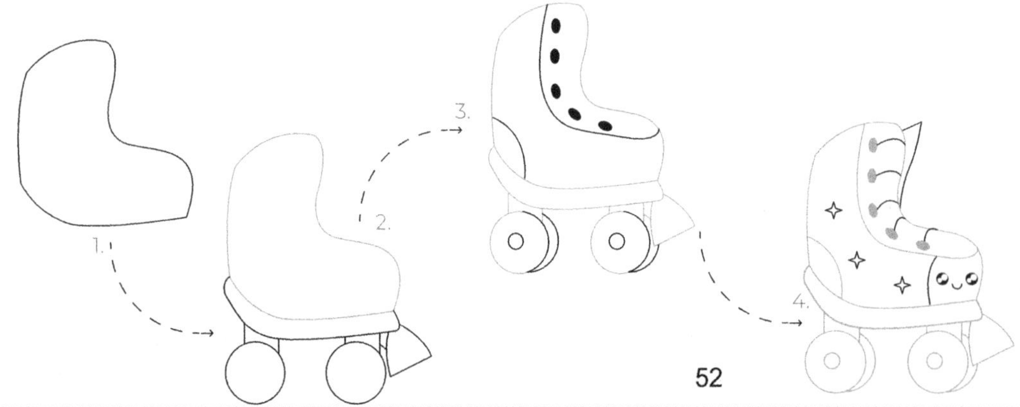

LIPSTICK

Start with a tall rectangle for the base. Stack more rectangles on top, then add the lipstick tip.
Tip: Keep the tip slanted so it looks ready to use!

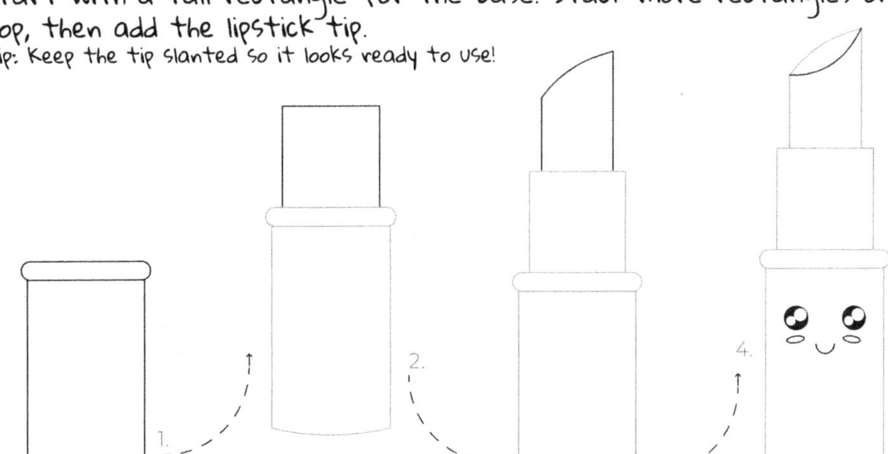

COWBOY

Begin with the hat and head, then build the body piece by piece!

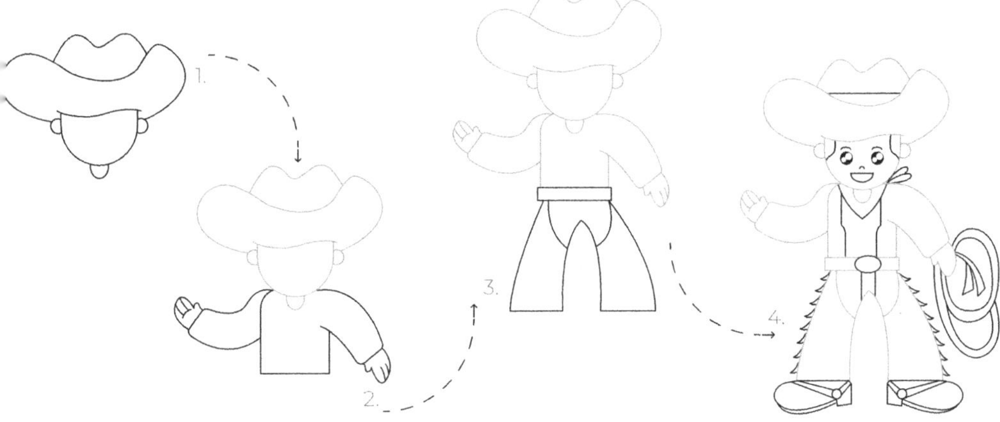

GHOST

Start with a round head, then draw flowing curves for the wavy body.

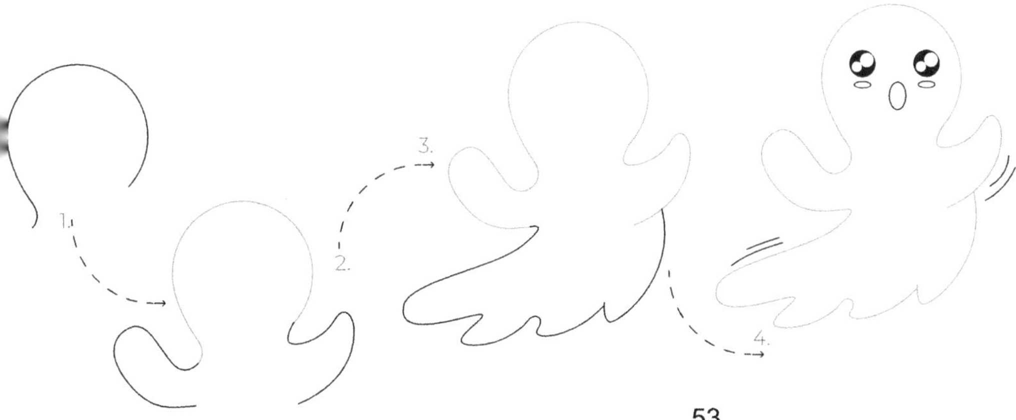

GIFT

Stack two rectangles and add a bow on top!

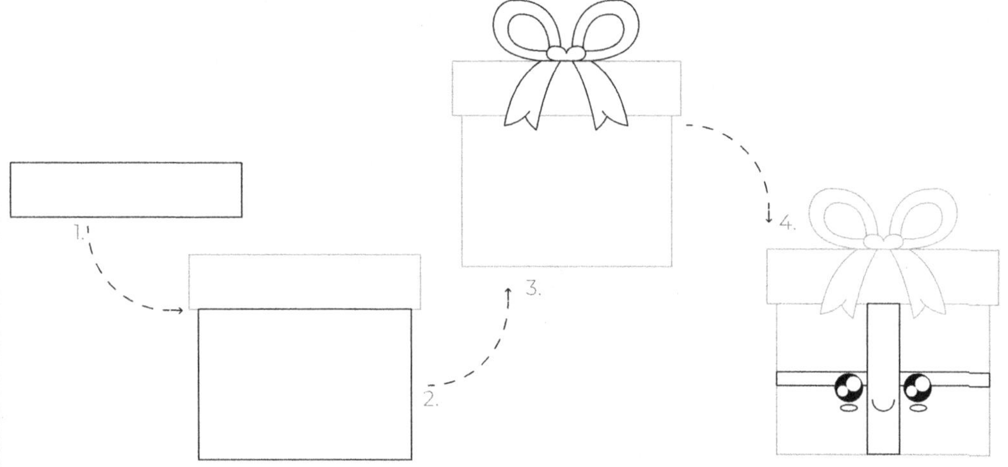

MOON

Begin with a curved C-shape, then add clouds.

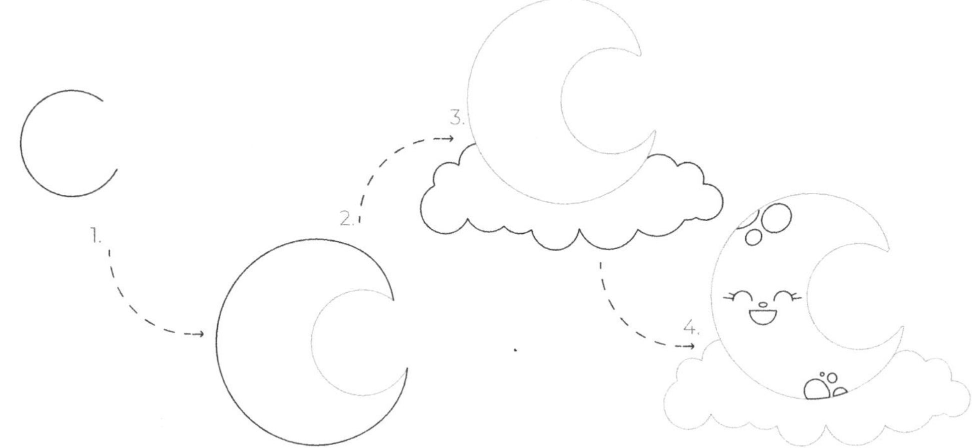

TREE

Start with the trunk and two branches at the top. Add leafy shapes above the branches.

Tip: Make the leaves fluffy for a full and happy tree!

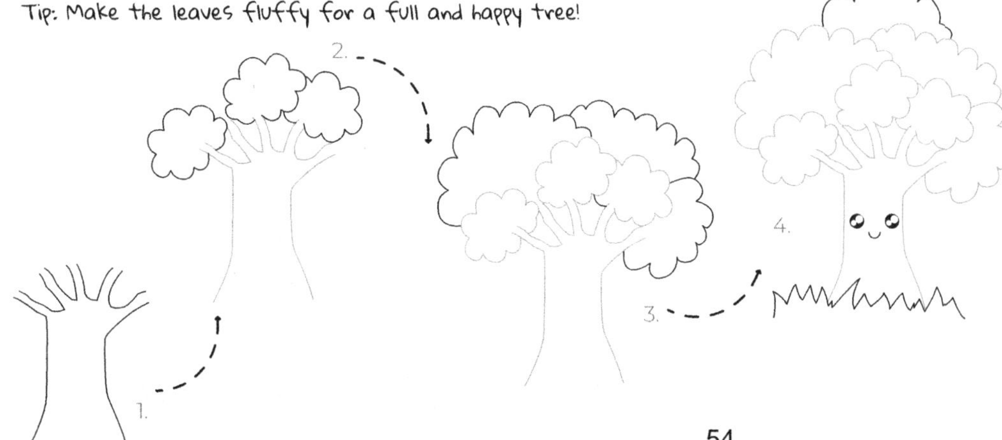

CHRISTMAS STOCKING

Draw a tall rectangle tilted sideways, then round the bottom into a sock shape.

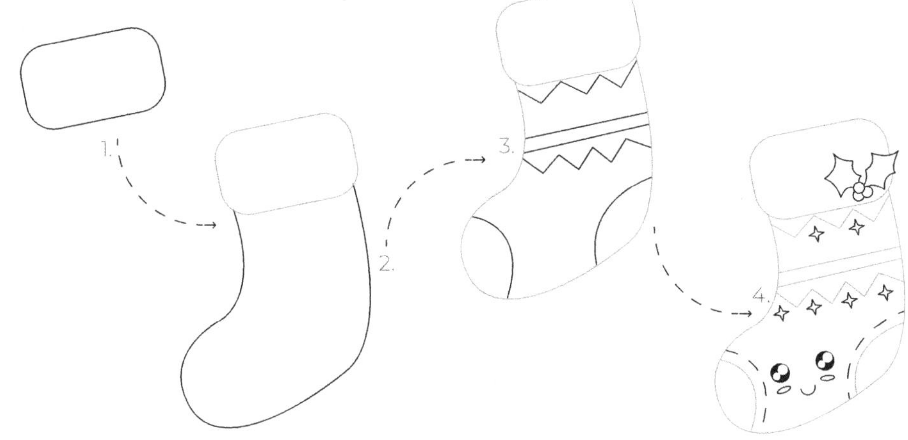

BALL PIT

Start with a wide shape like a box with rounded sides. Add the top edge, then draw the little round balls.
Tip: Fill it with lots of balls for extra fun!

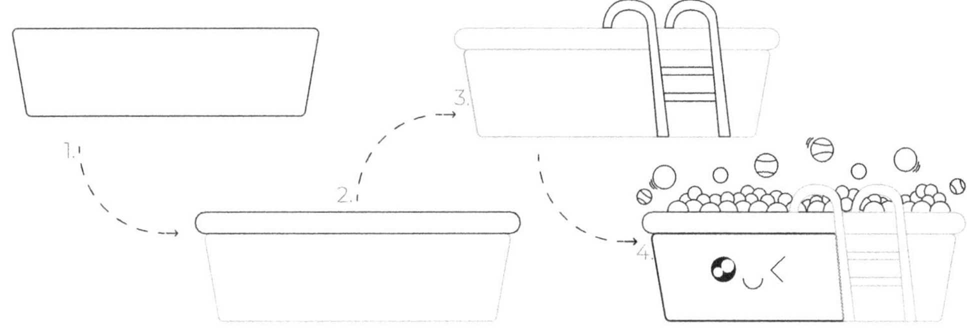

BRUSH

Begin with a skinny vertical tube, then draw the bristles as a soft triangle.

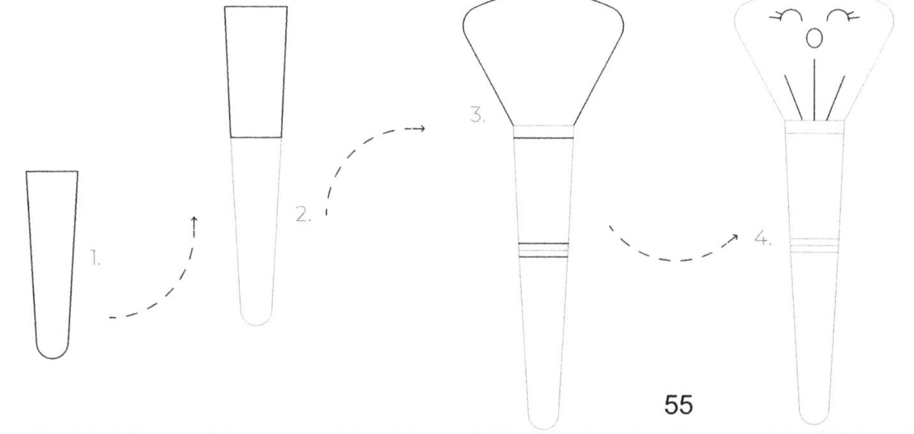

SURFBOARD

Draw a tall leaf shape with a pointed top and curved sides then add some fins.

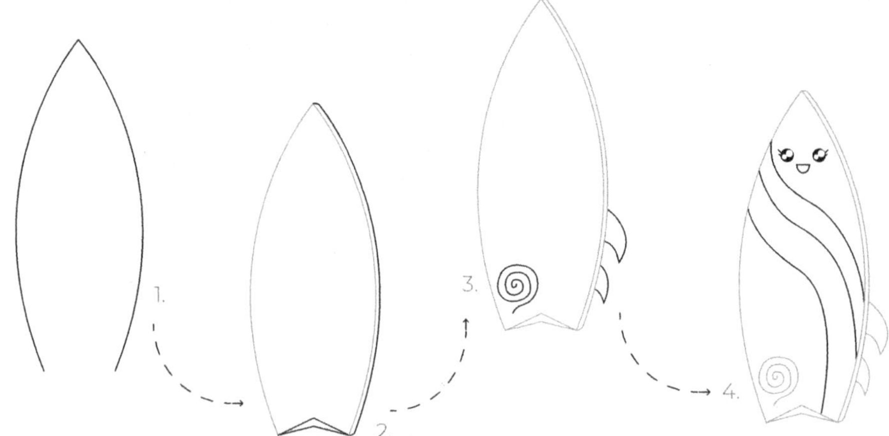

VIDEOGAME CONSOLE

Start with a wide rectangle, then round the corners and add a screen.

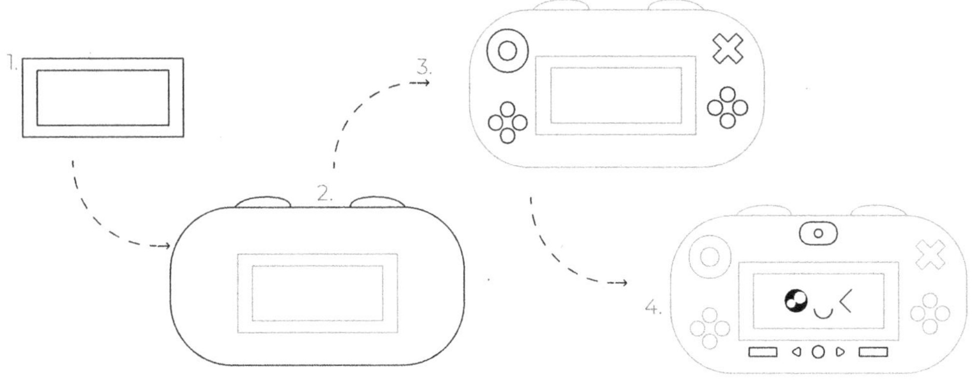

SUNGLASSES

Start with two connected ovals for the lenses. Then add the frame, arms, and fun details.

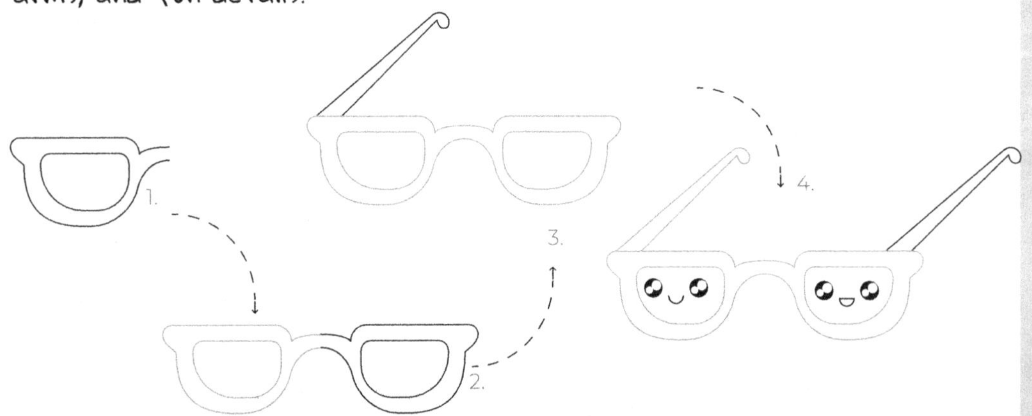

TOY ROBOT

Begin with a square head and round body parts.

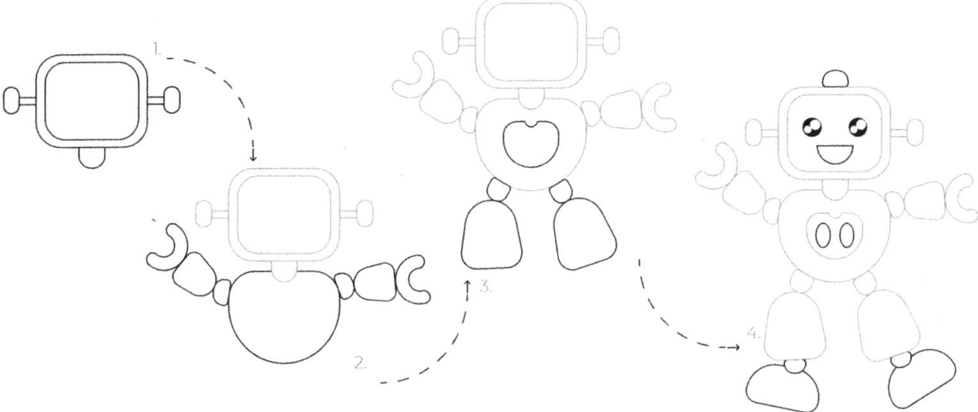

Yo-Yo

Start with two big circles side by side, then draw the string looping out.

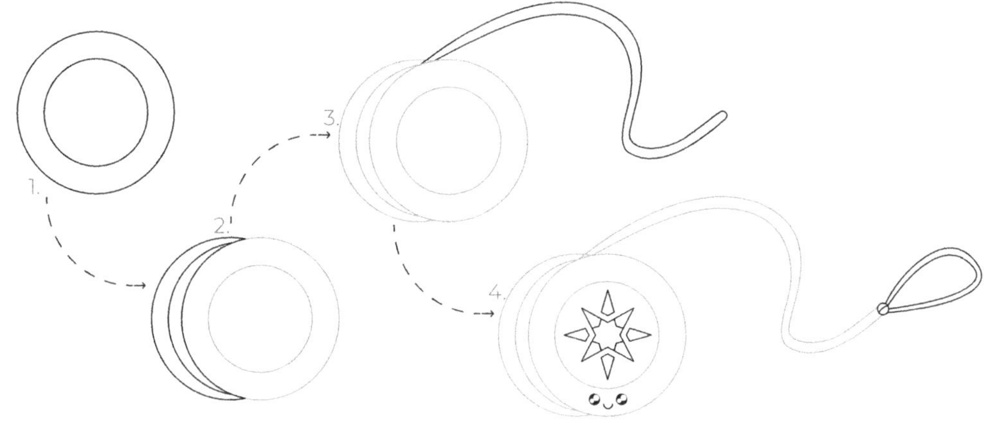

KITE

Draw a diamond shape tilted to the side, then add a tail.

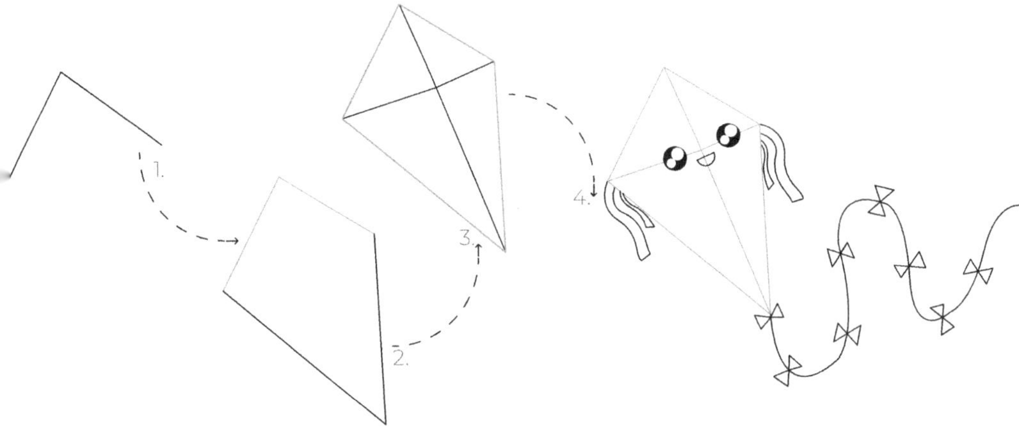

ROCKING HORSE

Start by drawing the horse's head and body. Add the base for balance.
Tip: Make the pole longer to rock backward and forward.

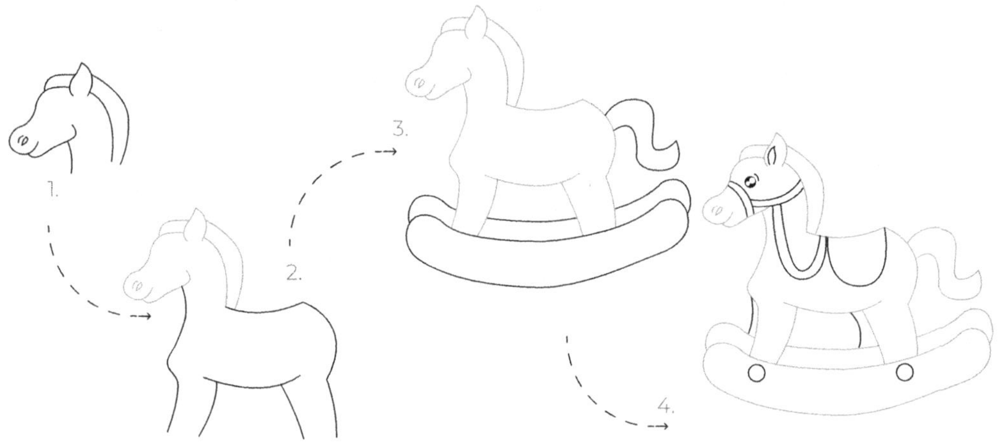

TRAMPOLINE

Draw a wide oval for the bouncy top. Add short legs and a second oval underneath.

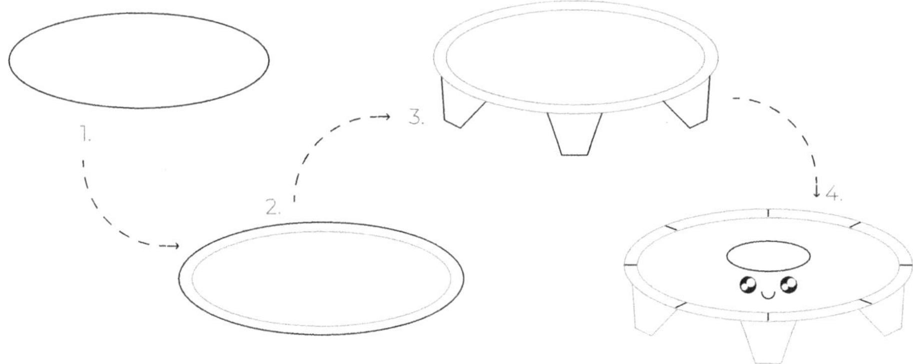

TOY DRUM

Start with a small oval and draw two straight lines down.
Finish the bottom with a curved line and add decorations.

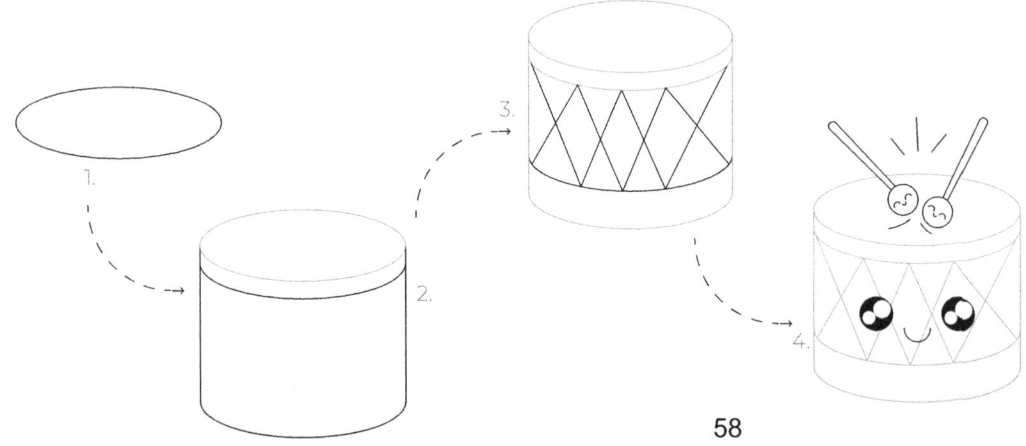

FRISBEE

Draw a big flat oval. Add one smaller oval inside it to show the top shape.

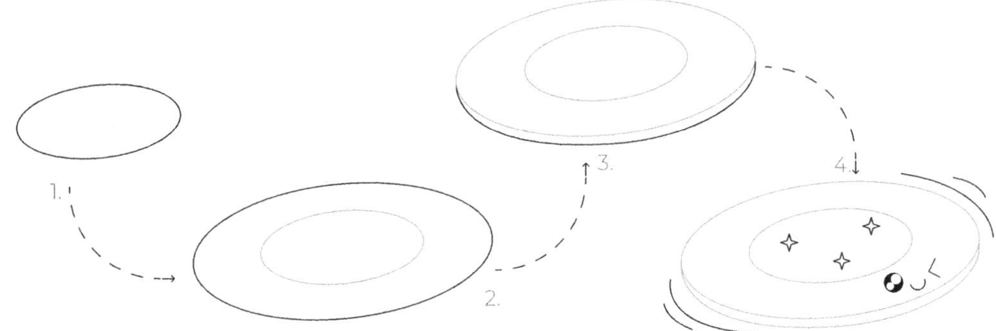

DARTBOARD

Start with a small circle in the center. Draw bigger circles around it to build the dartboard.

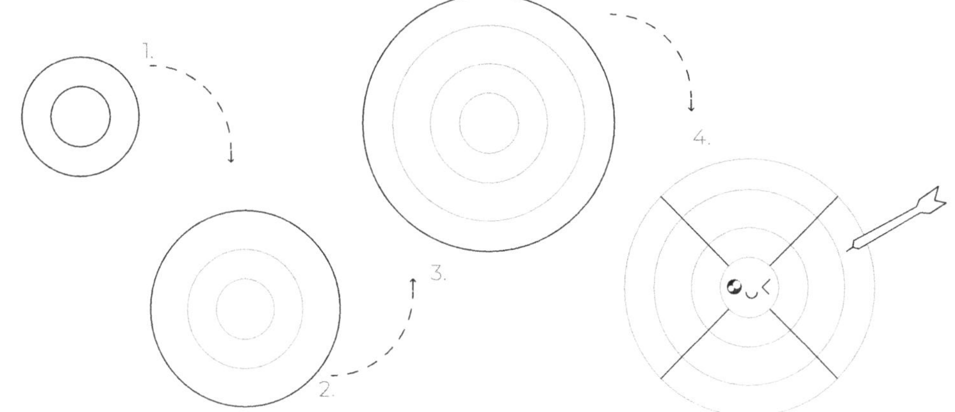

PLASTIC SWORD

Draw a long, straight triangle pointing up. Add a handle below with a circle and two flat lines.

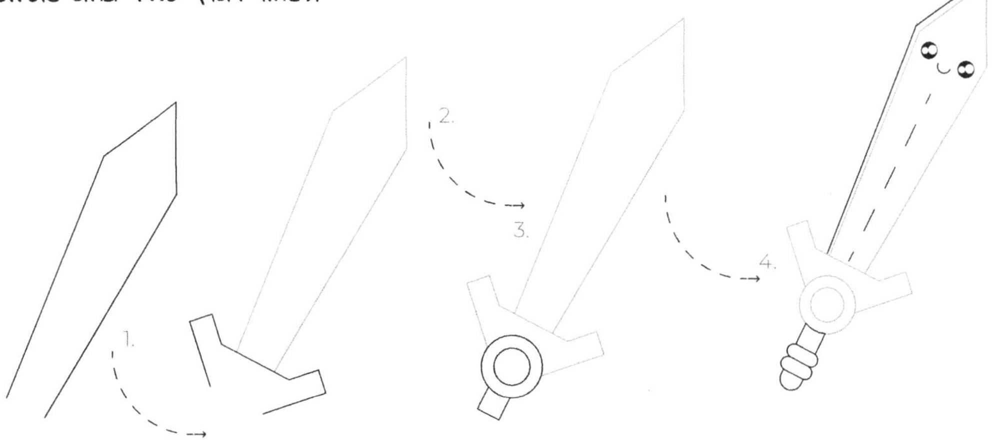

AMBULANCE

Start with a tall rectangle for the main body.
Add a square front and round the top corner for the cab.

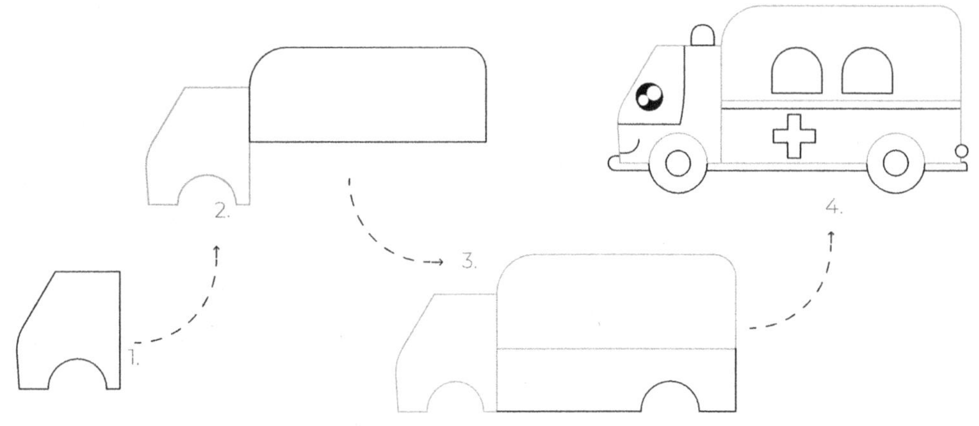

TRACTOR

Draw a small rectangle with a curved top for the cab. Then add a longer
rectangle for the body and a curved line at the back for the wheel arch.

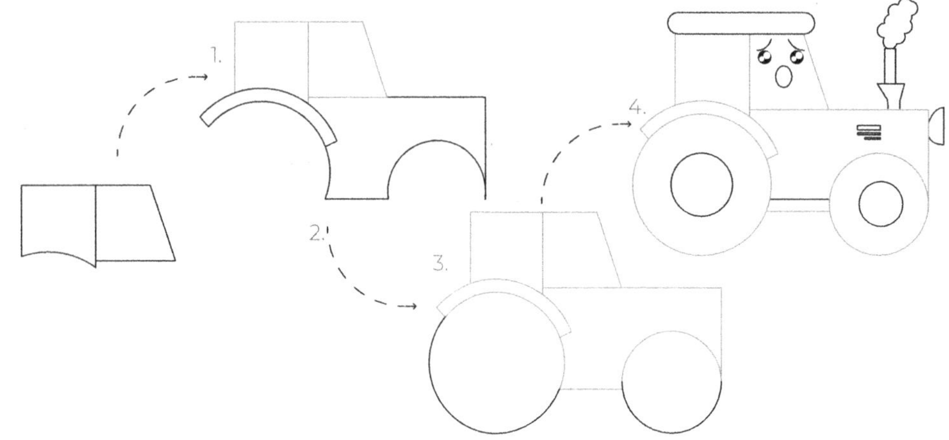

ICE CREAM TRUCK

Start with a big cab and a wide truck shape. Then add the ice cream
scoop and decorations.
Tip: Keep the base simple so the decorations stand out!

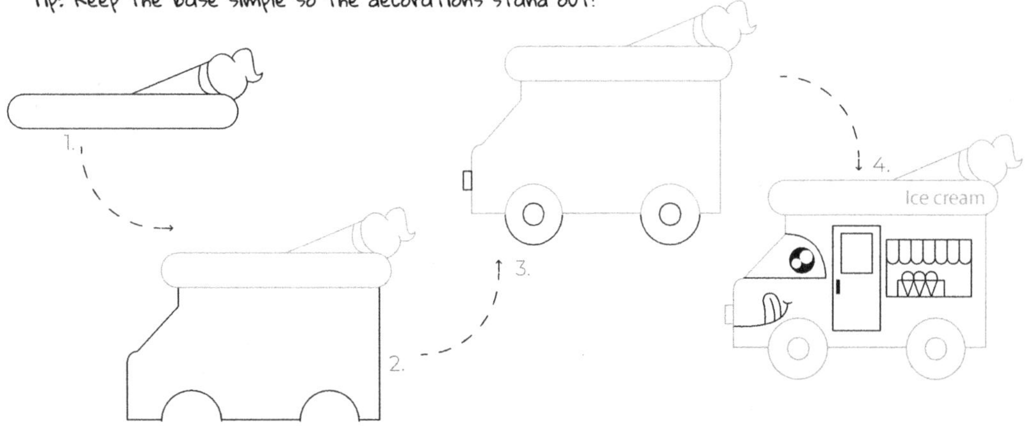

HELICOPTER

Start with a long oval for the body. Add two long ovals on top for the blades, then draw the tail.

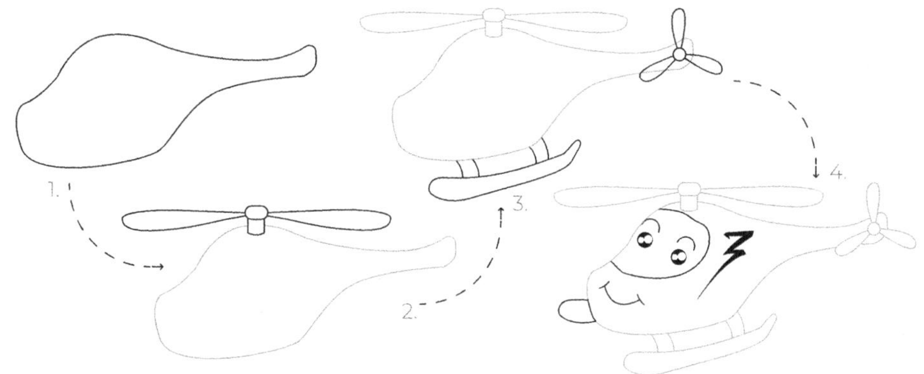

CRANE

Draw a tall cab shape and add wheels at the bottom. Then make a long arm with a round circle at the top, and finish with a hook.

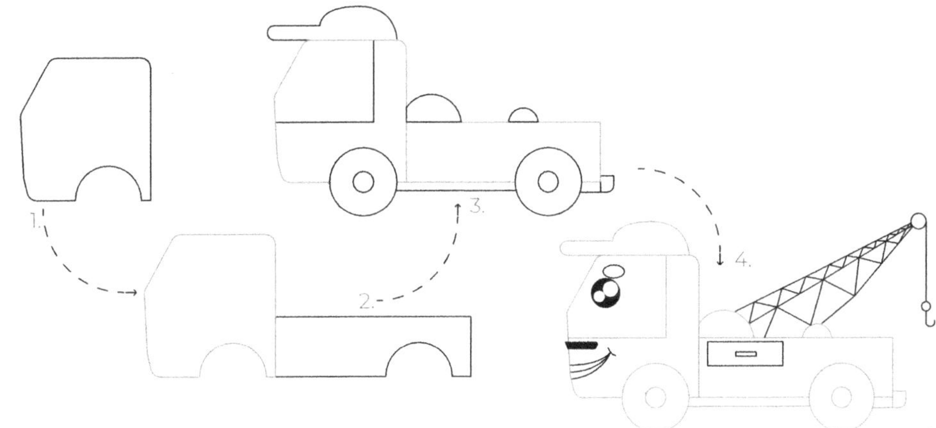

LOTUS FLOWER

Draw a rounded shape for the middle petal. Then add two more on the sides, making them tall and pointy. Finish with more petals behind.

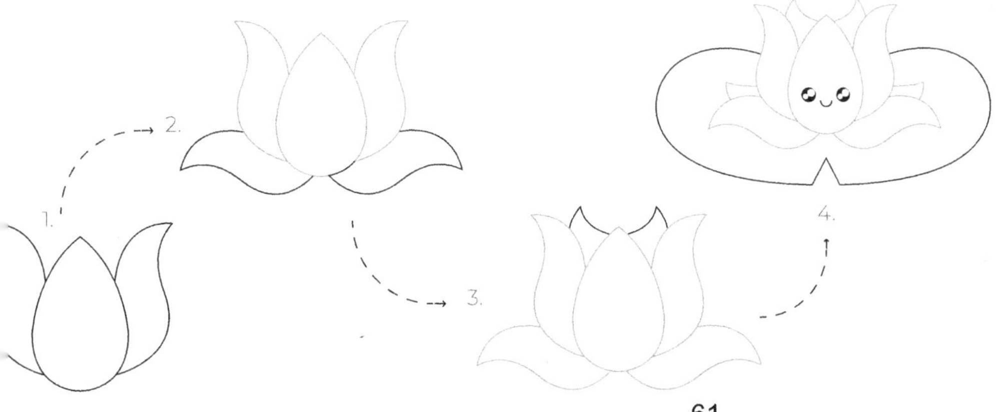

ROLLER COASTER

Start by drawing a simple cart shape with a curved front. To make the curve big enough to turn, widen the track below.

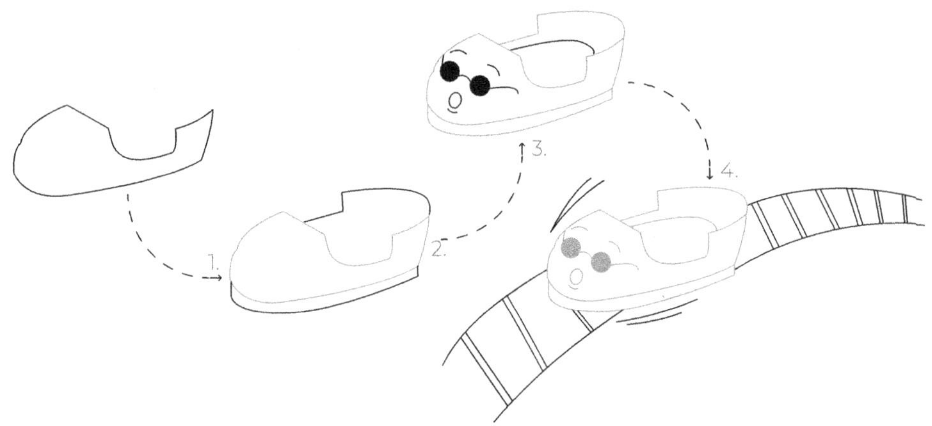

Your turn

FERRIS WHEEL

Draw a big circle for the wheel. Then add a smaller circle inside to guide where the seats will go.

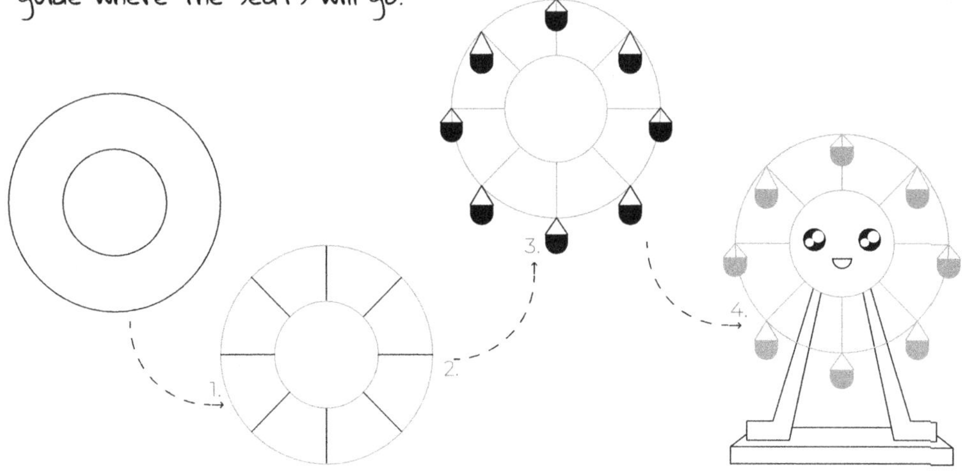

Your turn

CAROUSEL

Start by drawing the top canopy with a circle in the middle. Then add the center pole and base. Make the canopy tall so the horses can fit underneath.

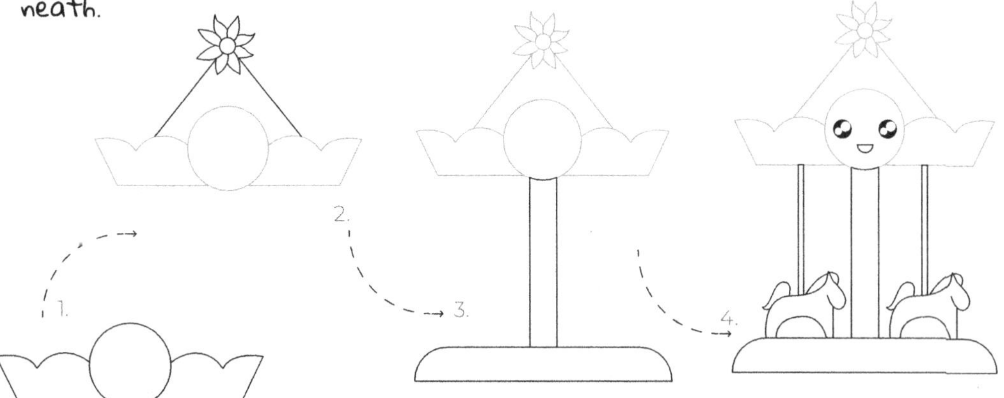

Your turn

TREEHOUSE

Start with a small square for the house.
Tip: Tilt it slightly back so it looks like it's sitting in the tree.

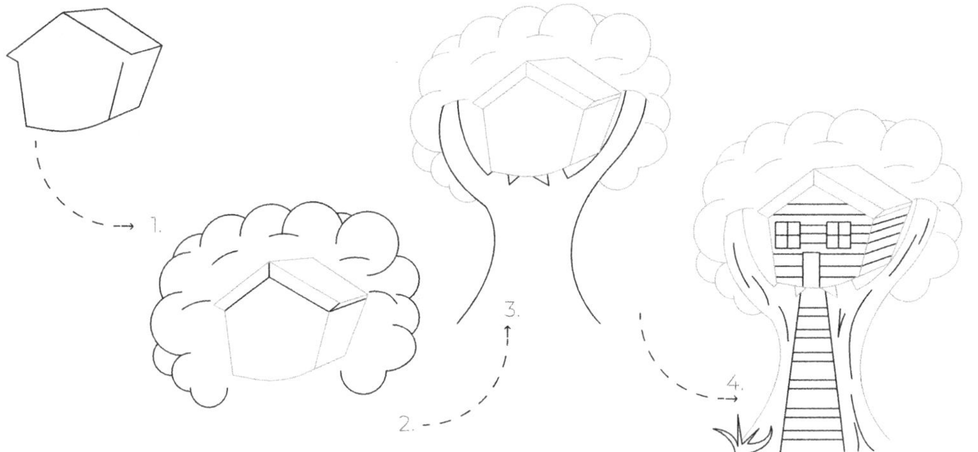

SLED

Draw a wide, curved shape like a shallow bowl. Then add smooth rails underneath so it looks ready to slide.

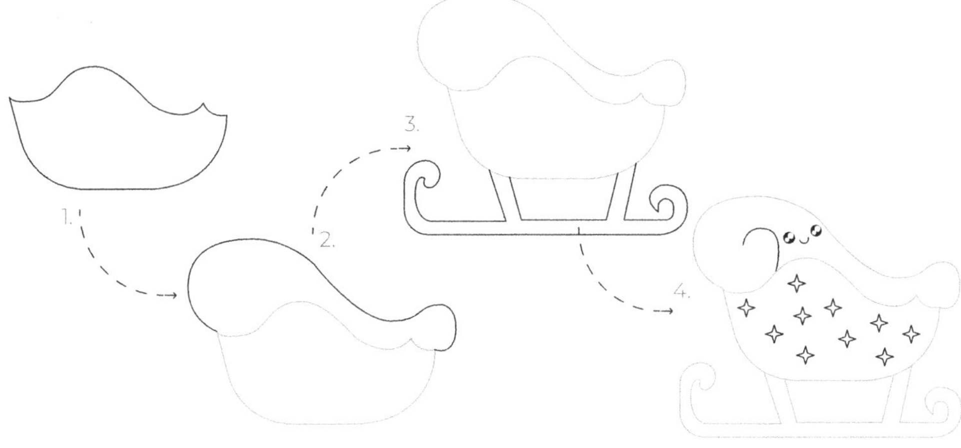

KAYAK

Start with a long kayak shape and add a curve at the back. Then draw the seat inside and the oars floating on the water.

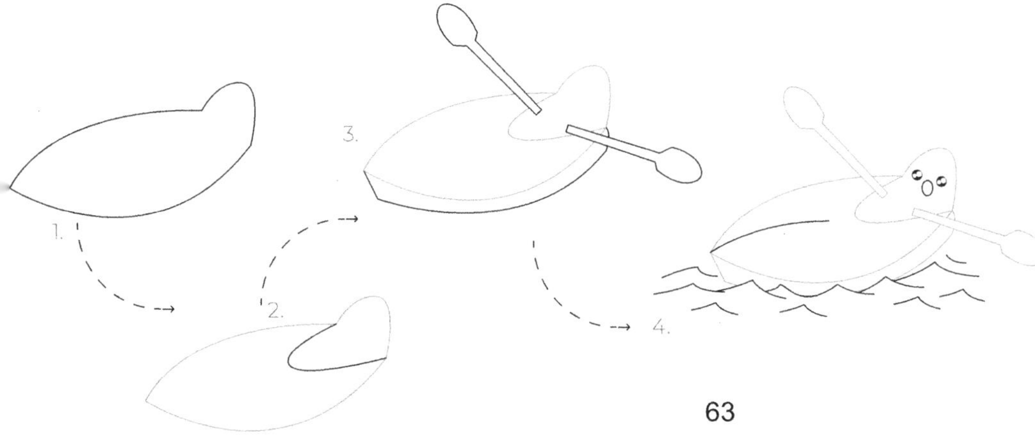

SNOWBOARDER

Start with a small circle for the head.
Tip: Leave space below for the body and snowboard.

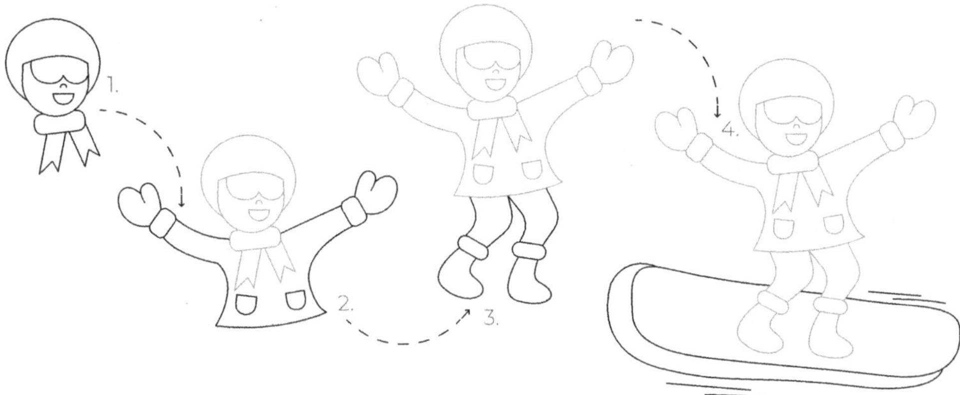

PARACHUTE

Draw a big curved line like a rainbow for the top. Add two short
curves below for the sides, then connect the strings to the person.

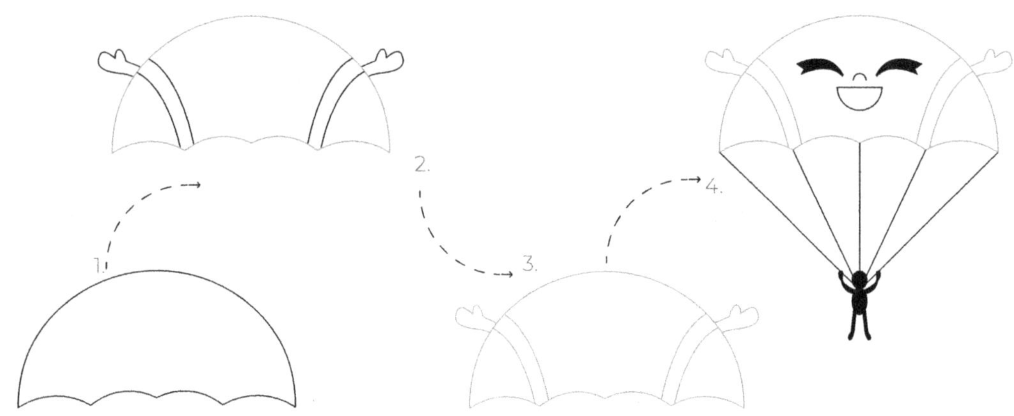

JETPACK

Start with a rounded rectangle. Then add engines on the sides and
flames at the bottom so it looks ready to fly.

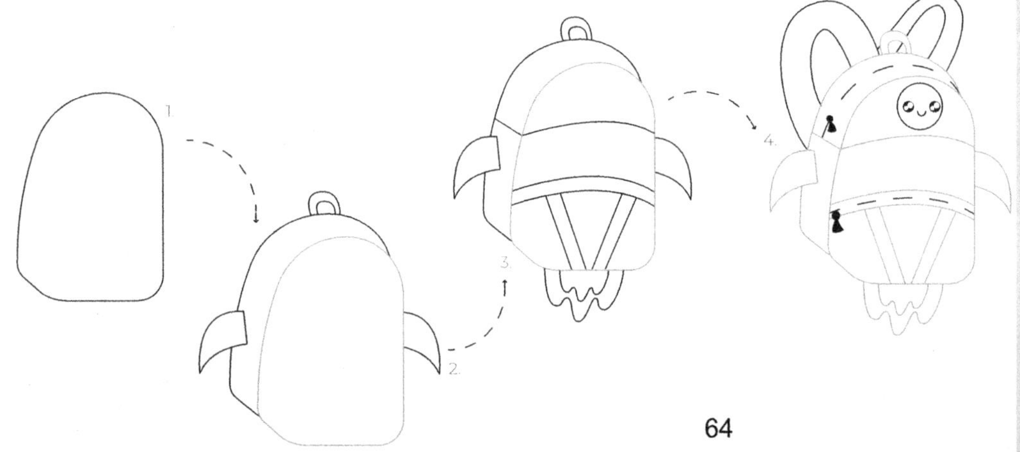

TELESCOPE

Start with a small rectangle tilted sideways for the eyepiece.
Tip: Tilt it slightly so the telescope looks pointed at the sky.

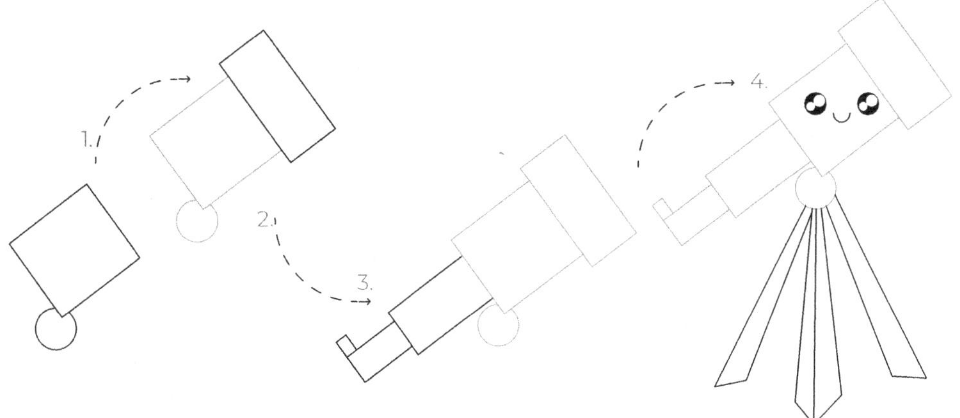

MICROSCOPE

Start with the eyepiece tube, then add the curved body and base.

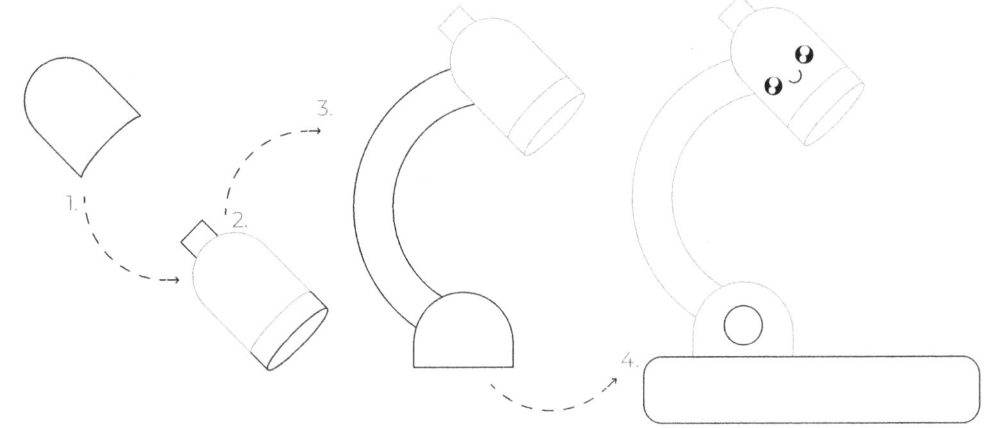

DRONE

Start with a hexagon shape for the body. Add four arms with small blades at the ends, plus legs underneath so it can land.

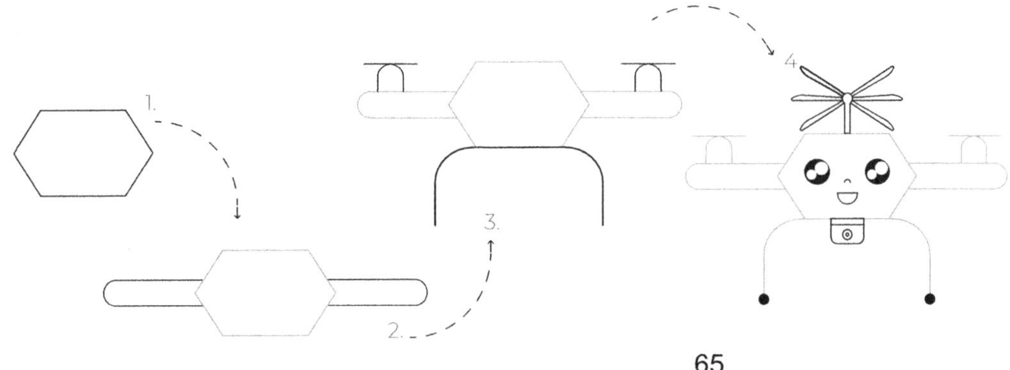

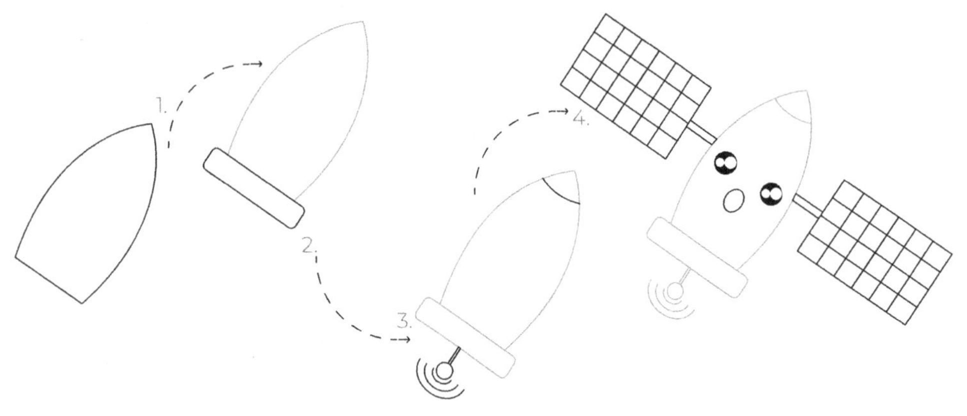

SPACE STATION

Start with a long oval for the module. Add solar panels on the sides to finish the space station.

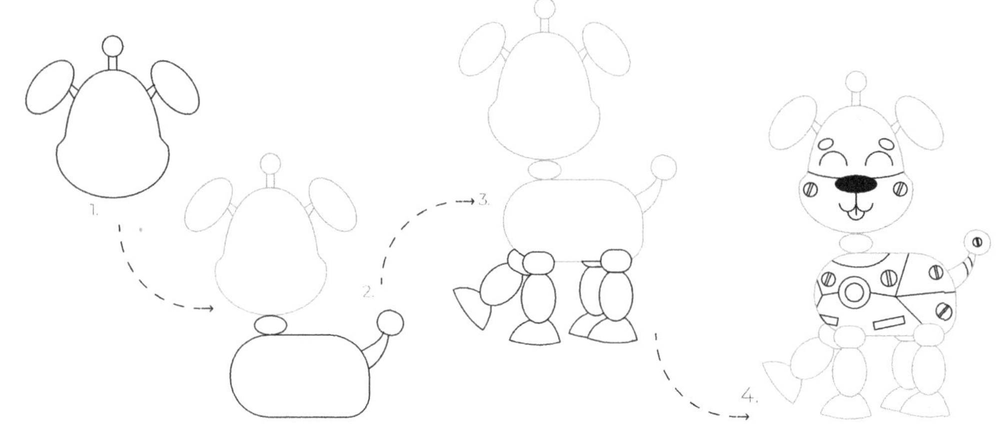

ROBOT DOG

Start with a round head and an oval body. Then add the legs and details to make it robotic.

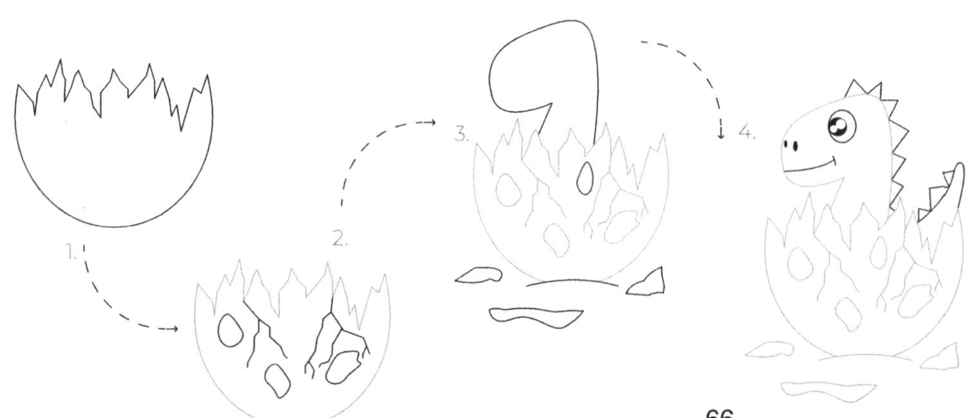

DINOSAUR EGG

Draw a cracked half oval for the bottom of the egg. Add tiny cracks on the top with a baby dinosaur peeking out.

SANDCASTLE

Start with one round tower and a flag on top. Then build the wide base and add more towers.

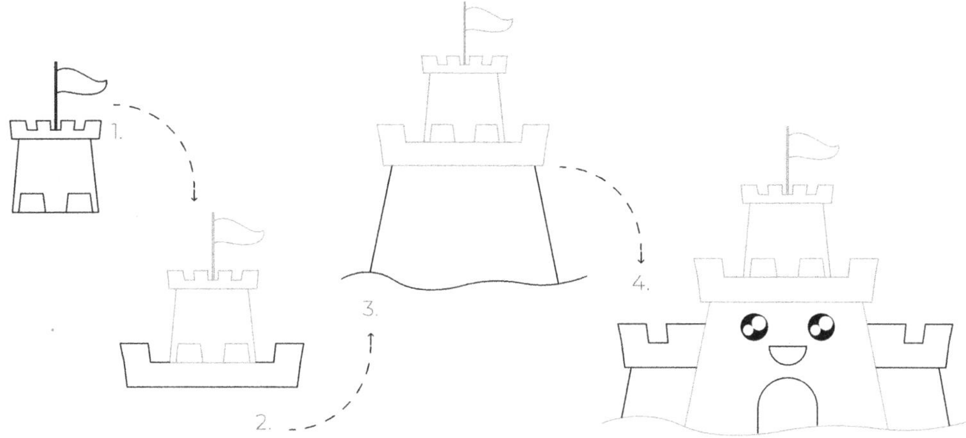

XYLOPHONE

Draw a row of vertical rectangles for the bars. Place the mallets beside them.

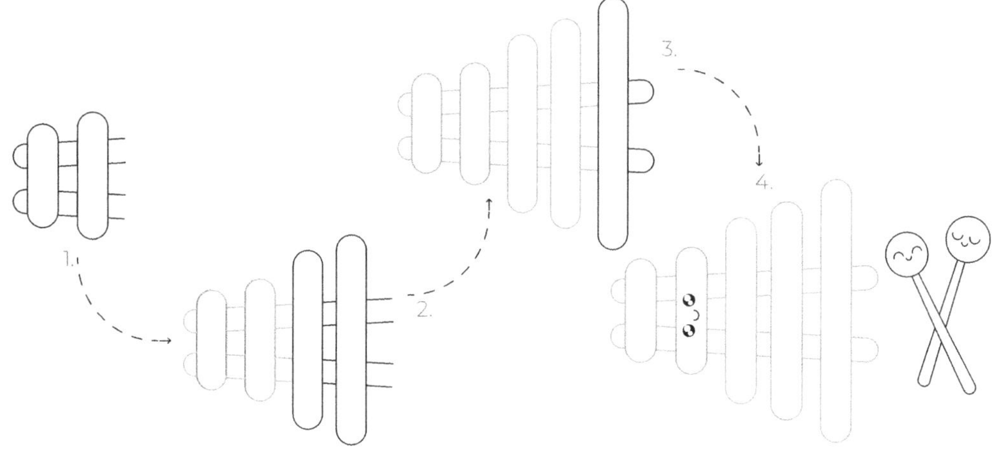

MAGIC KEY

Start with a flower shape on top, then draw the long stem and finish with the key teeth at the bottom.

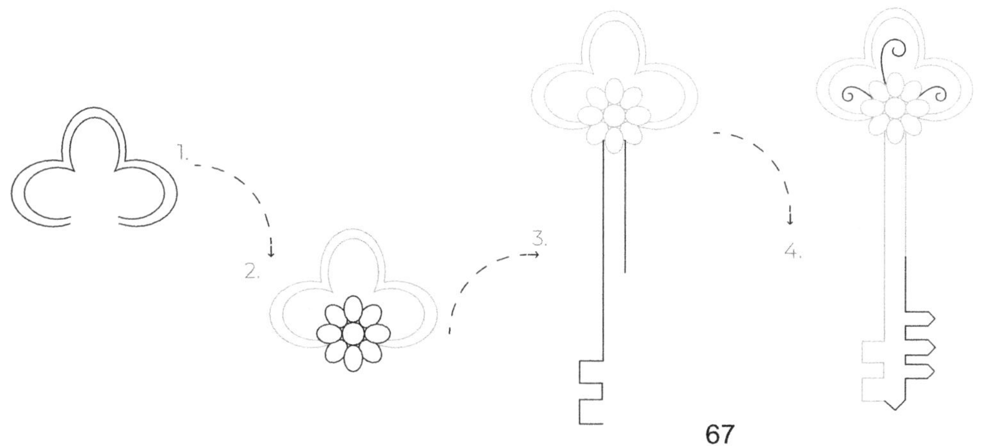

BOXING GLOVES

Start with a curved shape like a soft number 9. Then draw the wristband and closed glove on top.
Tip: Make them round and puffy like real gloves!

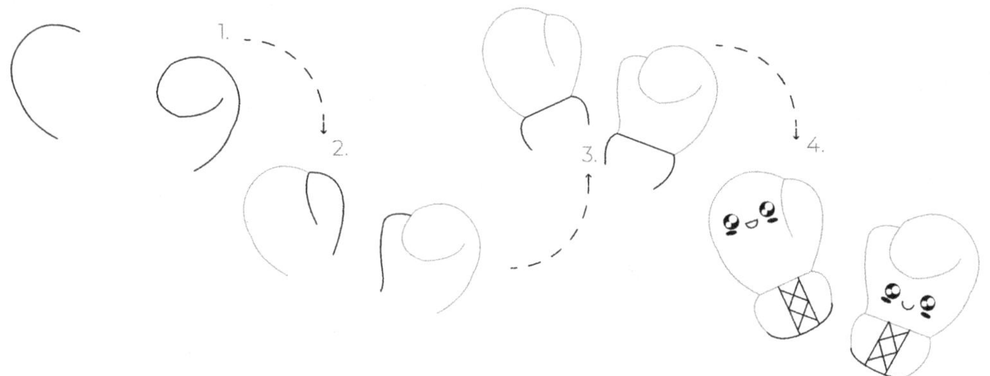

MUMMY

Start with the head and arms together in one round shape. Then draw the body and add bandages!

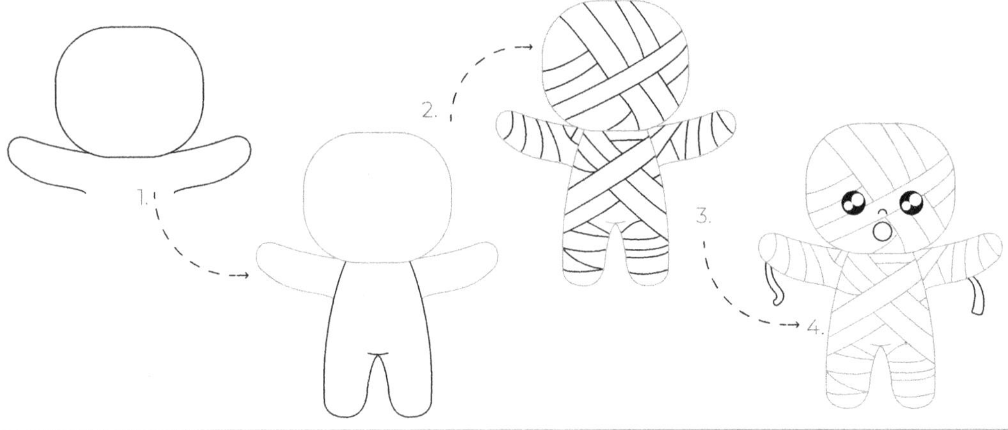

PUZZLE

Start with a small square for the first puzzle piece. Add bumps and notches on each side.
Tip: Keep the shapes round and close so the pieces fit together.

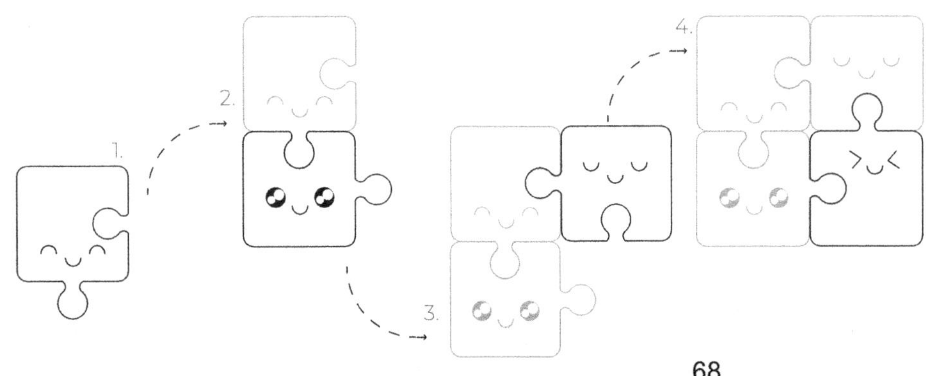

TRAIN

Start with the front engine and wheels. Then add the train cars and small connecting lines.
Tip: Use rectangles to keep each part neat and balanced!

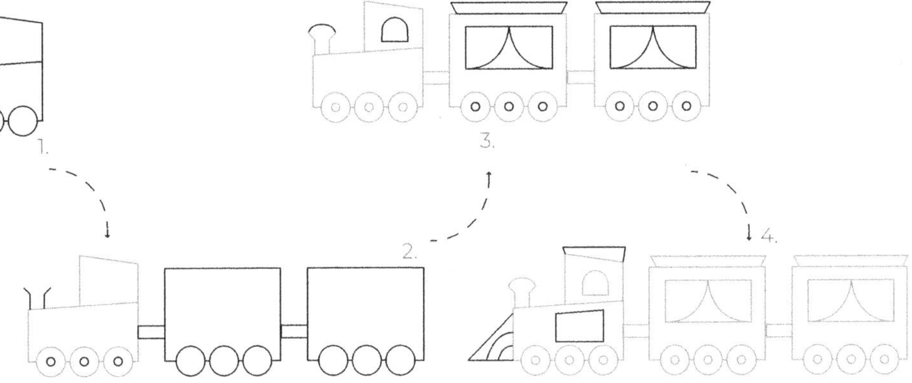

HOT AIR BALLOON

Start with a big oval for the balloon. Then draw the basket and connecting ropes.
Tip: Use smooth curves and straight lines for a real flying look!

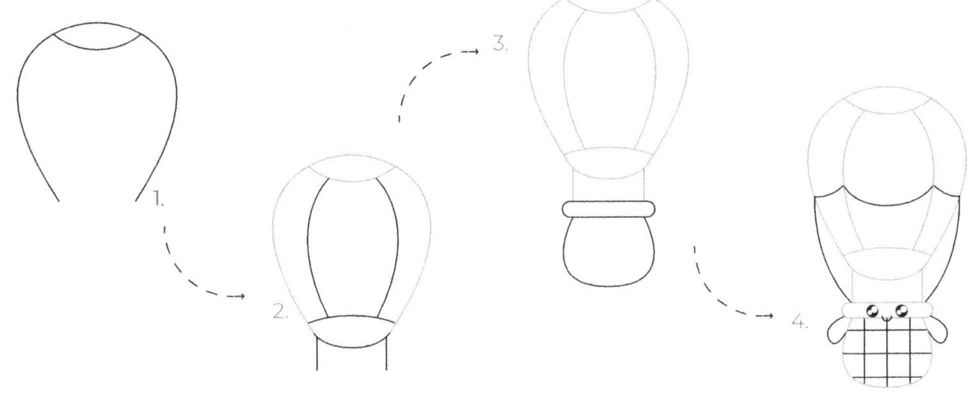

SUNFLOWER

Start with a big circle and petals around it. Then draw the stem, leaves, and a happy face!

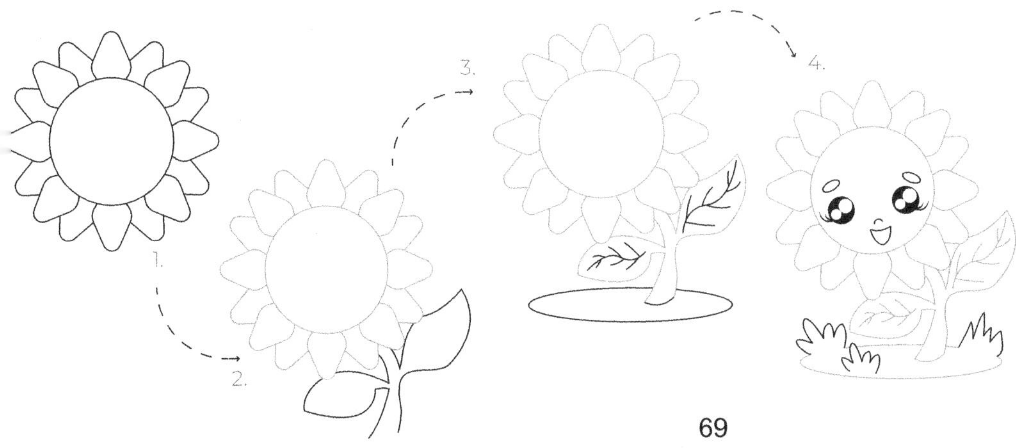

LEVEL 3:

AMAZING ANIMALS

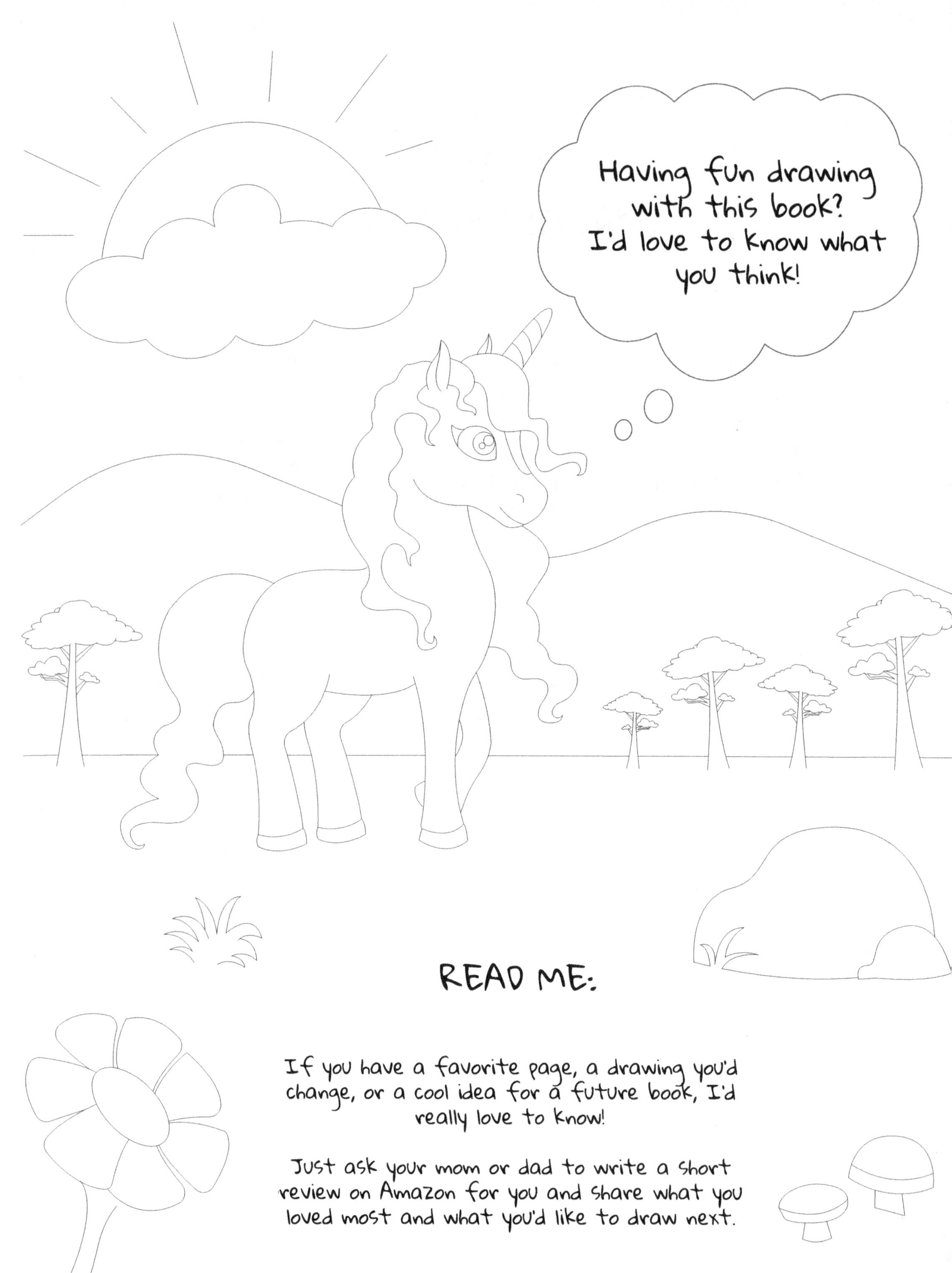

READ ME:

If you have a favorite page, a drawing you'd change, or a cool idea for a future book, I'd really love to know!

Just ask your mom or dad to write a short review on Amazon for you and share what you loved most and what you'd like to draw next.

PENGUIN

Start with the head. Then add the oval body below it.
Tip: Make the wings curved for a friendly look!

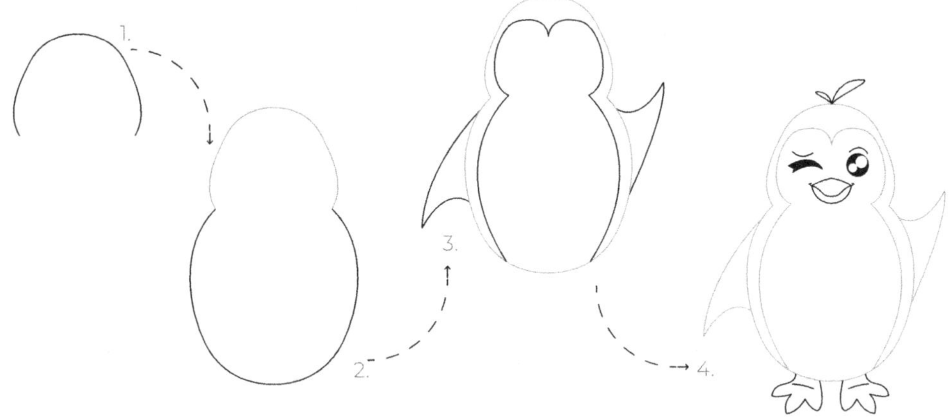

STINGRAY

Start with a wide, curved shape like a smile for the body. Add two big fins on the sides. Then draw the long tail and spots on top.
Tip: Keep the body wide so it looks like it's gliding through the water!

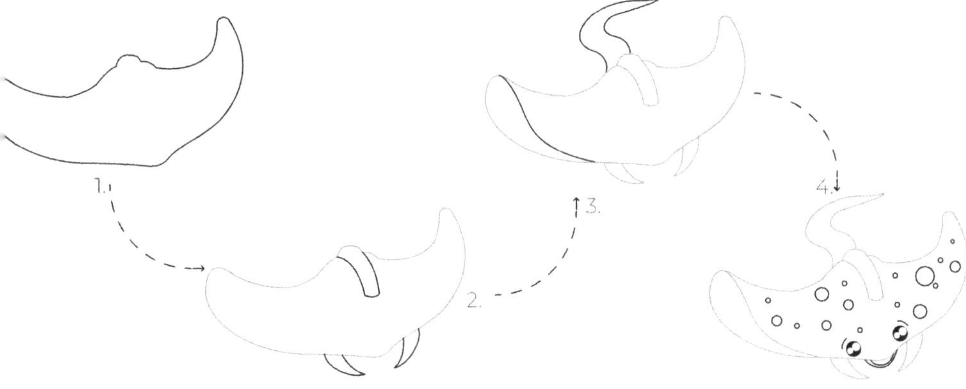

SEAL

Start with a small circle for the head and a tail on one side. Connect them with a long curved body. Then add flippers!

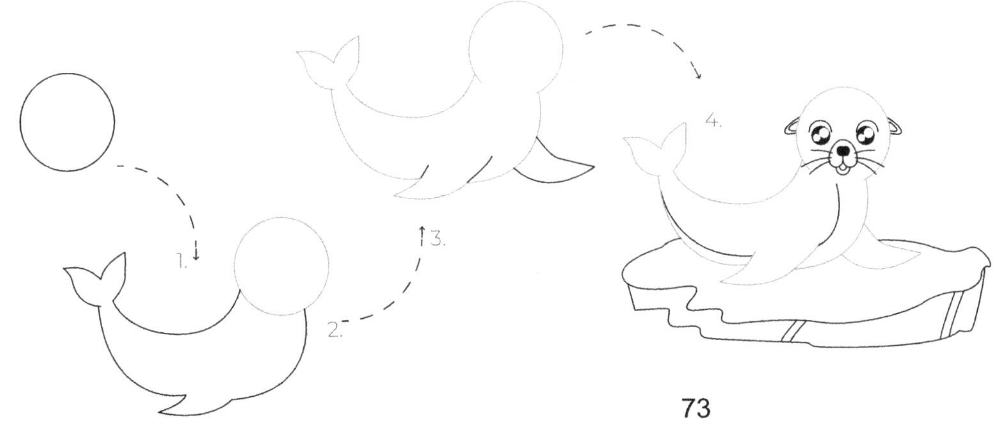

DOLPHIN

Start with a curved shape like a banana for the body.
Tip: Make the curve big so the dolphin looks like it's jumping.

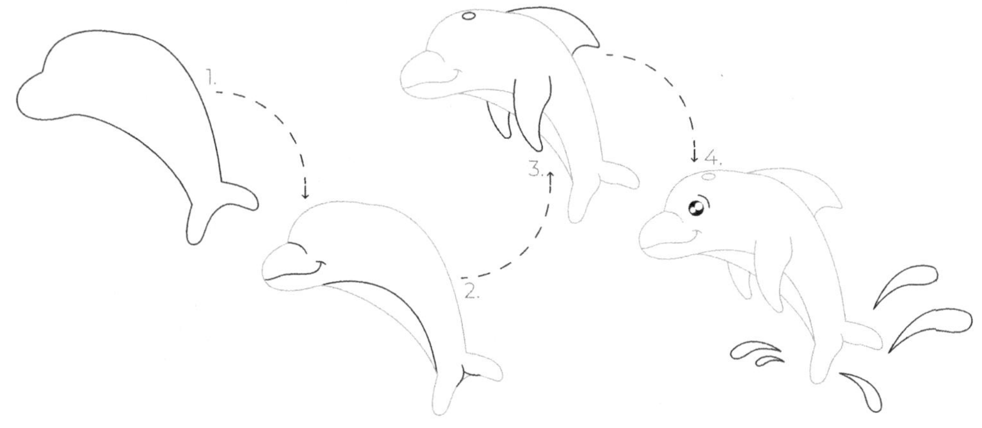

SNOWY OWL

Draw a fluffy crown shape for the head. Add a big oval body on a perch, then draw big round eyes.

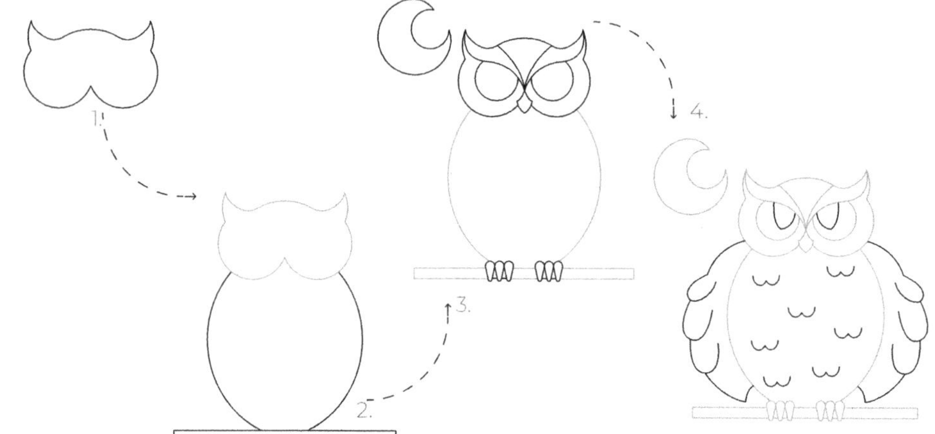

TIGER

Start with a rounded head shape with fur points on the sides. Add a tall rounded body underneath. Then draw the legs, tail, and ears.

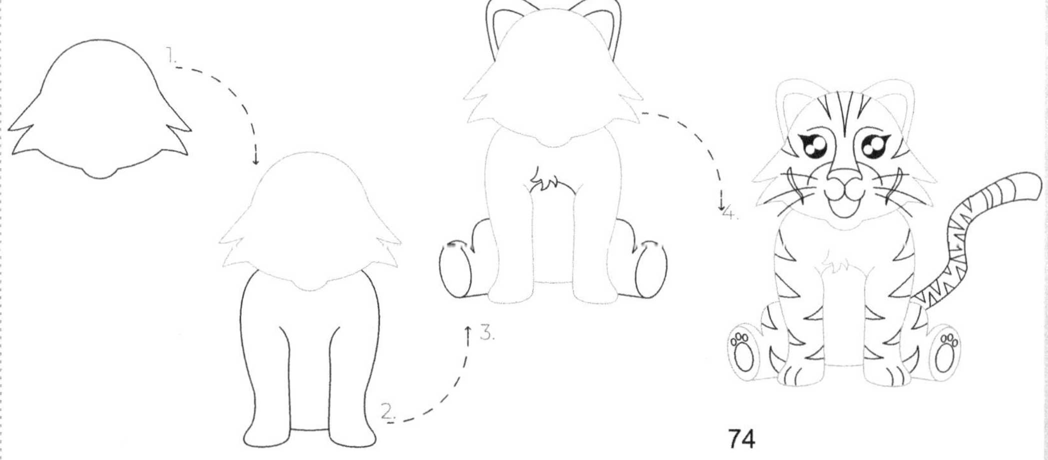

LION

Draw a circle for the head. Add a big spiky mane all around it.
Tip: Make the mane wider than the head so the lion looks extra fluffy.

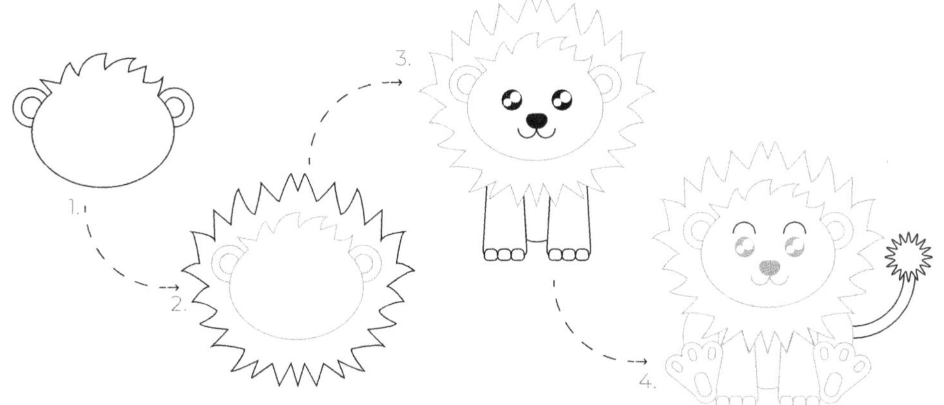

ELEPHANT

Start with a wide head with wavy sides. Add a tall body underneath, then draw the big ears, trunk, legs, and tail.
Tip: Make the ears almost as big as the head for a realistic look!

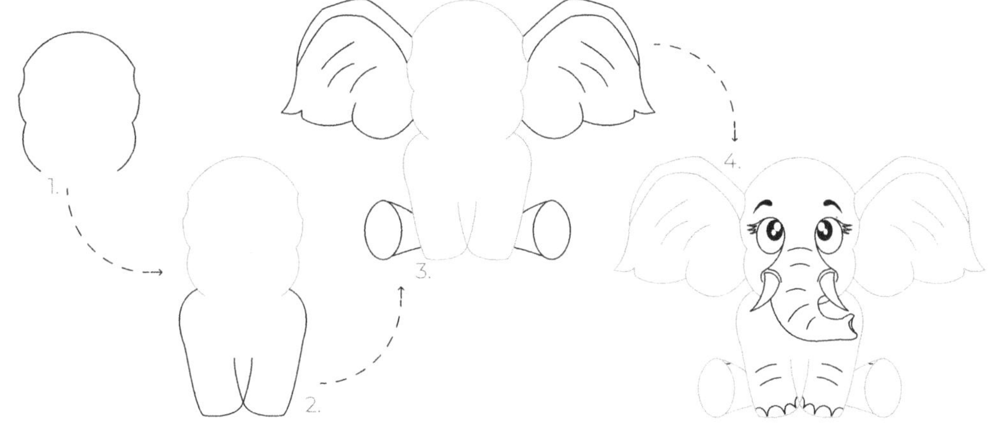

GIRAFFE

Draw a small oval for the head. From there, add a very long, thin neck, then the body and legs.
Tip: Make the neck extra tall to leave space for the spots.

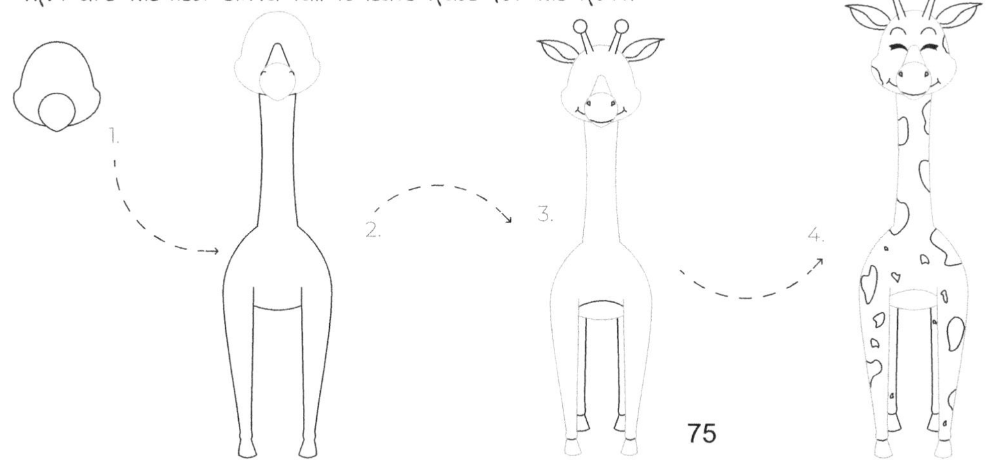

CHEETAH

Draw a small rounded shape for the head. Then add the thin body, legs, and long tail.

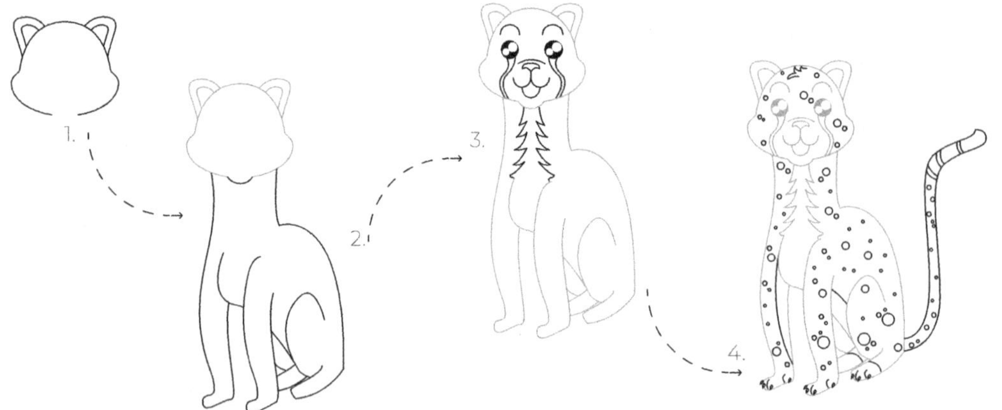

MEERKAT

Draw the head with small round ears, then a long curved body standing upright. Add arms, legs, and tail to finish.
Tip: Keep the body tall so it looks alert and watchful!

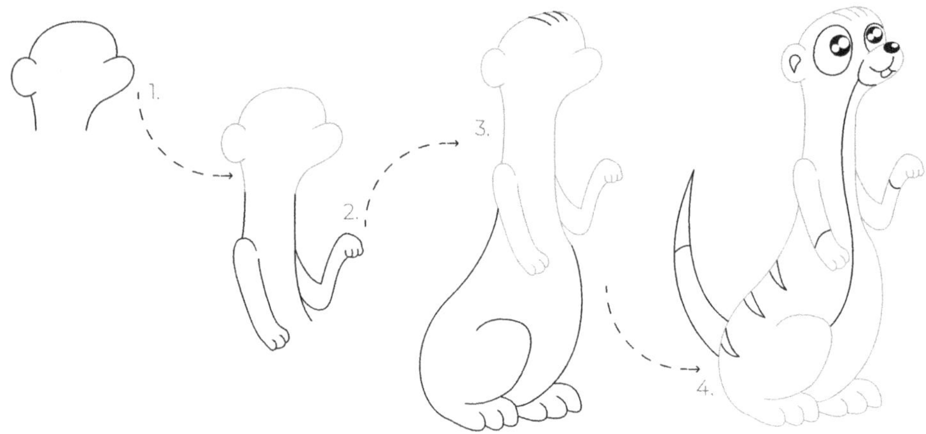

LEMUR

Draw a wide head with a small curved body and two legs. Add ears, long striped tail, and face.

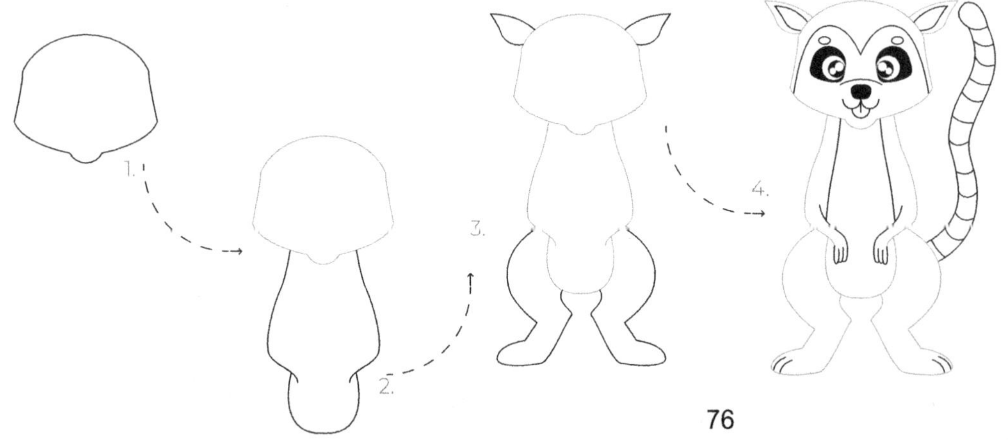

RHINOCEROS

Start with a big round head shape and a small bump for the horn base.
Add a large oval body behind it, then draw the horn, legs, and tail.

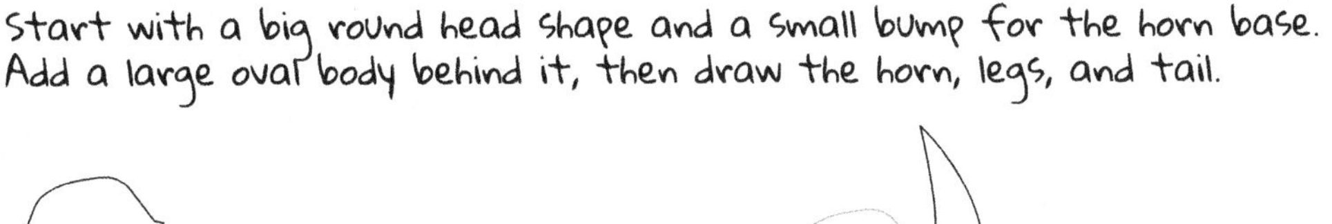

CROCODILE

Start with a bumpy oval shape for the head.
Tip: Make the back and tail bumpy to show the crocodile's rough skin.

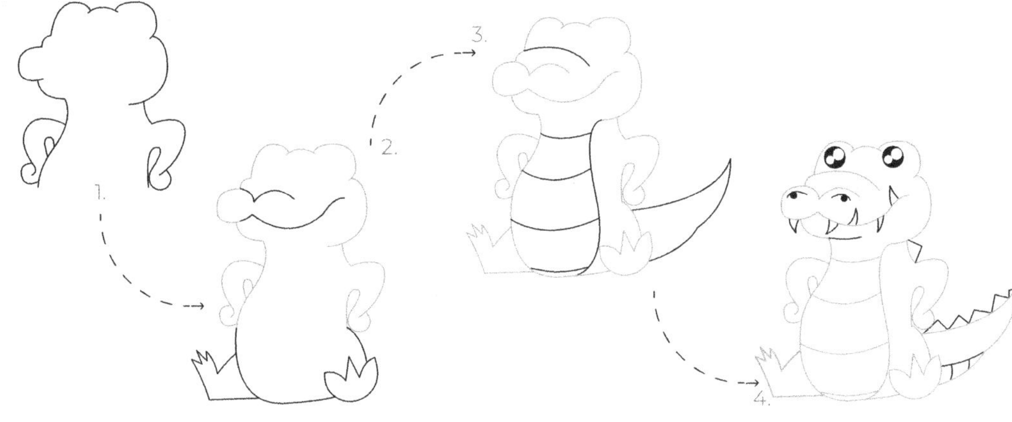

BABY HIPPO

Draw a round head with two small ears on top. Add a wide oval body
with short, chubby legs. Finish with big eyes, a nose, and a happy smile.

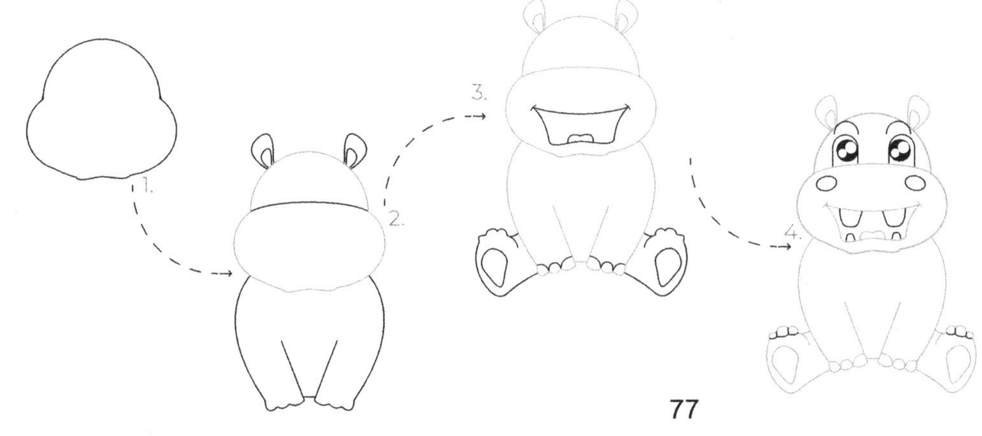

COBRA

Draw a wide mushroom shape for the head. Add a long curved neck and a rounded body below. Then add the eyes, fangs, and a wavy tail.

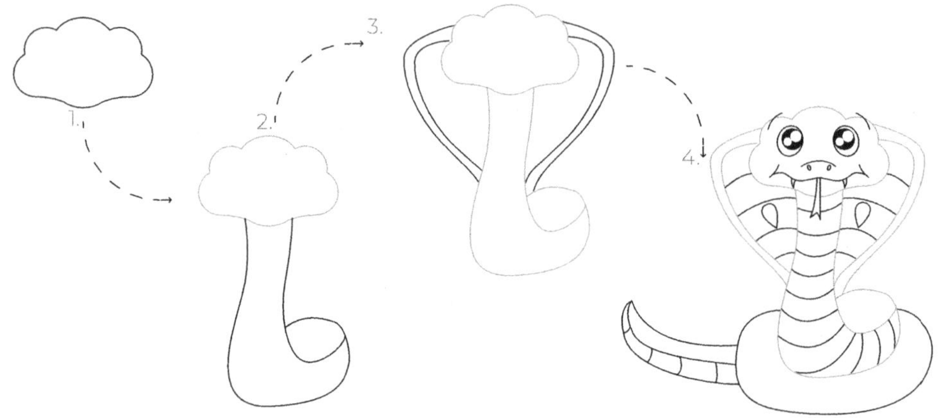

GORILLA

Start with a cloud shape for the head.
Tip: Make the arms longer than the legs so the gorilla looks strong and powerful.

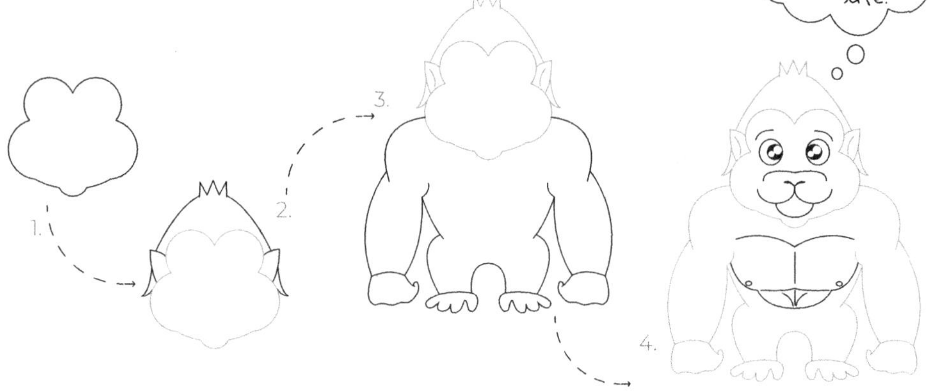

OSTRICH

Start with a small oval for the head and a long skinny neck.
Tip: Stretch the neck tall and keep the body puffy like a ball.

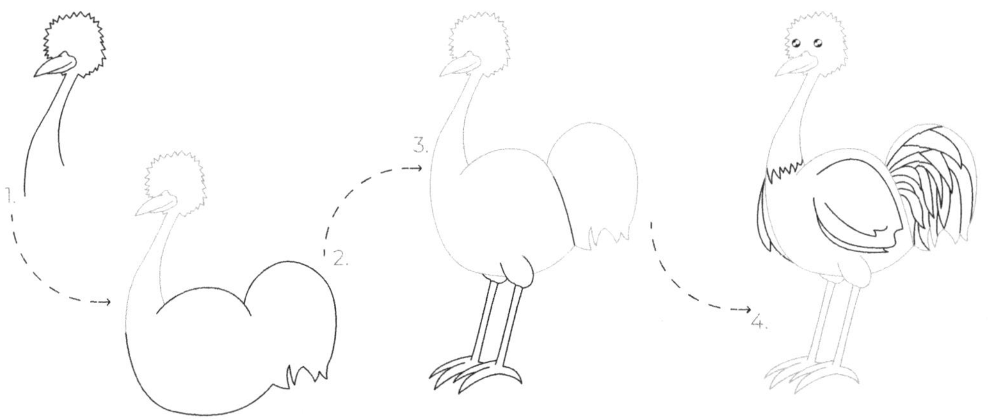

KOALA

Start with a round shape for the head and two big fluffy ears.
Tip: Make the ears very big and round to show the koala's cuteness.

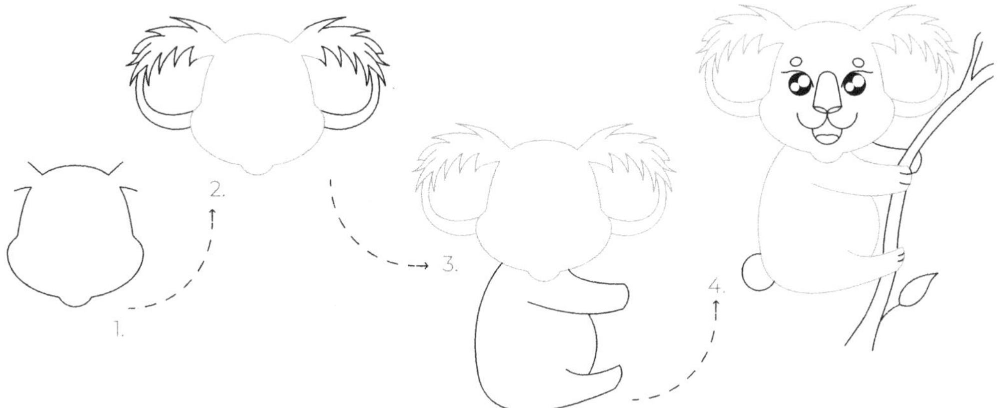

PLATYPUS

Draw a long oval body with a flat bill at the front. Add short legs and a wide, textured tail.
Tip: Make the tail big and crisscrossed to look like a real platypus!

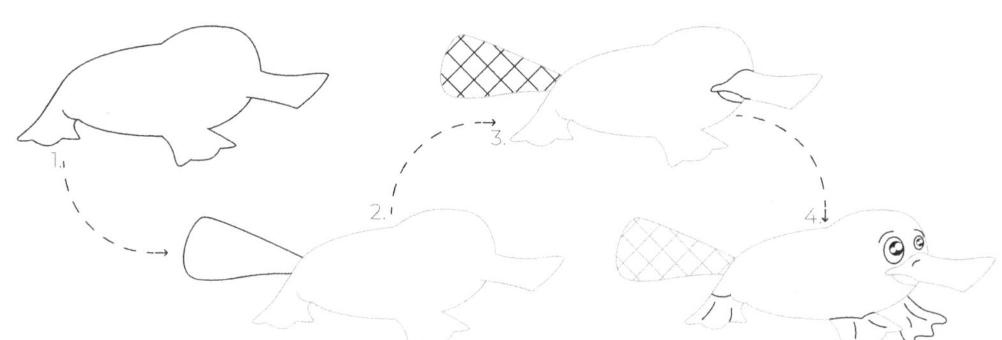

KANGAROO

Draw the head with two tall ears. Add a large pear-shaped body, then strong back legs and a long tail for balance.
Tip: Make the pouch in the middle so it looks like it can carry a joey!

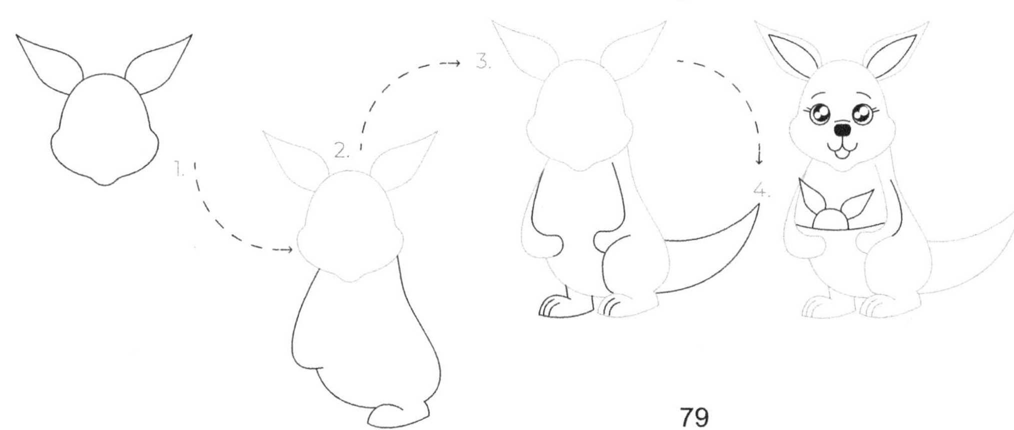

PEACOCK

Draw a tall teardrop body with a small round head on top. Add thin legs, a crown of feathers, and a wide fan tail filled with oval patterns.
Tip: Make the tail big and round so it looks proud and beautiful!

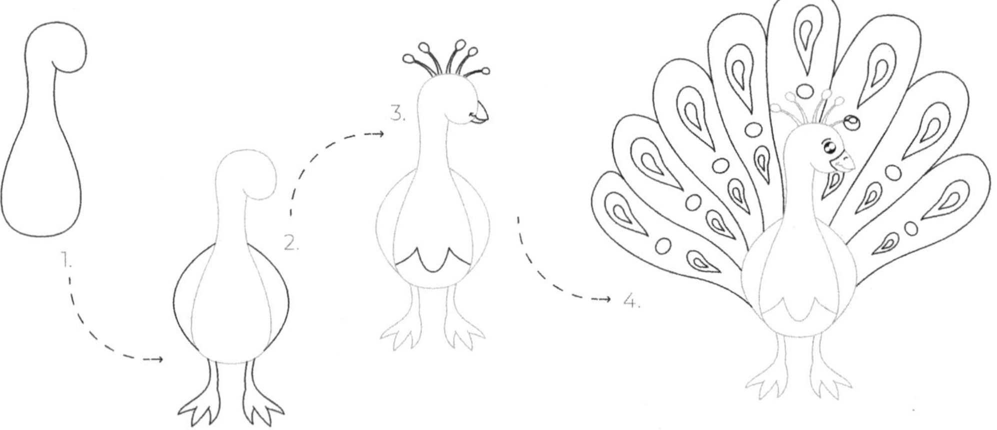

BABY ELEPHANT

Start with two round shapes, one for a wide ear and one for the head with a short trunk in front. Then add the body, short legs, and tail!

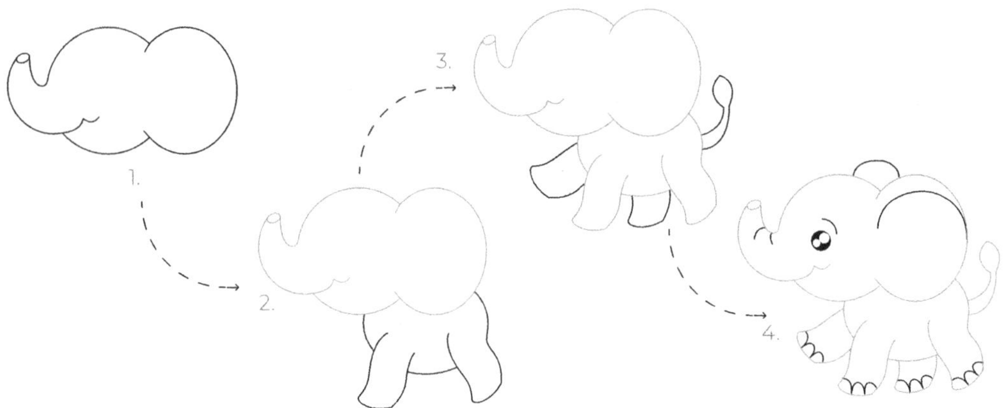

KOMODO DRAGON

Start with a small oval for the head. Draw a big rounded body and a long curving tail attached to it.

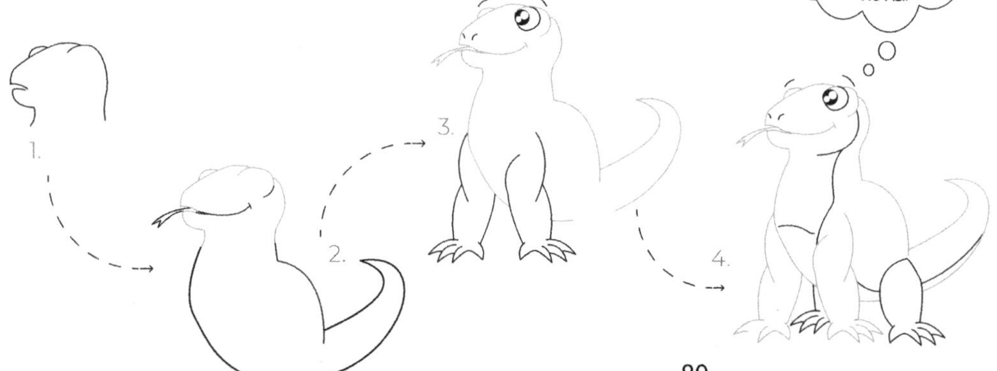

CAPYBARA

Draw a small rounded rectangle for the head, then draw the body underneath.

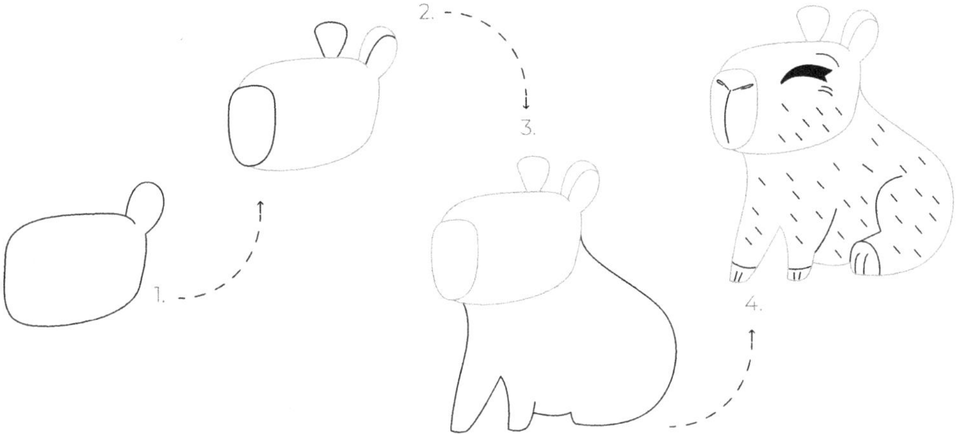

ANTEATER

Draw a long curved shape for the snout and head.
Tip: Stretch the nose long and low so it really looks like an anteater.

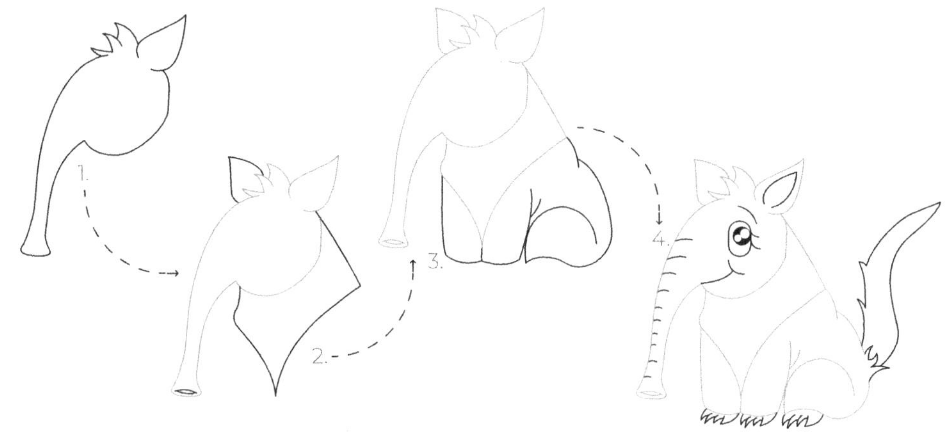

SLOTH

Draw a wide U-shape hanging down for the body.
Tip: Make the U nice and round so the sloth looks cozy on the branch.

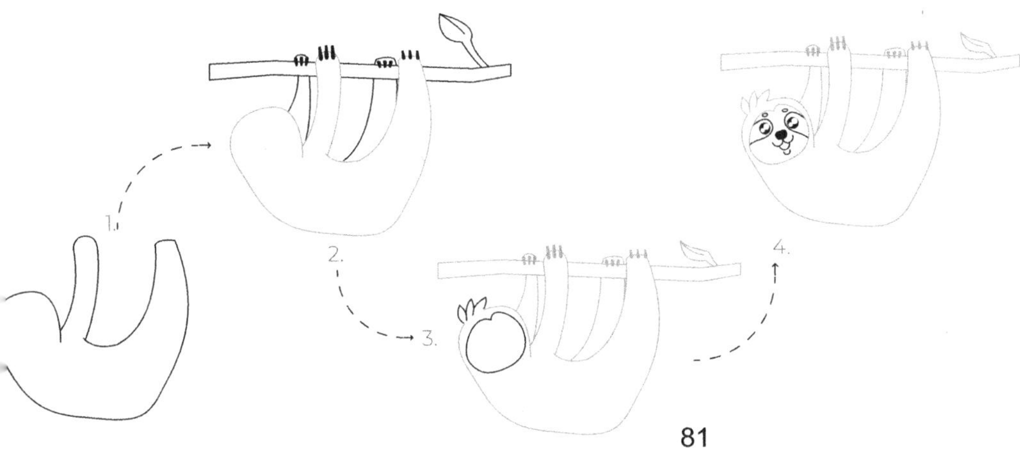

BLACK PANTHER

Draw a small round head with two short ears. Underneath, draw a large smooth shape for the body. Add the legs, tail, and face.

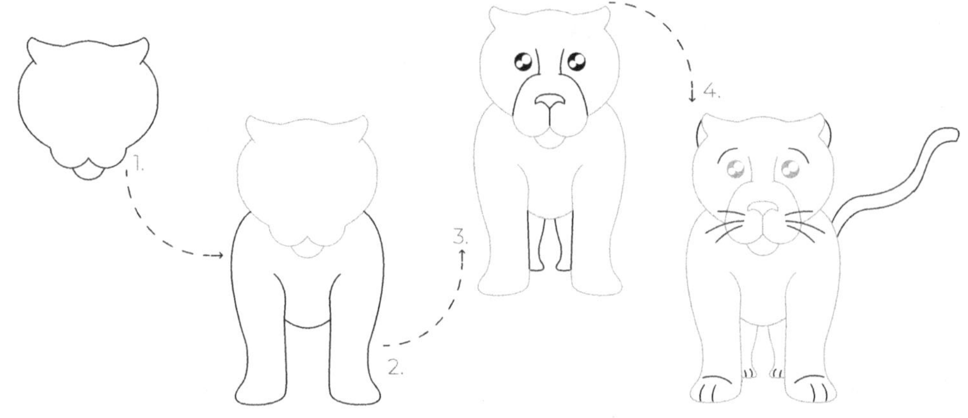

TOUCAN

Draw a long, curved banana shape for the beak, then add the rounded head and body!
Tip: Make the beak almost as long as the body for a real toucan look.

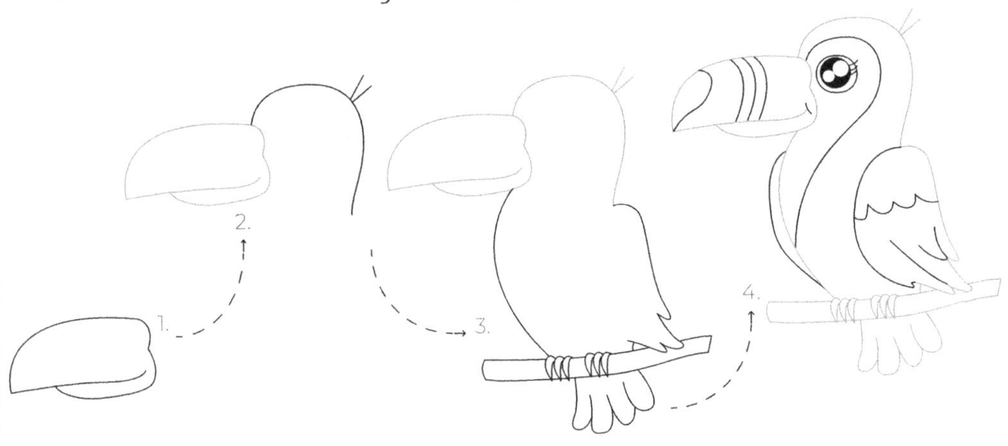

ARMADILLO

Draw a rounded oval for the head. Draw a bigger oval for the body, slightly pointed at the back.
Tip: Leave space on the back to add the curved armor lines.

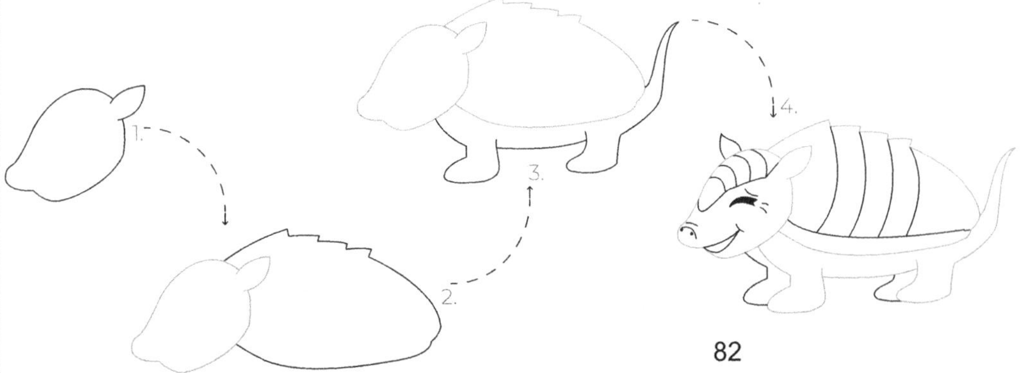

CHAMELEON

Draw a rounded head with a small bump on top for its helmet shape. Add the curved body and tail to make it look like it's resting on a branch.

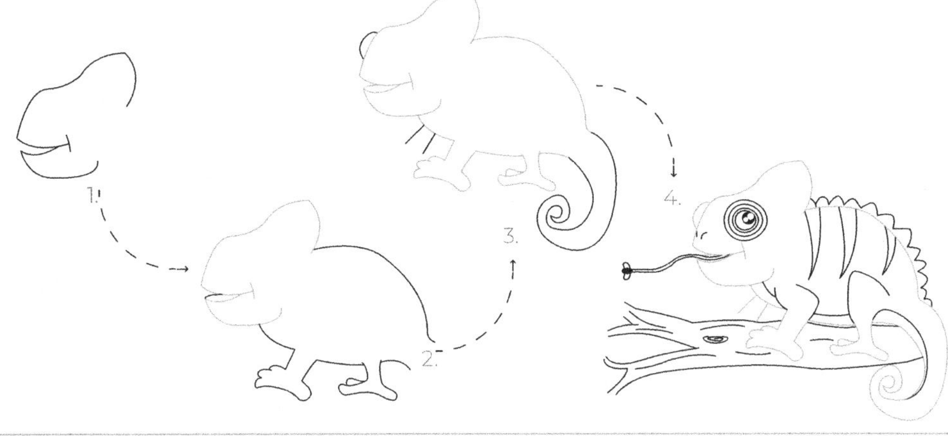

PARROT

Start with a round head and a curved beak. Add a long body with a tail pointing down!

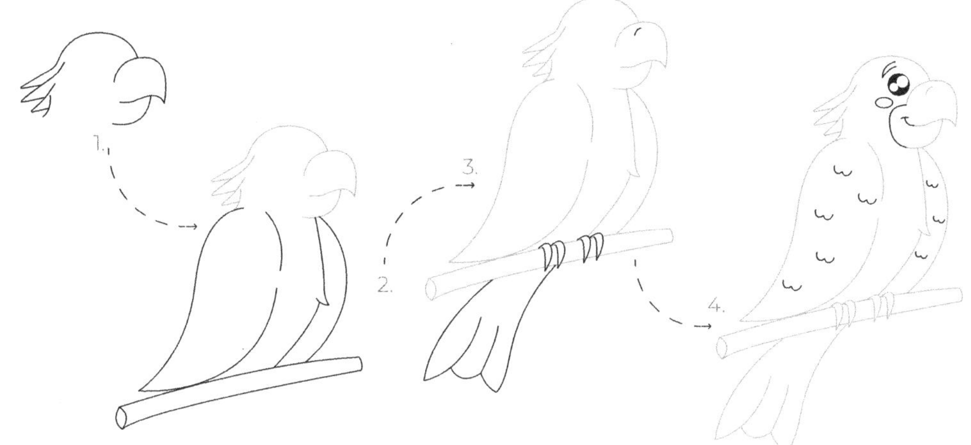

TURTLE

Draw a small oval for the head and a big oval behind it for the shell. Add four flippers and a little tail.

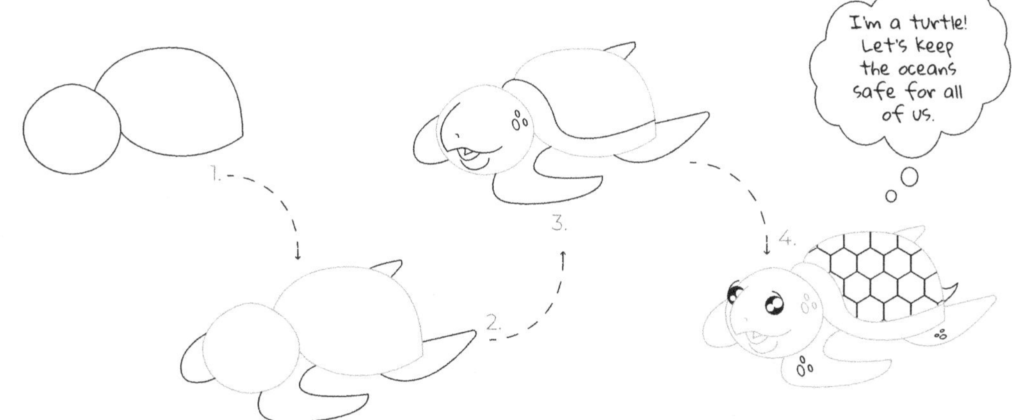

DODO

Draw a rounded head with a big curved beak.
Tip: Keep the body low and wide to match the dodo's chunky shape.

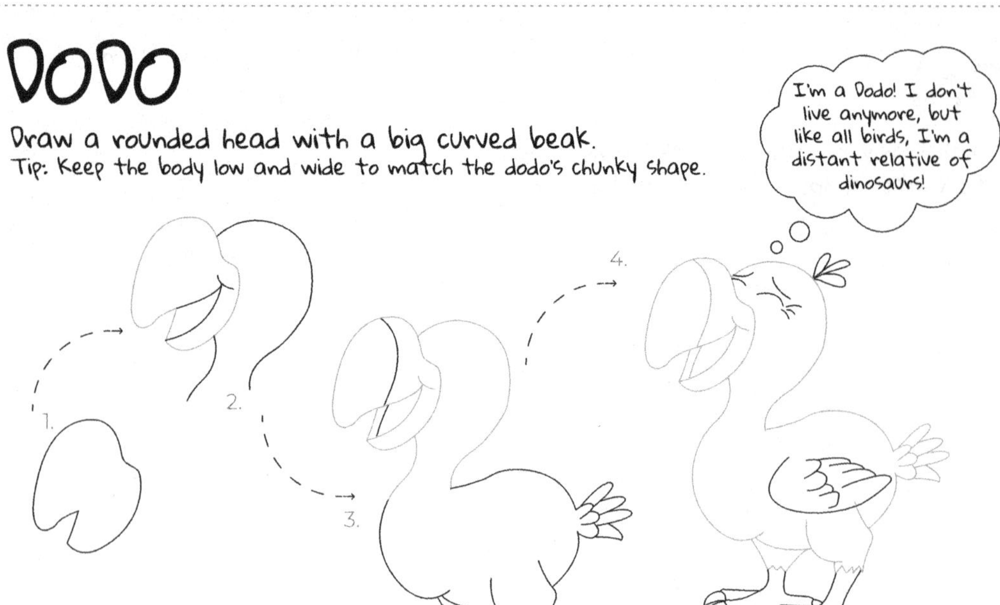

PELICAN

Draw a wide banana shape for the beak. Then draw a big oval body and small legs.
Tip: Keep the beak large and round to fit the pelican's pouch.

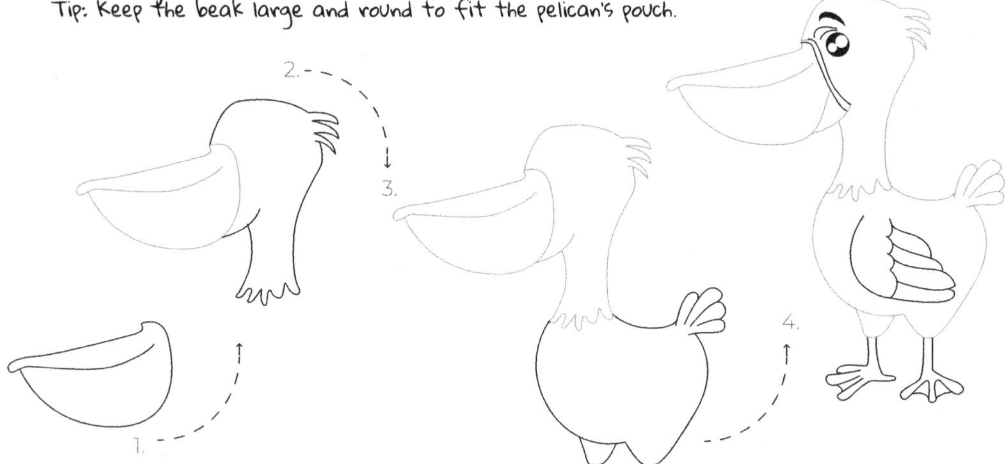

BEE

Draw one small circle for the head and a bigger circle for the body. Add two antennas on the head, then draw wings on top and stripes on the body.

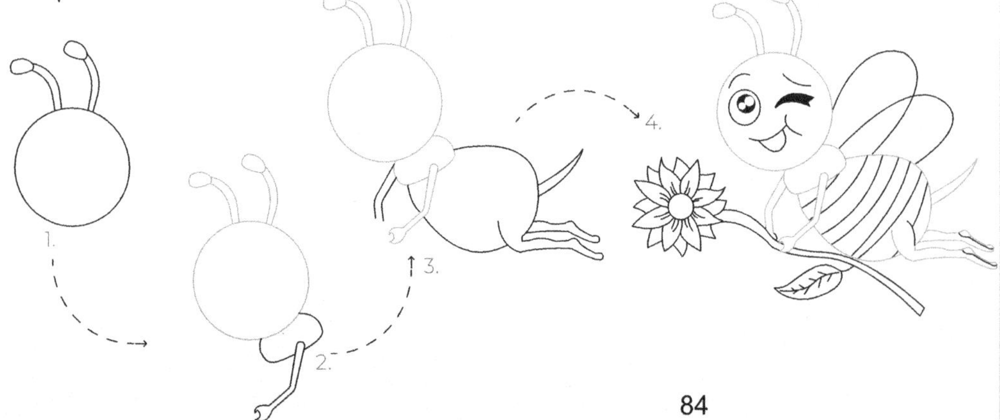

EAGLE

Draw a small round shape for the head and a hooked beak in front. Add the body with strong curved wings and pointed tail feathers.
Tip: Draw the neck feathers pointing down to make the eagle look powerful.

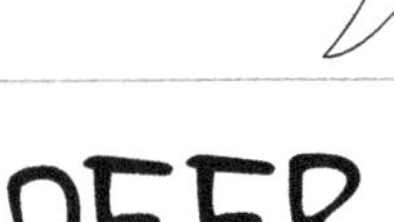

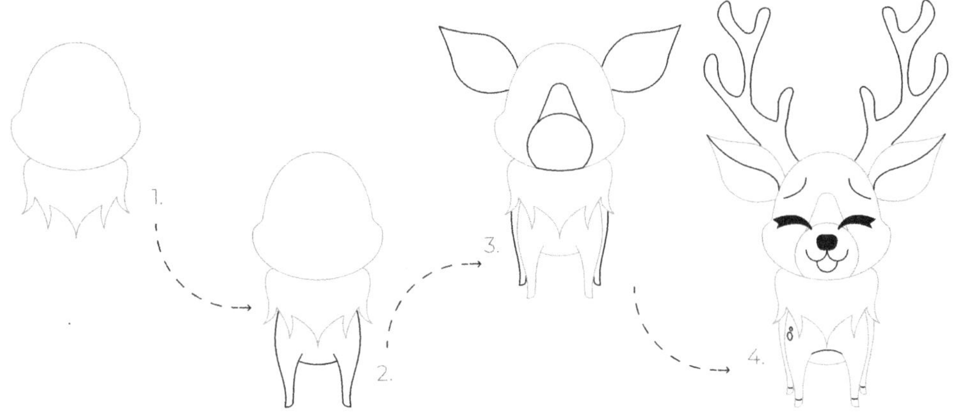

DEER

Draw a rounded head on top of a fluffy chest shape!
Tip: Leave room on top for the big antlers.

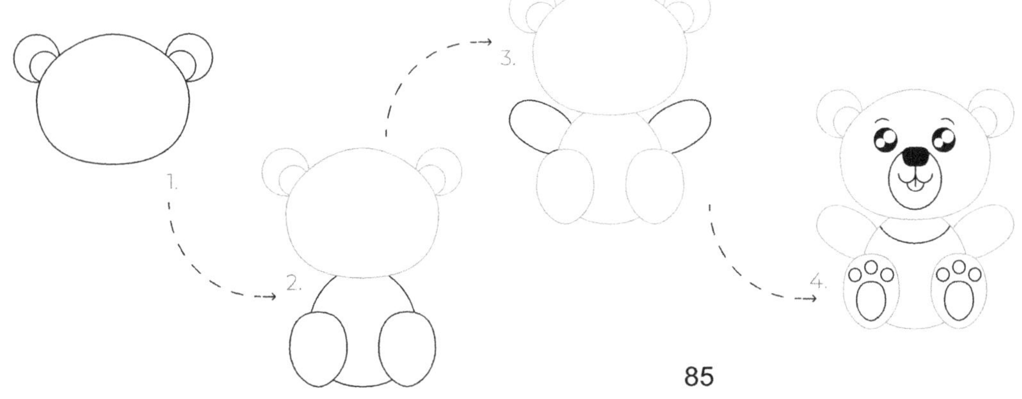

BEAR

Draw a big circle for the head and two small round ears.
Draw a smaller oval for the body with short arms and legs.

WOODPECKER

Start with a small head and a long pointy beak. Add a slim body leaning forward so it looks ready to peck the tree.

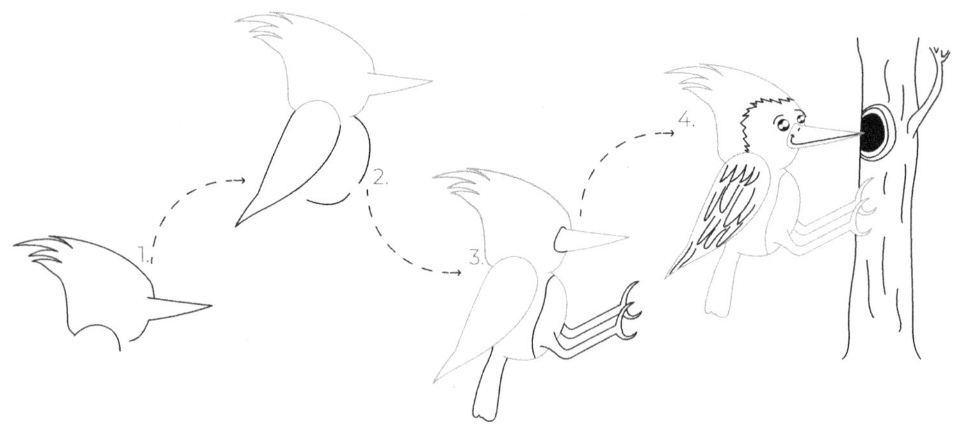

WILD BOAR

Draw a round head with two pointy ears. Don't forget the wild boar's spiky mane on top and the two tusks at the front!

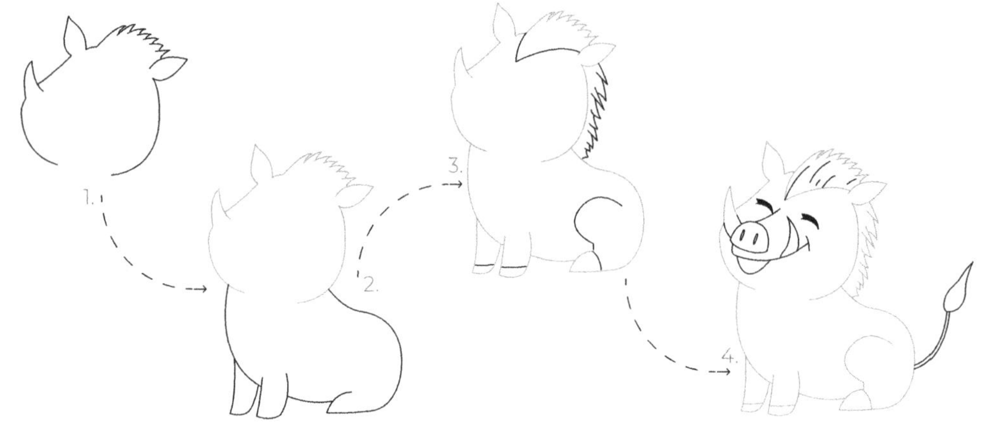

BAT

Draw a small circle for the head, an oval for the body, two big wings curving out, and big ears on top.

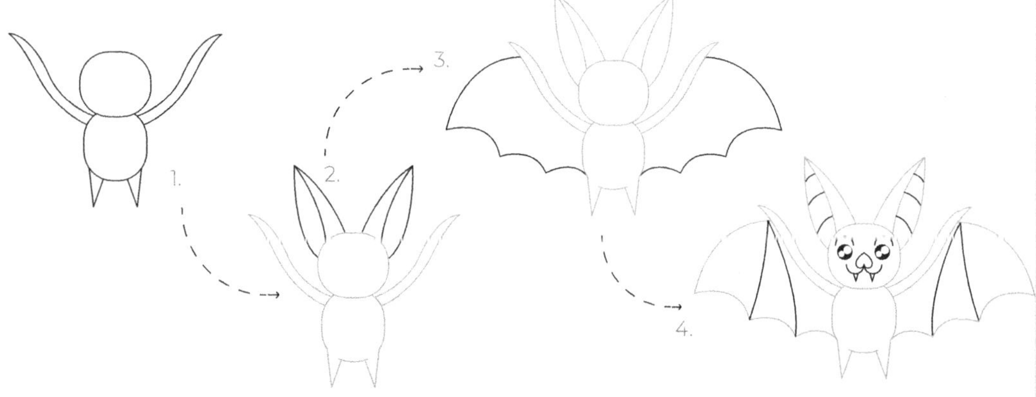

FOX

Draw a wide head with two big, pointy, triangle-shaped ears.
Tip: Make them tall and sharp so the fox looks alert.

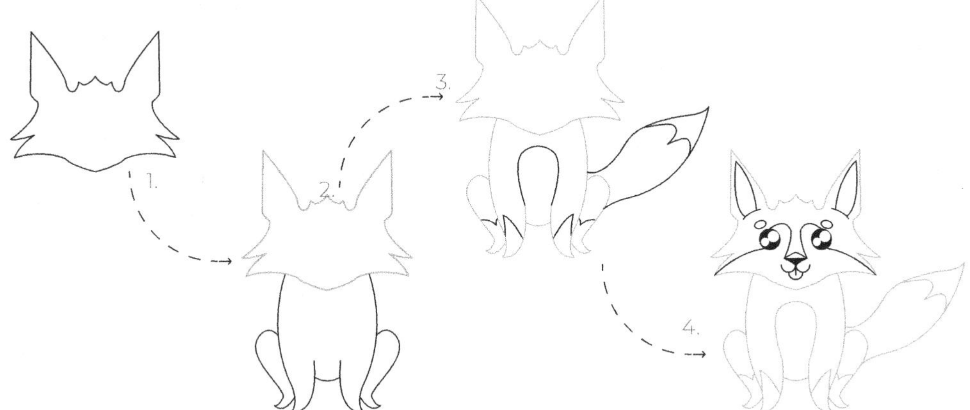

RACCOON

Draw a head shaped like a bell with two small ears on top.
Tip: Leave space for the fluffy tail and mask details later.

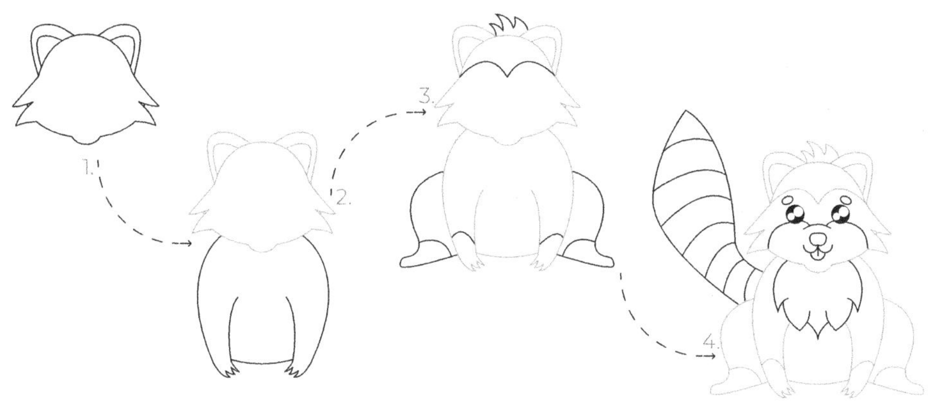

SKUNK

Draw a rounded head and two tiny ears. Add a big, fluffy tail curving over the back.
Tip: Don't forget the white stripe running from the head to the tip of the tail.

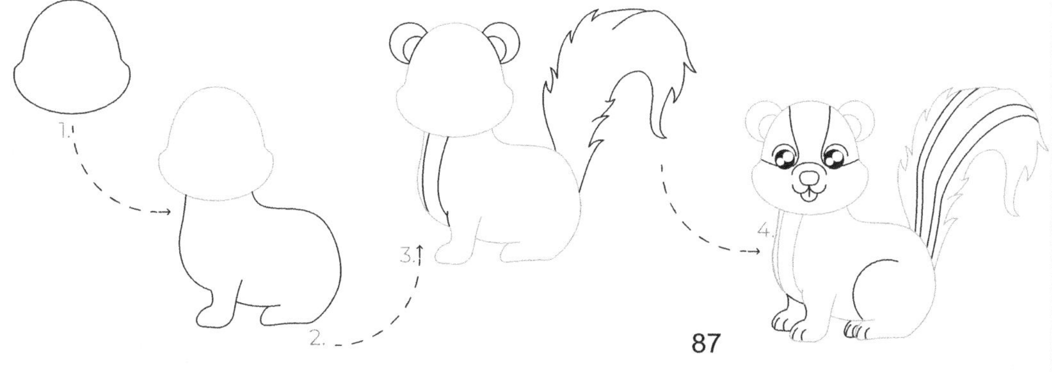

BEAVER

Draw a furry head shape. Add a wide, rounded body underneath, then put two small round ears on top.
Tip: Leave space on one side for the big flat tail with its crisscross pattern.

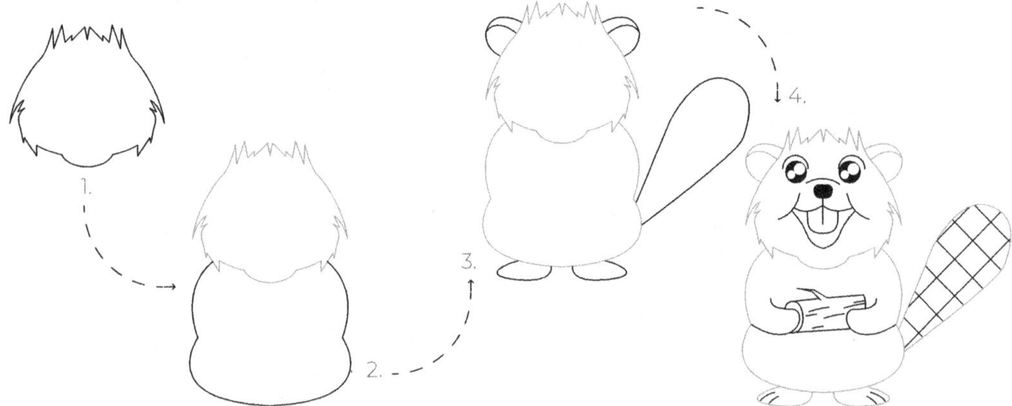

CRAB

Draw a half-circle for the shell. Add three thin legs on each side, pointing outward. On top, draw two big claws and finish with two tall eye stalks.

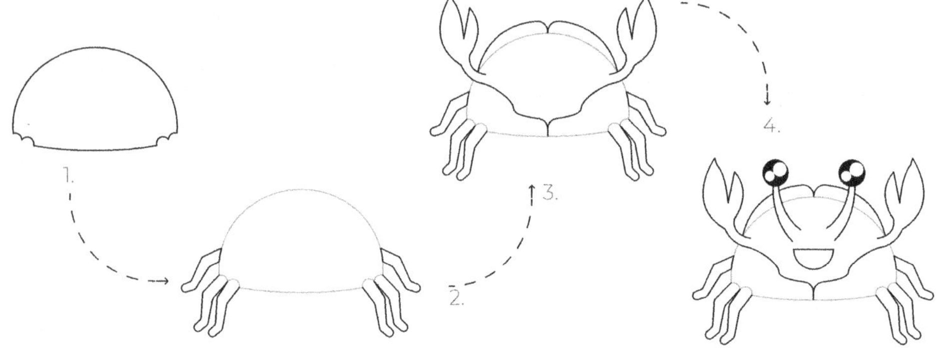

SQUIRREL

Draw a rounded head and an oval body with two small feet at the bottom. Add two tall, pointy ears on top, then draw a big, curly tail on the side.

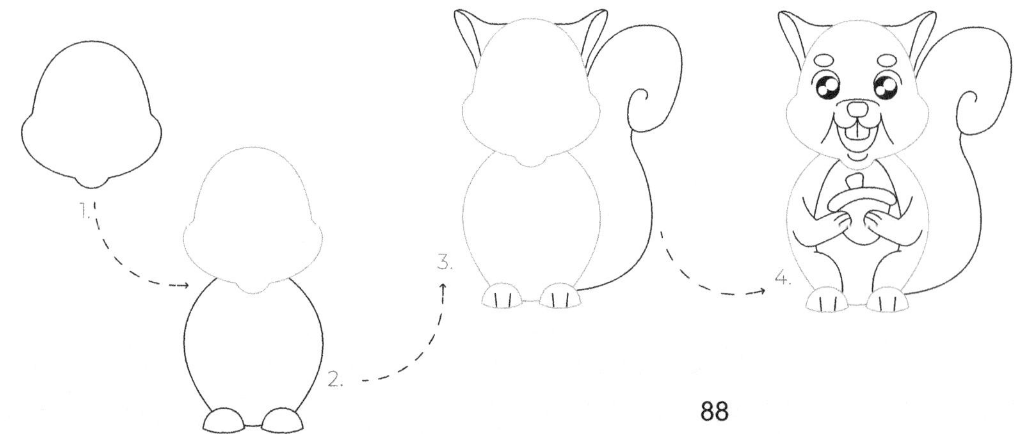

BUFFALO

Draw a rounded head and a wide, furry body underneath. Add a small spiky tuft of hair on top, then draw two big curved horns on the sides.

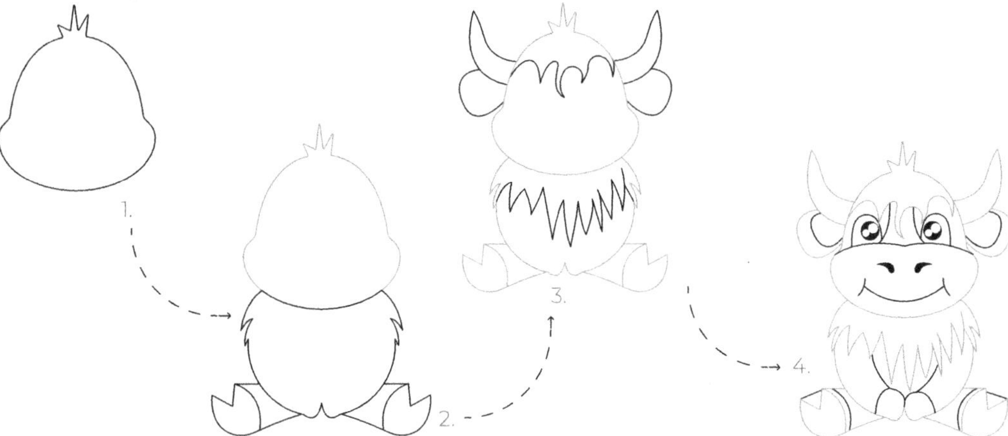

REINDEER

Draw a round head with two small ears on the sides. Leave space above the head to draw tall branching antlers, then finish with the tail and chest fur.

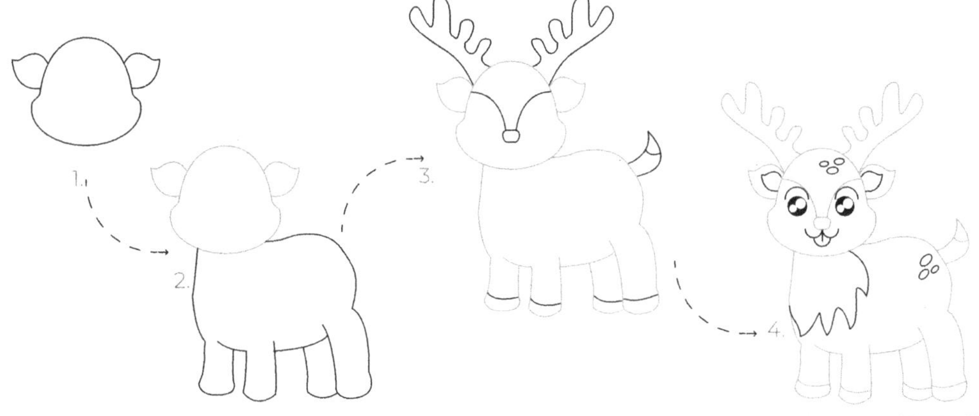

LYNX

Draw the head with two tall, pointy ears. Add the body underneath, then draw the fluffy fur on the cheeks and small tufts on top of the ears.

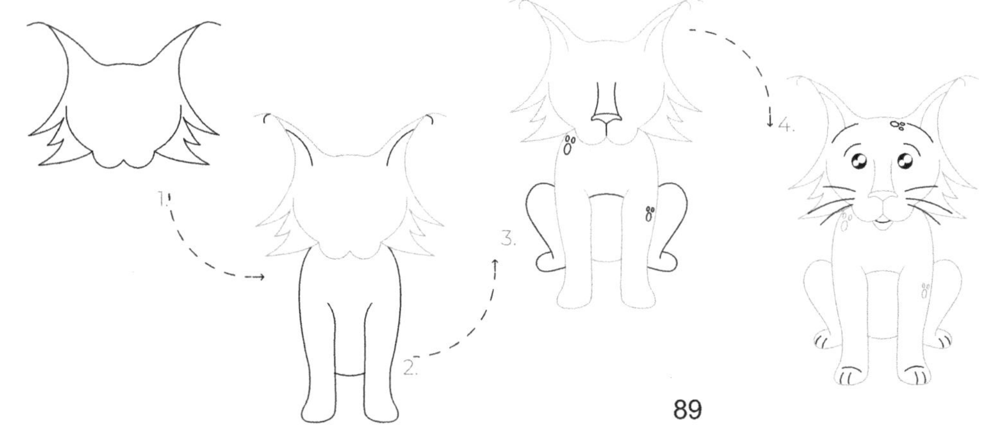

POLAR BEAR

Draw a round head with two small ears on top. Add a wide body underneath, then draw the arms and cute legs.

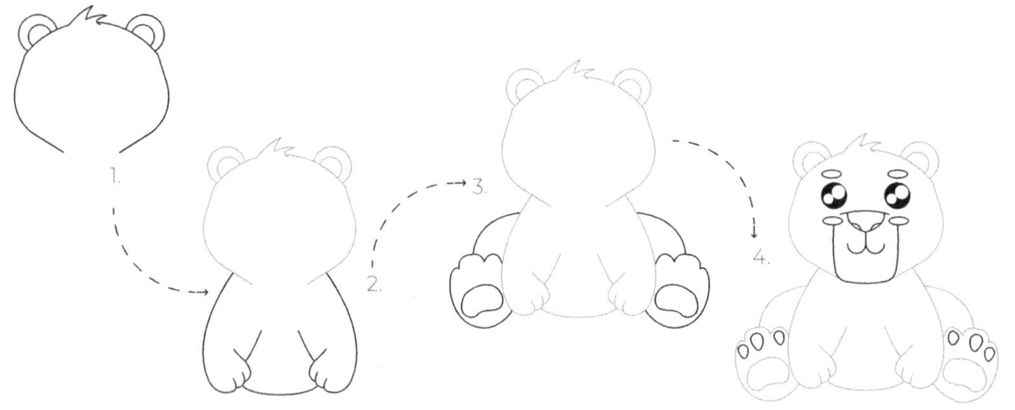

ORCA

Draw a long curved body with a pointed tail.
Tip: Curve the back smoothly to show the orca swimming.

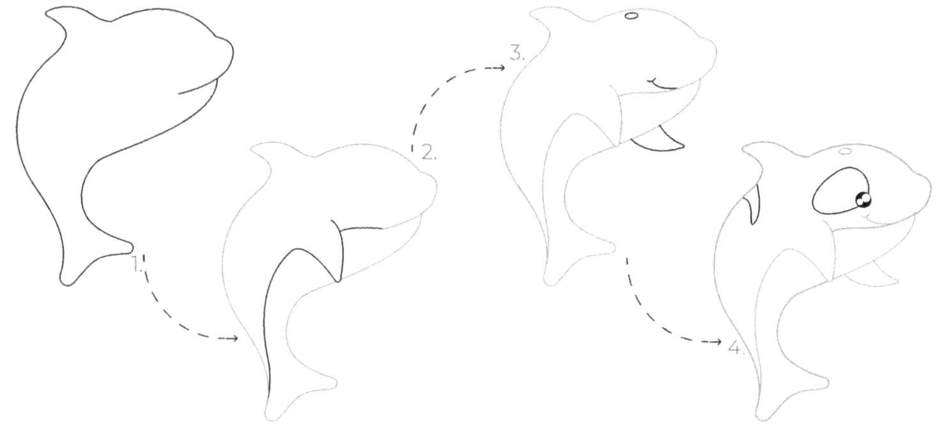

WALRUS

Draw two circles together for the mouth, then add a small circle on top for the nose. Draw a bigger circle above for the head. Add a large round body, flippers, and two long tusks.

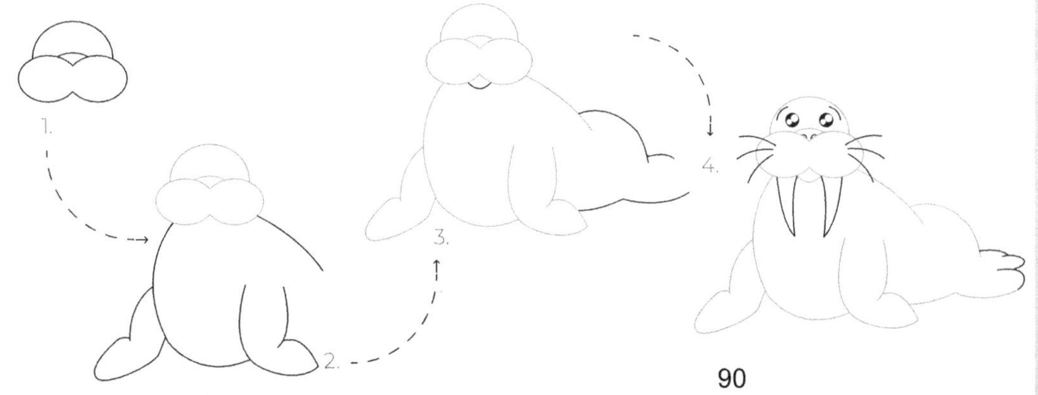

DOG

Draw a wide head shape with two floppy ears. Add fluffy fur, then draw a small sitting body, a curved tail, and details for the paws.

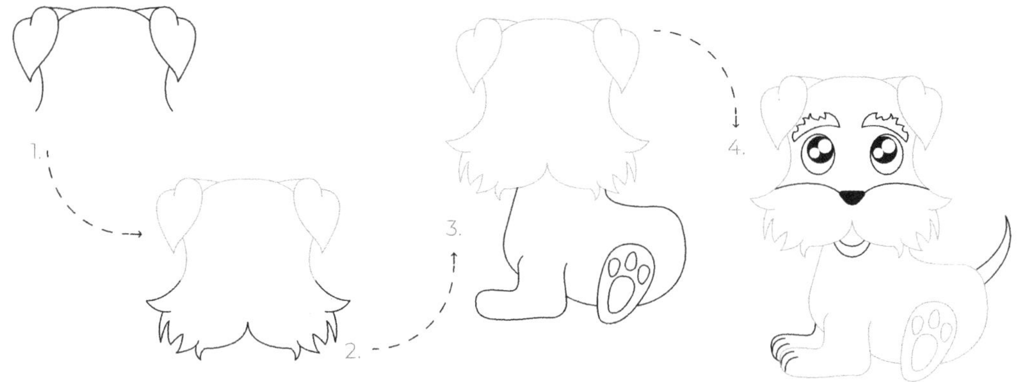

RABBIT

Draw a round head with two tall ears.
Tip: Make the ears long and close together to look like a real bunny.

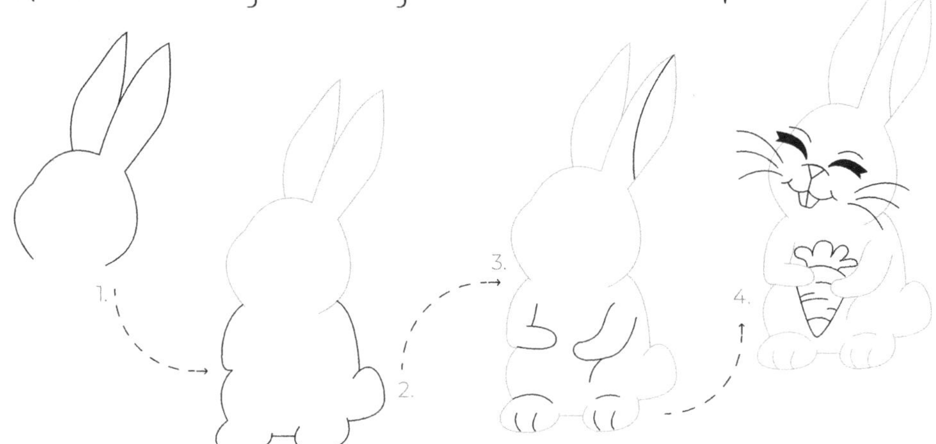

CAT

Draw a round head with two pointy ears on top. Add a small sitting body with round front paws and a curved tail.

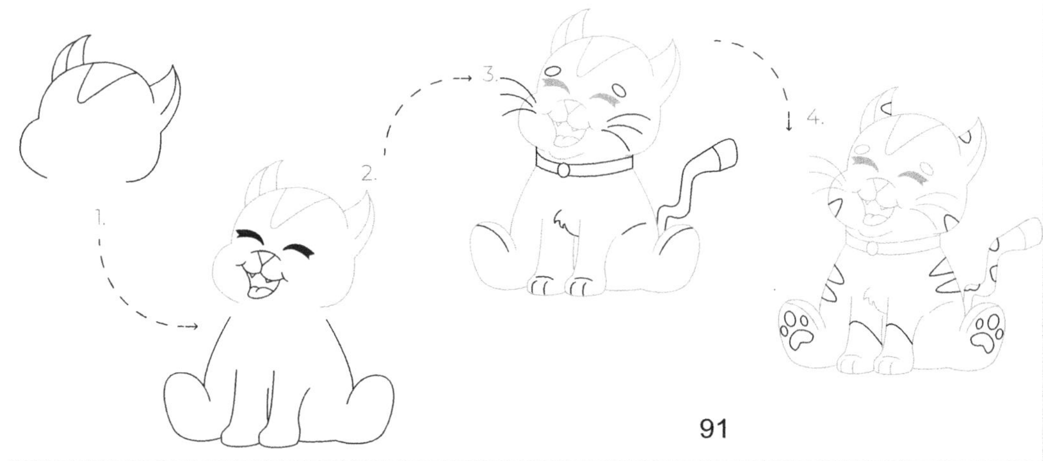

PIG

Draw a round head with two small ears on top. Add a big oval body on its side and four short legs. Finish with a tiny curly tail at the back.

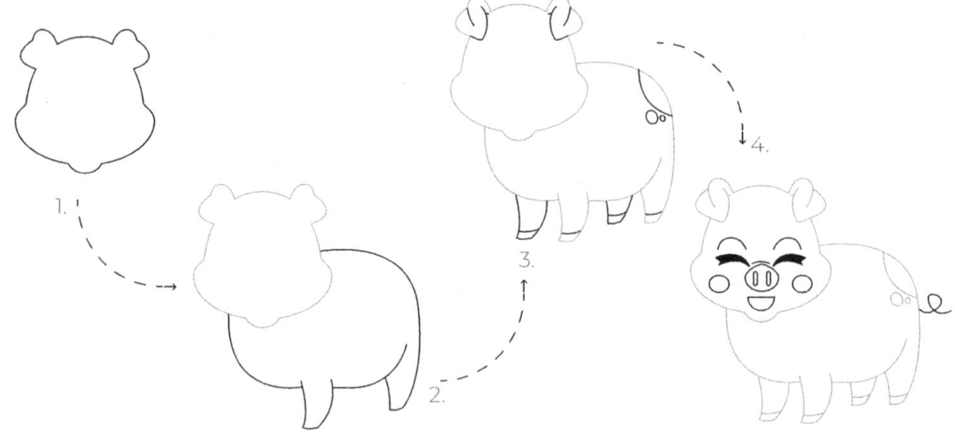

SHEEP

Draw a rounded shape for the head. Add a big fluffy cloud shape underneath for the body. Draw two ears on the sides and four legs at the bottom.

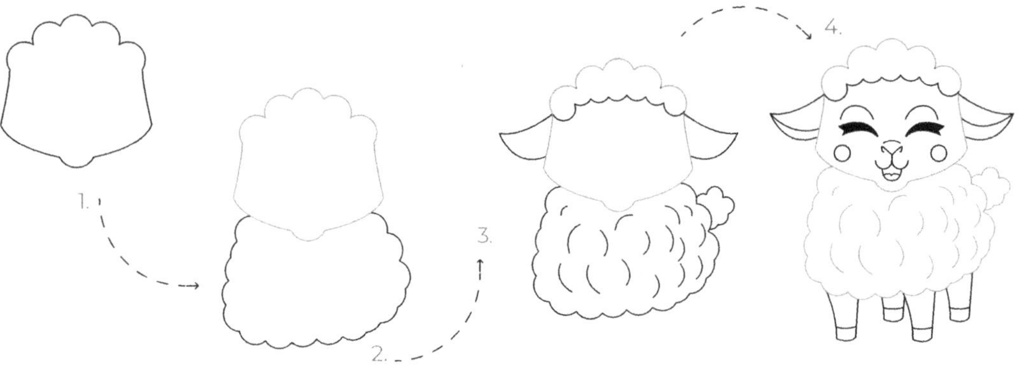

GOAT

Draw a rounded head and a wide body underneath. Add two curved horns on top and pointy ears on the sides.
Tip: Don't forget the little beard under the chin!

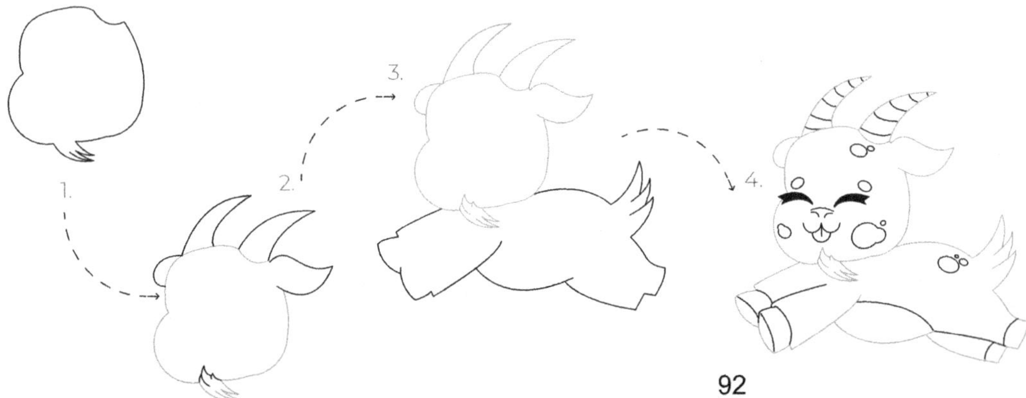

DONKEY

Draw a long head with two tall ears.
Tip: Make the ears extra tall so it looks different from a horse.

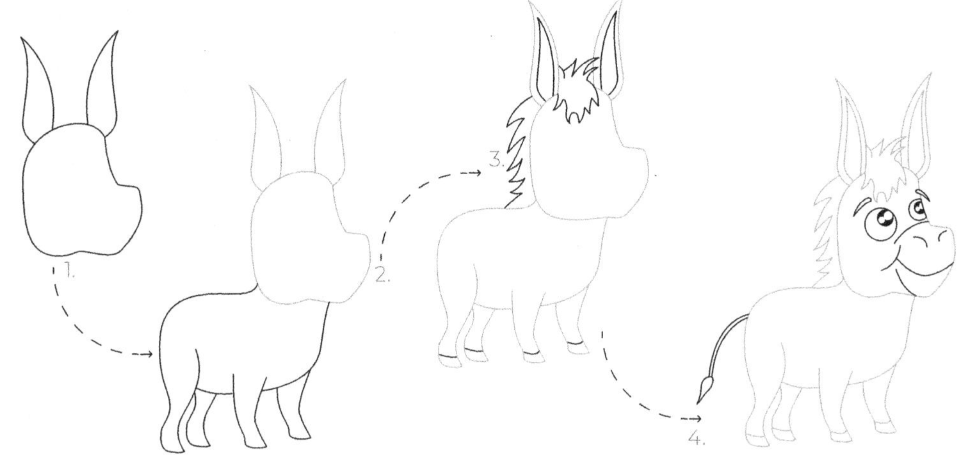

HEDGEHOG

Draw a small round head with a long nose.
Tip: Curve the back and fill it with short, spiky lines for the quills.

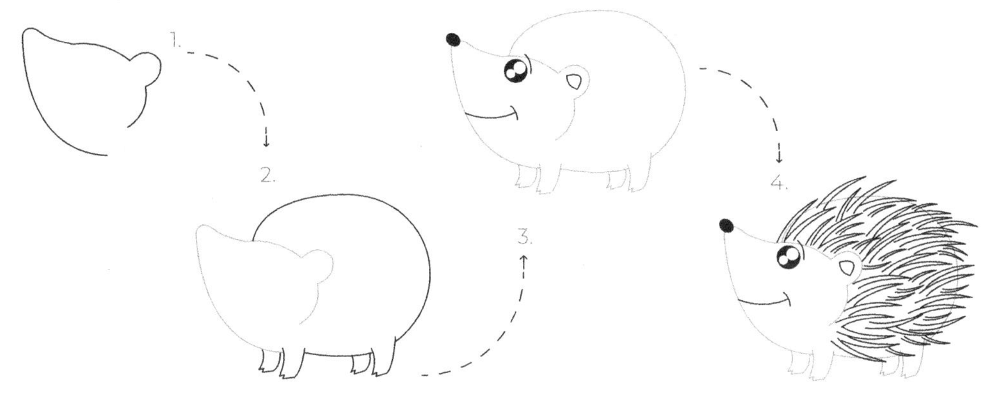

MOUSE

Draw two circles for the ears and a small round head.
Tip: Keep the body tiny so the ears look extra big and cute.

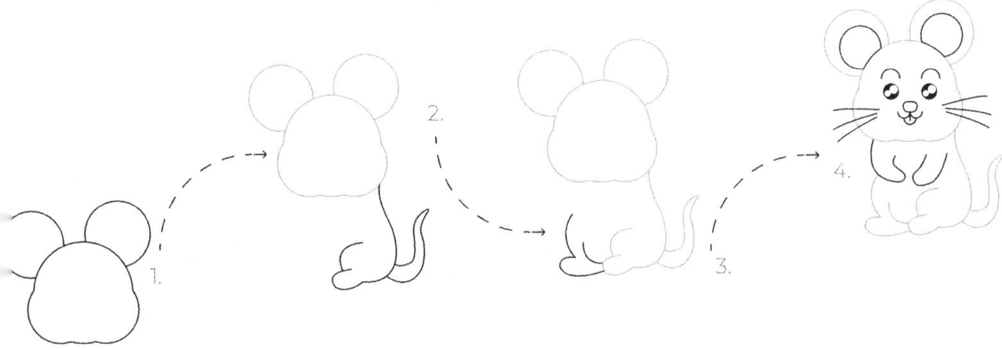

Your turn

Your turn

Your turn

DUCKLING

Start with a circle for the head and a tuft of feathers on top.
Tip: Make the wings curve out so it looks like it's flapping.

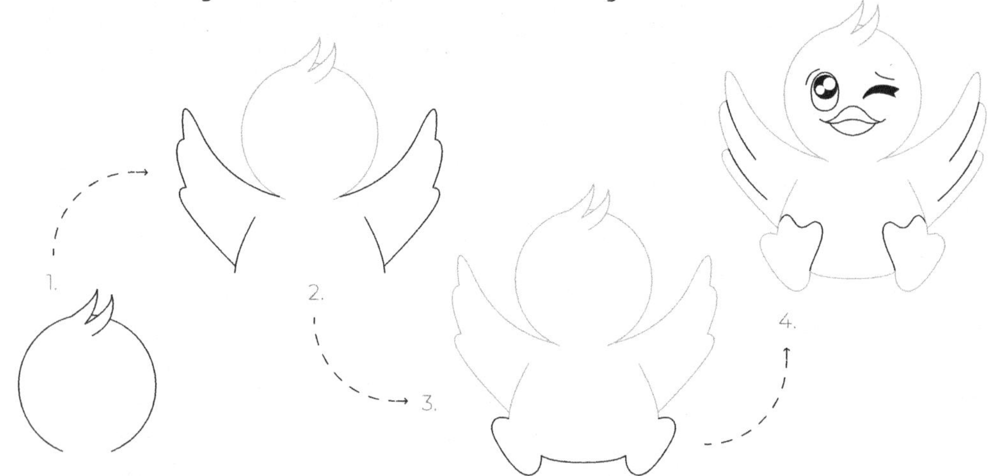

CATERPILLAR

Draw a row of small connected circles for the body.
Tip: Make each circle slightly smaller as you go to show it bending forward.

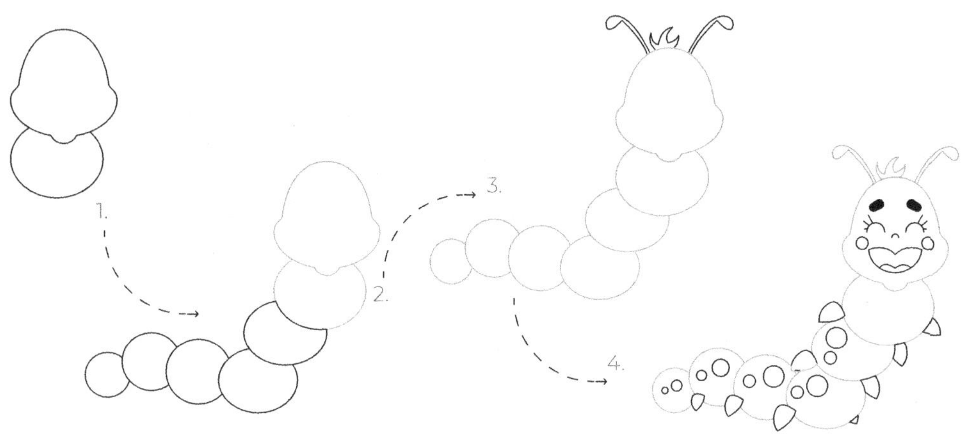

TOAD

Draw two round eyes on top of a wide head shape.
Tip: Leave space under the head for the big legs and toes.

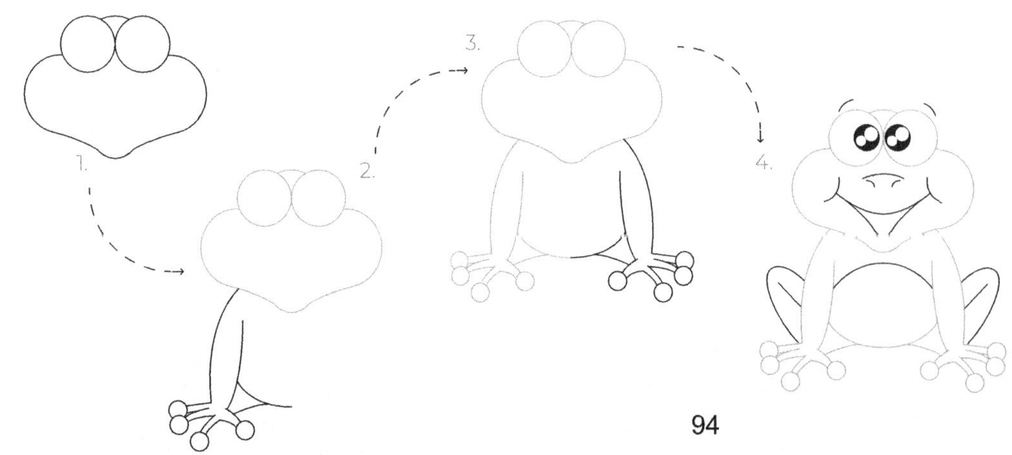

BUTTERFLY

Draw a small oval for the body and two big wings on each side.
Tip: Decorate the wings with patterns or shapes to make your butterfly look unique.

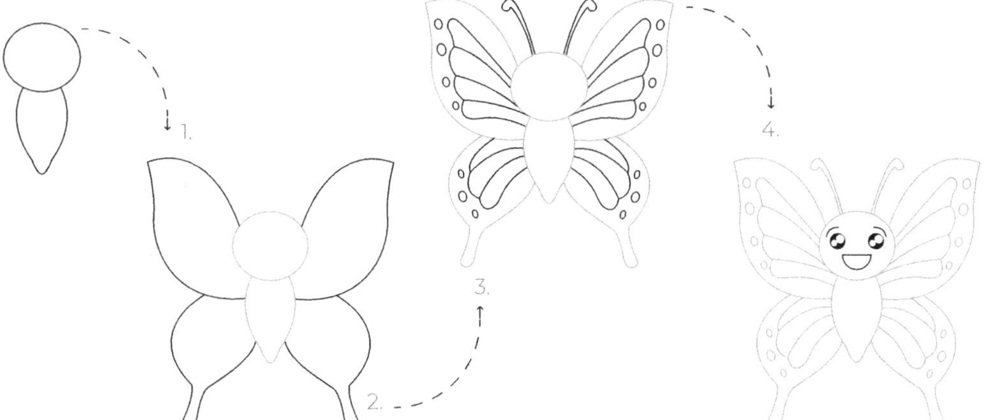

SNAIL

Start with a spiral for the shell. Add a long, curved body stretching forward, then draw two eye stalks on top.
Tip: Make the body look stretched to show the snail slowly moving.

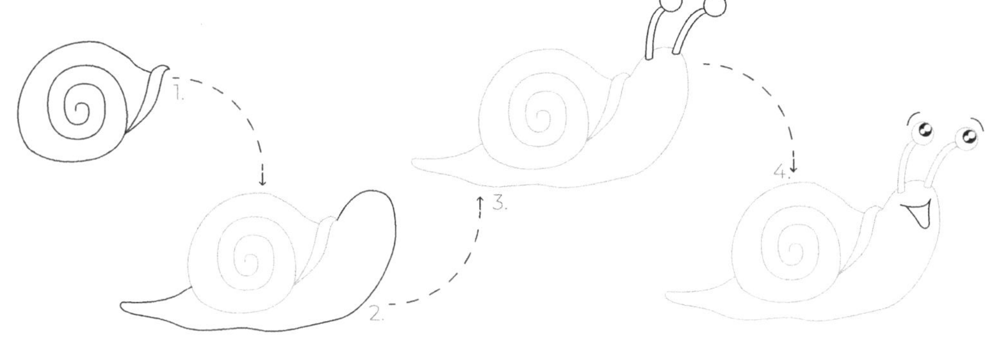

CRICKET

Draw a small circle for the head and a long curved oval for the body. Add two long back legs pointing backward, and two small front legs close to the head.

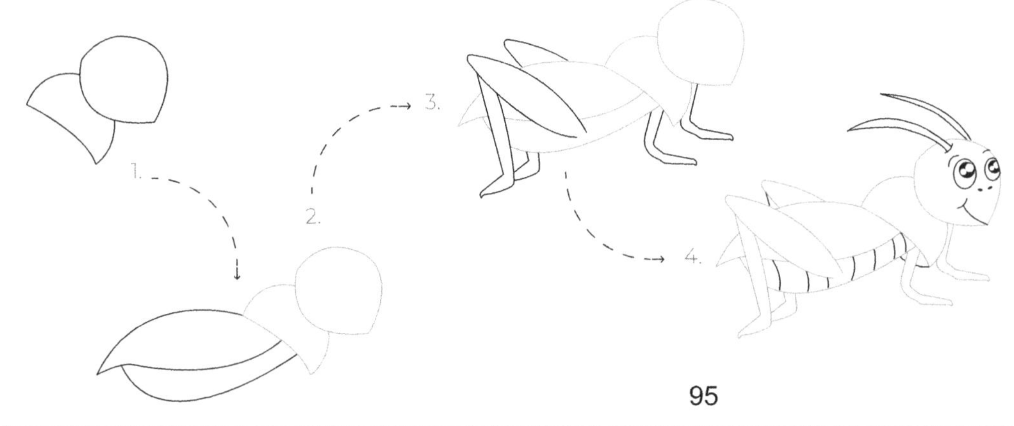

DRAGONFLY

Draw a small round head and a long thin body made of little sections.
Add two pairs of long wings so it looks light and fast.

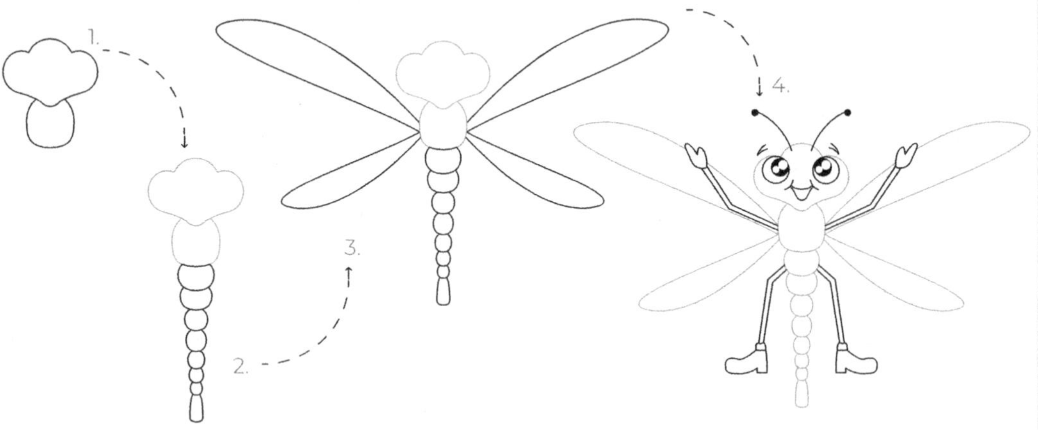

TARANTULA

Draw one big round shape with small bumps on top for the head and body
together. Add eight legs, bending them so they spread out wide!

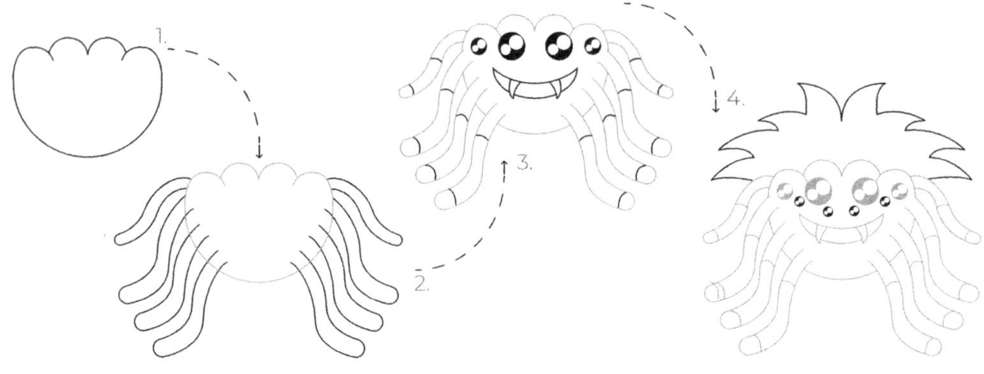

ANT

Draw three ovals in a row for the head, middle, and back.
Tip: Make the middle oval smaller so it looks like a skinny waist.

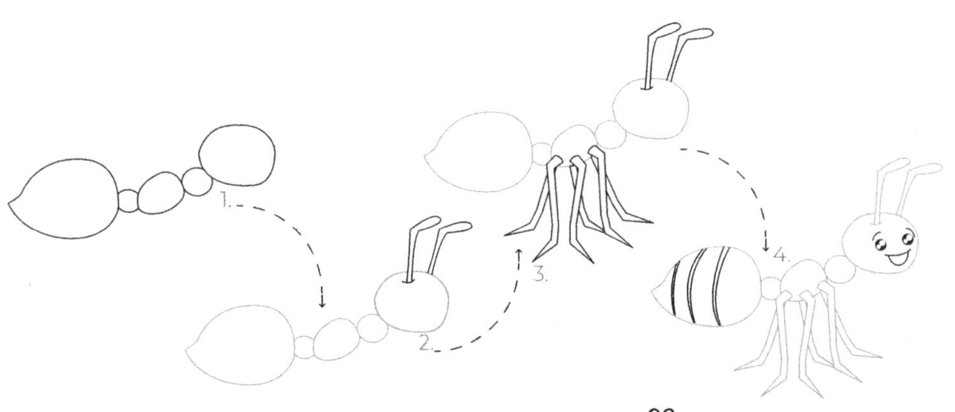

PRAYING MANTIS

Draw two big eyes and a small pointed face. Add long front legs, a curved body with wings, back legs, and antennae.

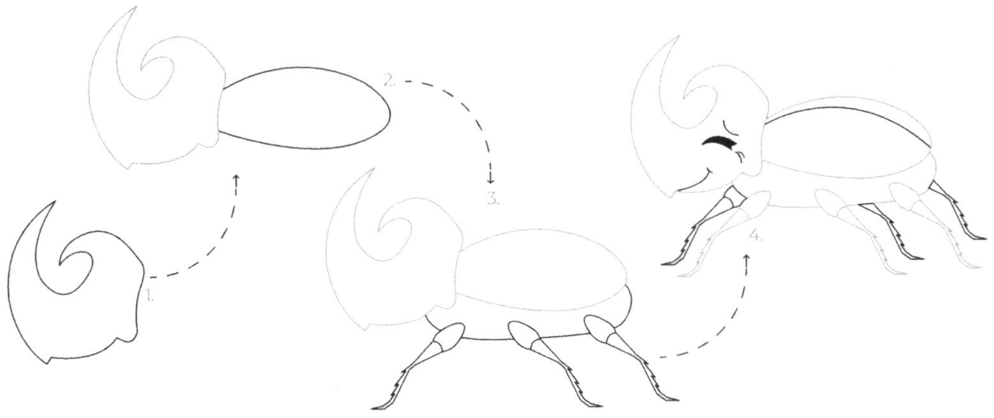

RHINOCEROS BEETLE

Draw a head with a big curved horn on top. Add a long oval for the back and connect them. Draw six legs, keeping the front ones closer to the horn.

LADYBUG

Start with a small circle for the head. Add a big round shell behind it. Finish by adding spots and antennae.

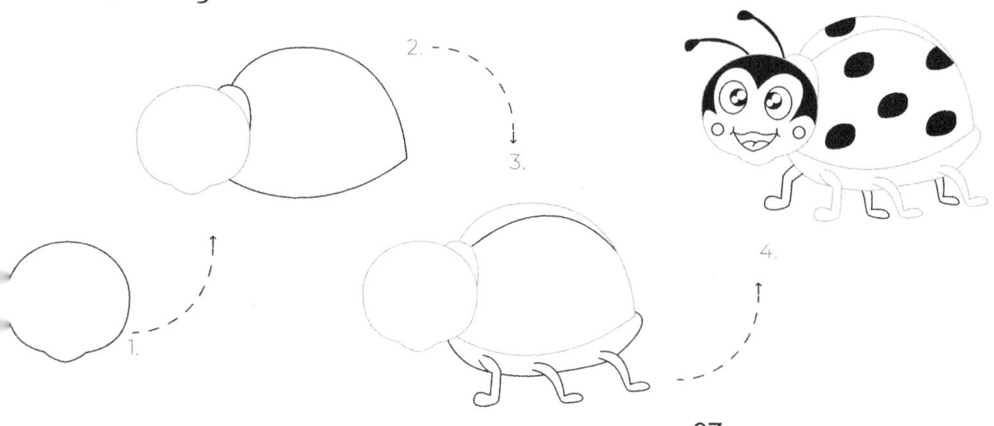

SEAHORSE

Draw a small round head and a long curved body.
Tip: Add a curl at the tail to make it look like a real seahorse.

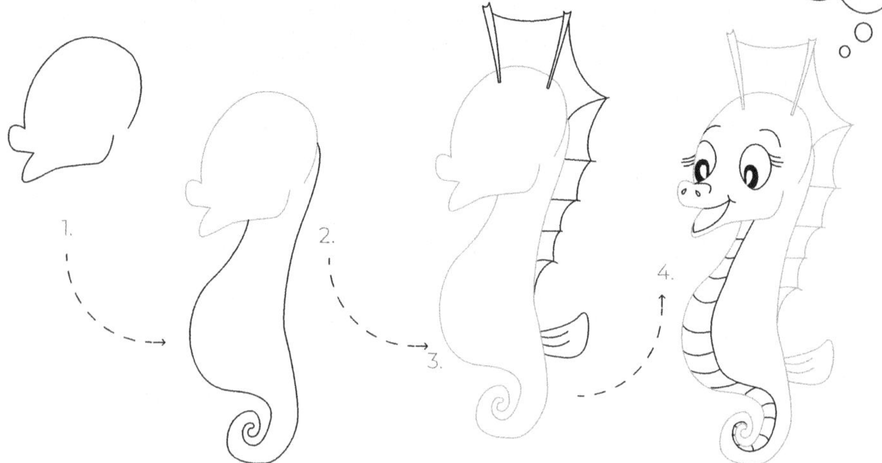

Your turn

STARFISH

Draw a big star shape with soft, rounded arms!

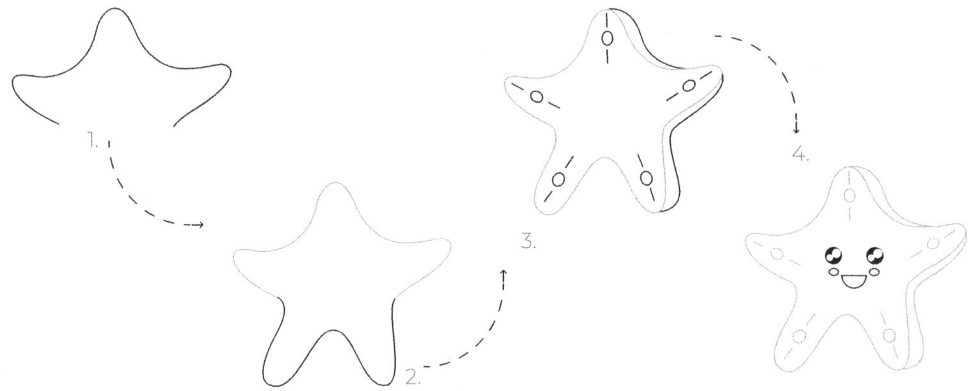

Your turn

OCTOPUS

Draw a round head and start adding long wiggly arms.
Tip: Curve the arms in different directions so they look playful and flowing.

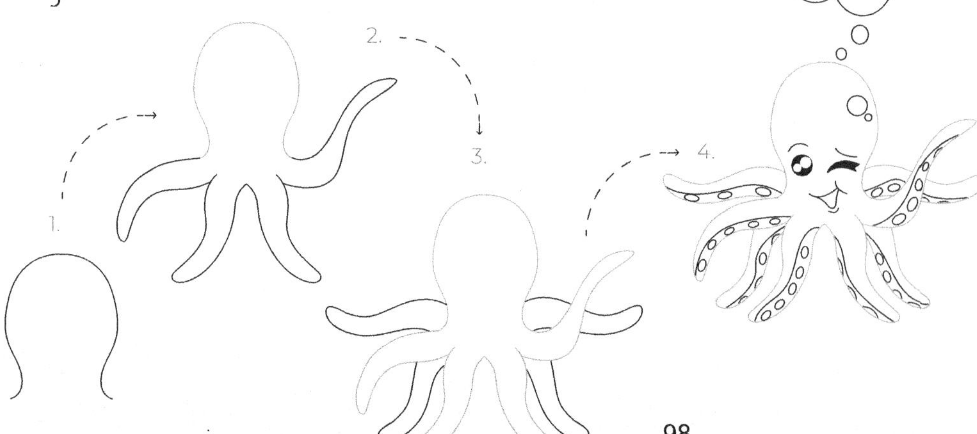

Your turn

Create Your Own Animal Scene!

Use this whole page to draw a big scene with your favorite animals from this level.
Make them play, explore, or go on an adventure together!

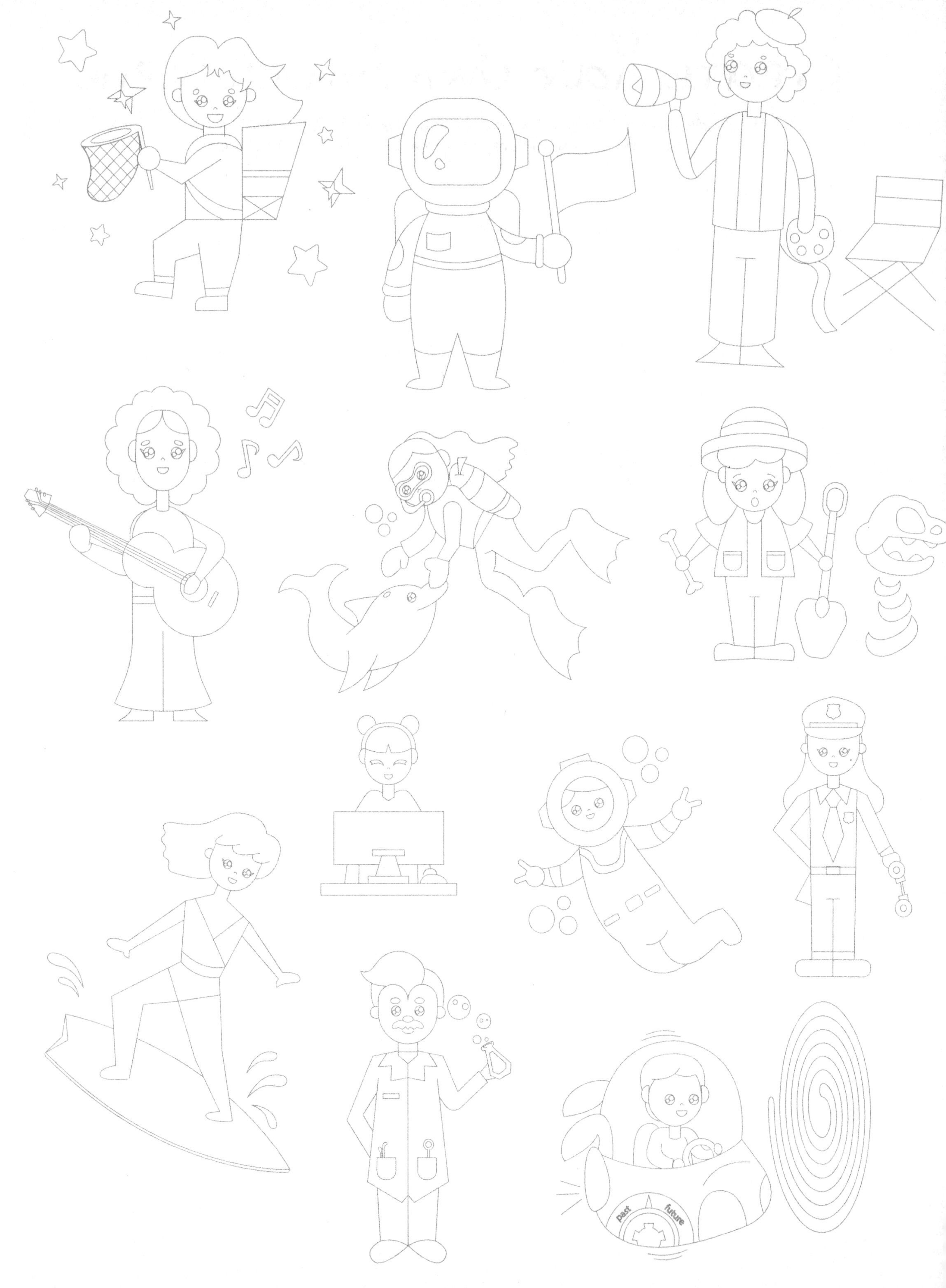
past
future

LEVEL 4:

BIG DREAMERS, BIG JOBS

DANCER

Draw a circle for the head, then add a rectangle body underneath. Next, draw two curved arms on the sides. Add two legs, one crossed or tilted to make it look like it's dancing.

Tip: Move the legs in different directions so it looks full of energy!

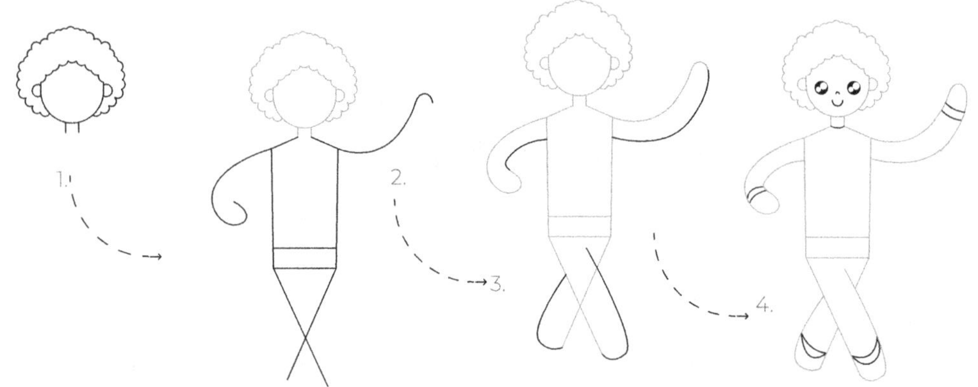

BAKER

Draw a puffy chef hat and a wide body shape underneath.

Tip: Put a whisk, spoon, or a yummy cake in the hands so everyone knows it's a baker!

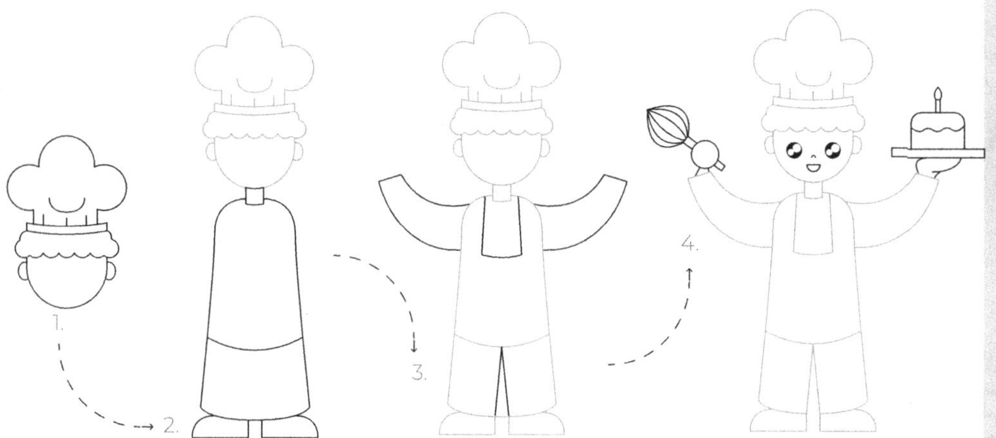

MARINE BIOLOGIST

Start with the dolphin's body, from the nose to the tail. Add the swimmer's body above the dolphin.

Tip: Don't forget the mask and the air tank, they make it look like a real diver!

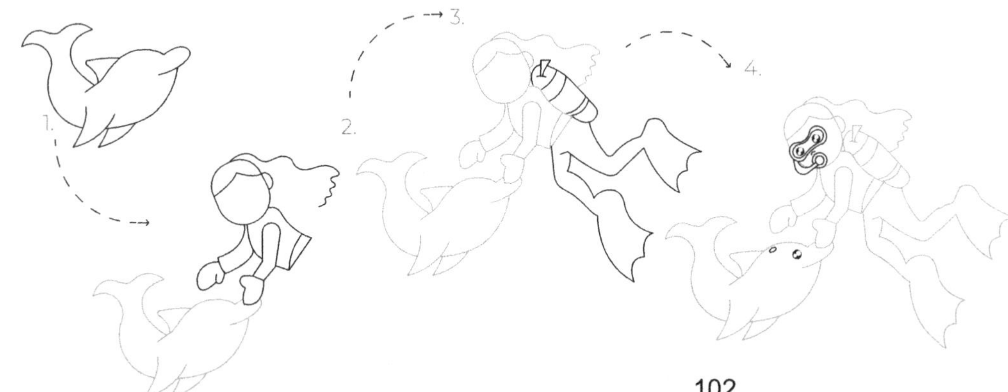

CHEF

Start with a big puffy cloud shape for the chef's hat.
Tip: Make the hat tall so the chef looks extra important!

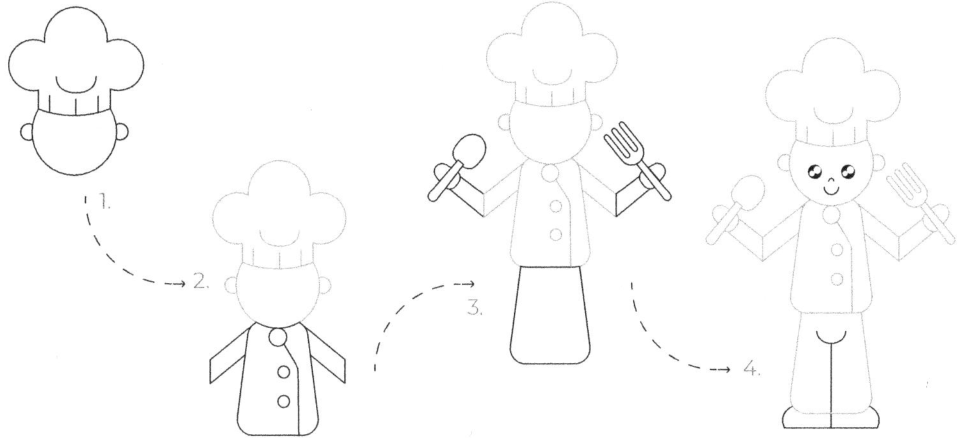

DOCTOR

Draw a round face with a wide headband and a mirror on top.
Tip: Curve the stethoscope gently so it fits around the neck.

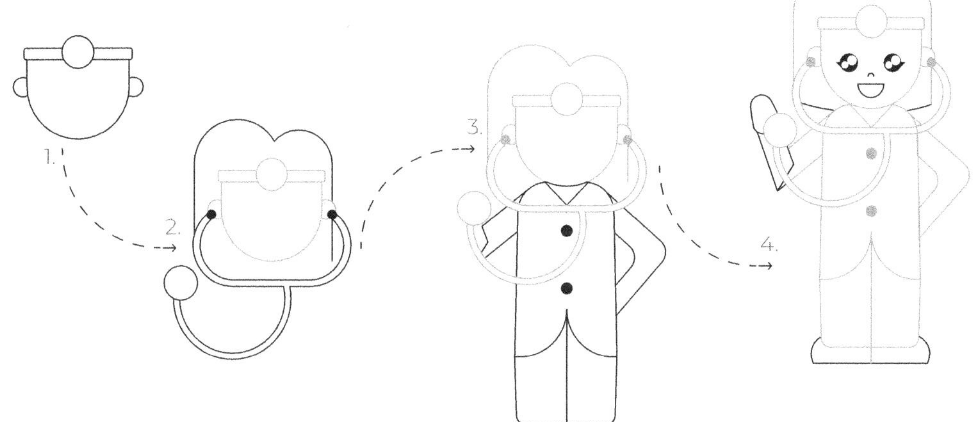

TEACHER

Draw a round face with simple hair on both sides.
Tip: Add a book in one hand so it looks like the teacher is teaching.

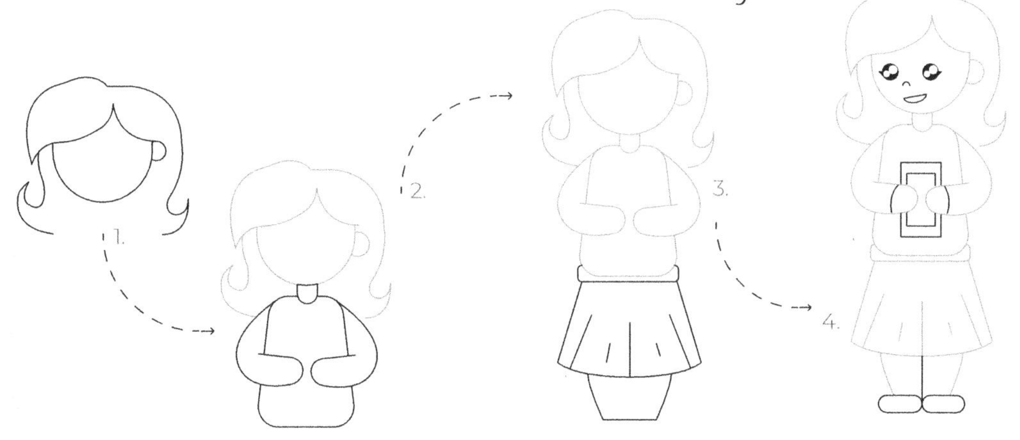

POTION BREWER

Draw a wizard hat with a round face below. Add a robe and curved arms. Finish with a potion bottle or cauldron.
Tip: Make the hat wide so it feels magical!

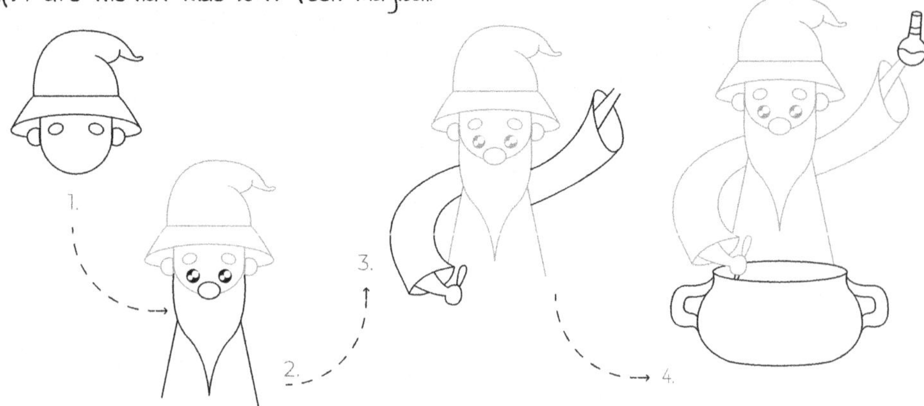

STAR CATCHER

Start with a circle head and add simple hair swoops. Add the body with arms reaching up.
Tip: Scatter stars everywhere so it looks like they're floating in the sky!

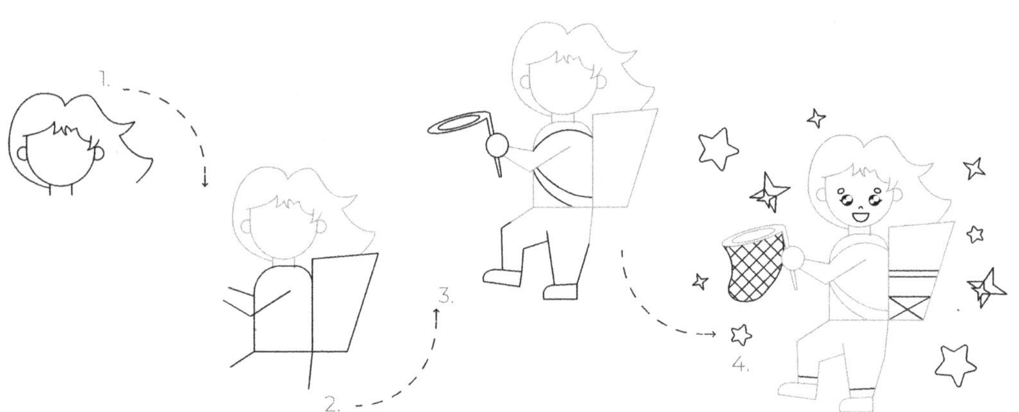

ICE SCULPTOR

Begin with a round head and a tall rectangle for the body.
Tip: Draw the ice block tall so it looks ready to be sculpted!

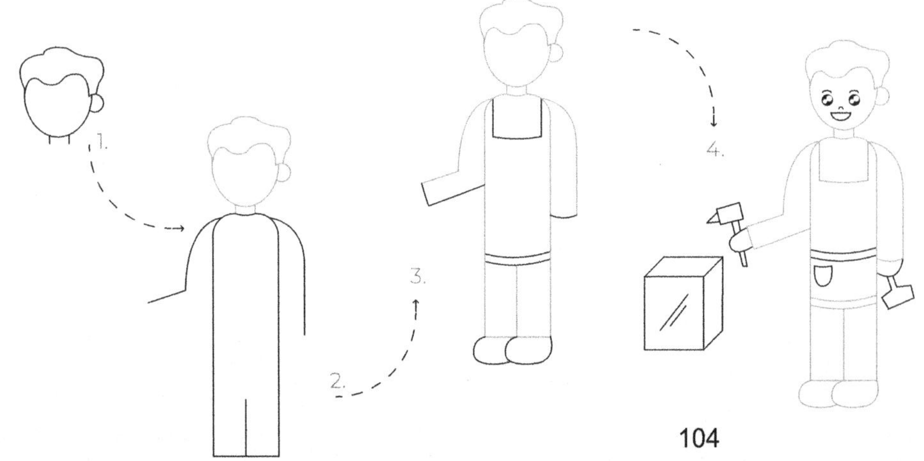

ROCKET PILOT

Draw a round helmet with a face inside. Add a space suit with arms and legs.
Tip: Leave extra room for the big suit so it looks super spacey!

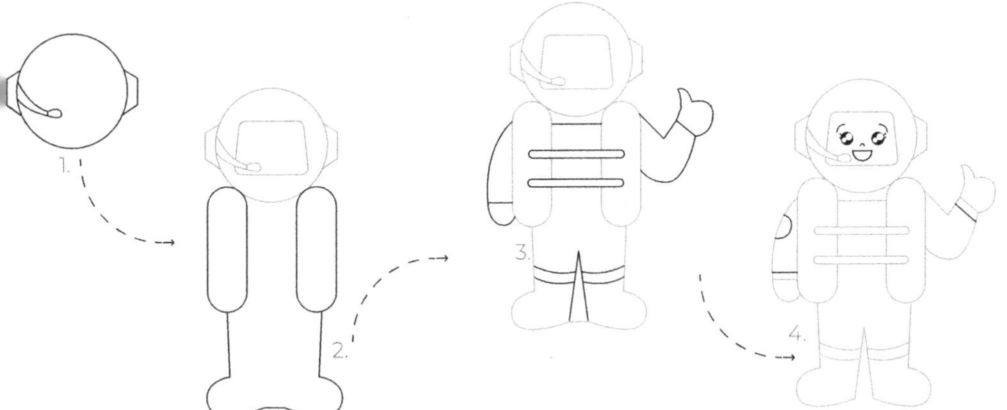

FIREFIGHTER

Draw a helmet with a small badge on top. Add a long coat with arms and legs. Finish with stripes and a water bucket.

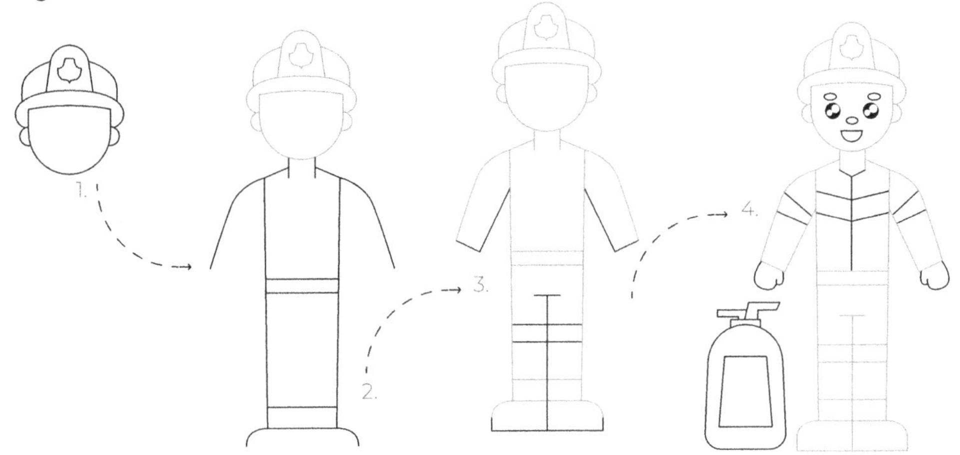

POLICE OFFICER

Start with a round head and a cap with a badge. Finish with details like buttons and a whistle.

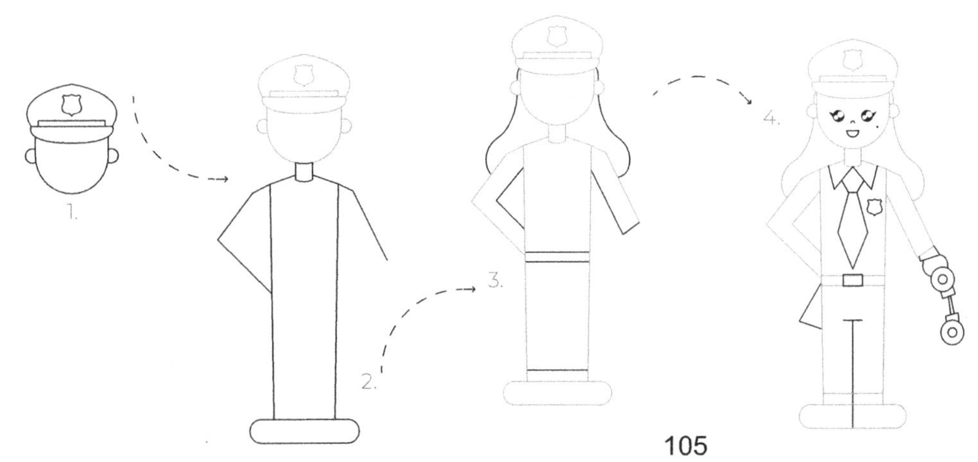

ASTRONAUT

Draw a big round helmet, then add a suit with a patch on the side.

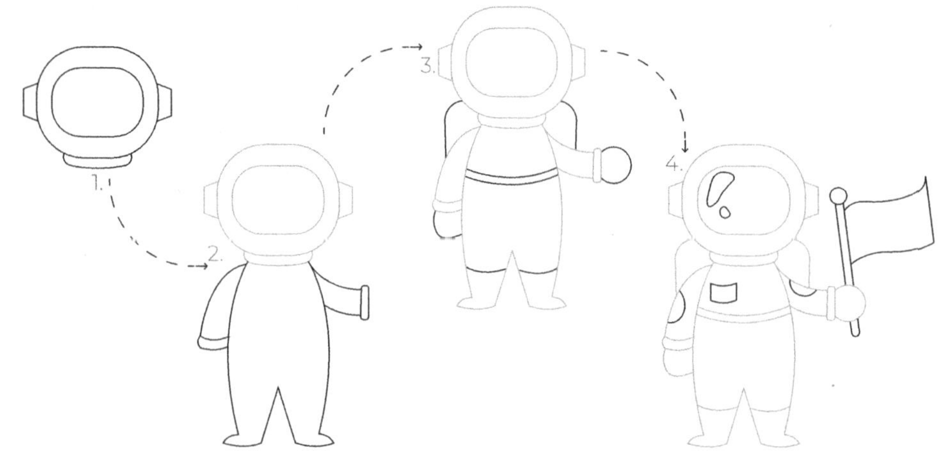

BALLET DANCER

Start with a round head and a bun on top.
Tip: Spread her arms wide so she looks like she's dancing!

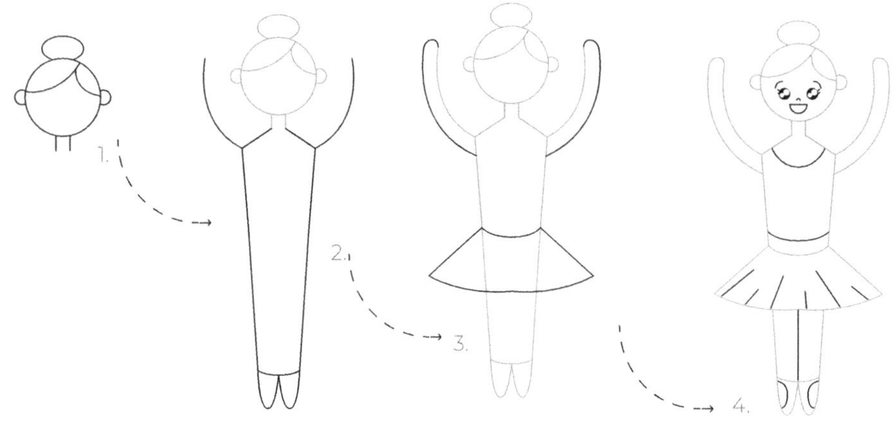

ZOMBIE ACTOR

Draw a round head with a little bite missing to make it spooky.
Tip: Add scars or stitches so it looks like a real zombie actor!

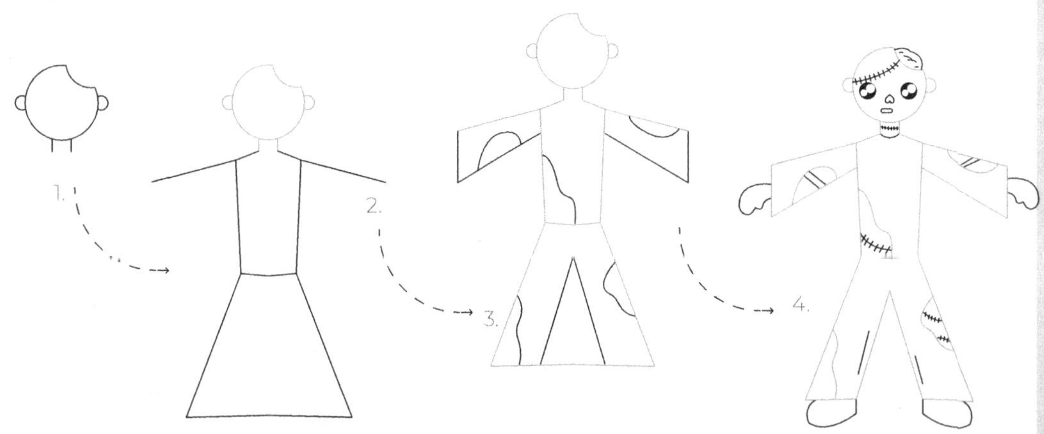

MUSIC TEACHER

Draw a round head with a bun on top. Add a long coat body with arms.
Tip: Don't forget the baton so everyone knows she's the music teacher.

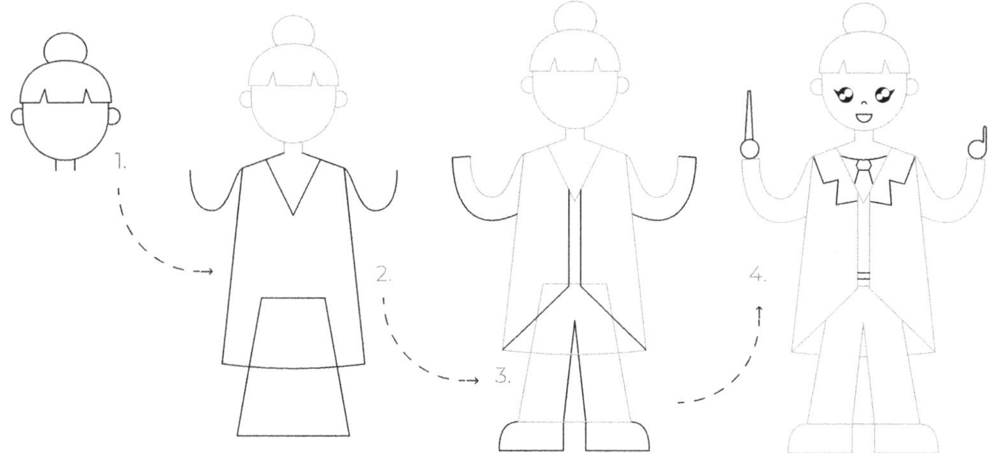

SCIENTIST

Draw a round head with curly hair.
Tip: Big round glasses make her look extra smart!

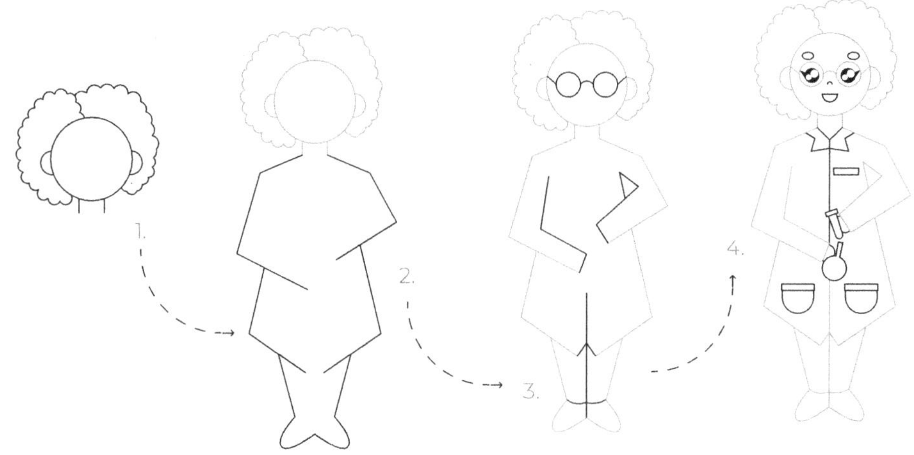

NURSE

Draw a round head with a nurse's cap.
Tip: Put a syringe in her hand so she looks ready to give medicine!

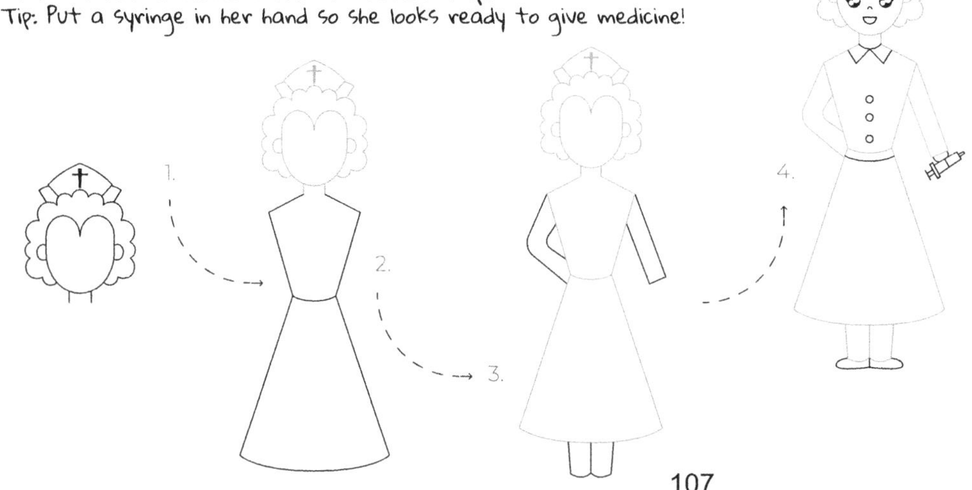

REPORTER

Draw a round head with neat hair.
Tip: Don't forget the microphone and notebook so everyone knows they're reporting news!

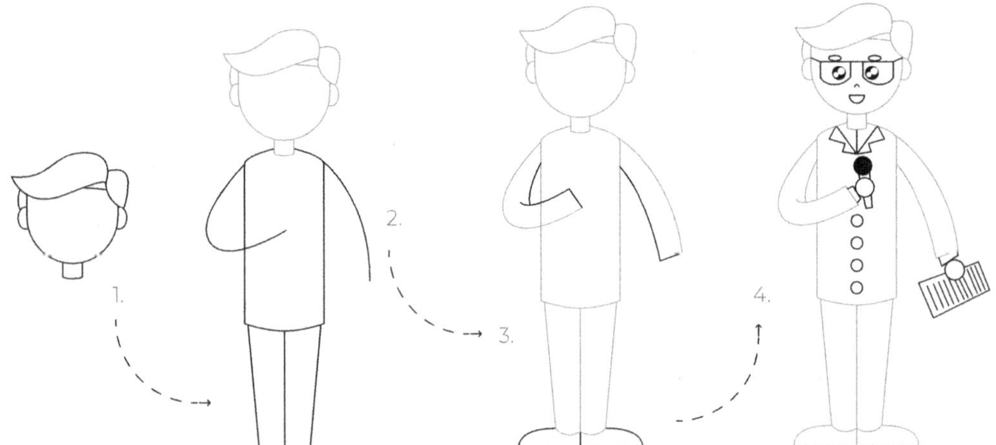

LIFEGUARD

Draw a round head with a cap on top. Add a body with arms and rescue gear.

Tip: A big float or buoy makes the lifeguard look ready to save the day!

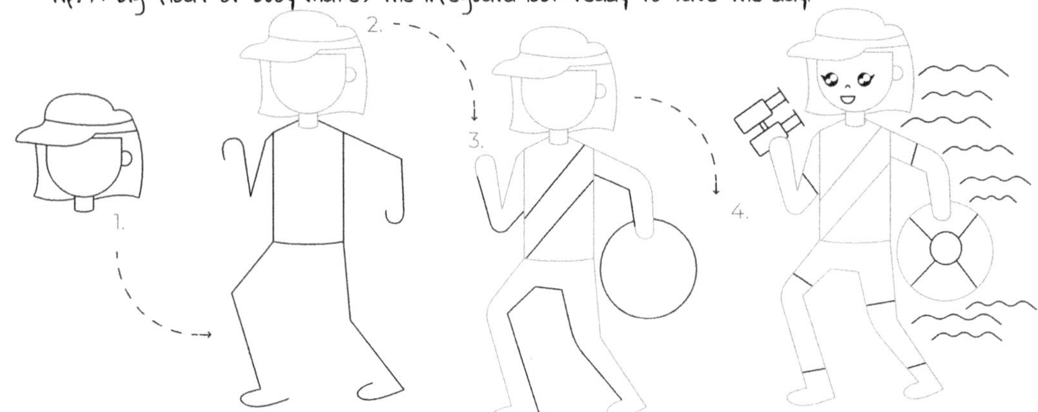

SINGER

Draw a round head with big curly hair.
Tip: A microphone in her hand makes her look like a superstar on stage!

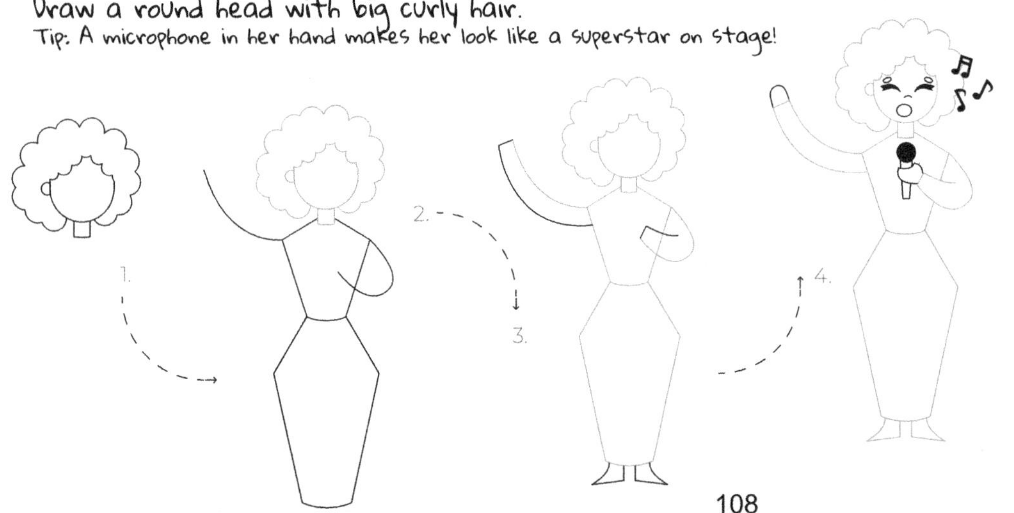

MODEL

Start with a round head with straight hair.
Tip: Add sparkles around her so she shines like on the runway!

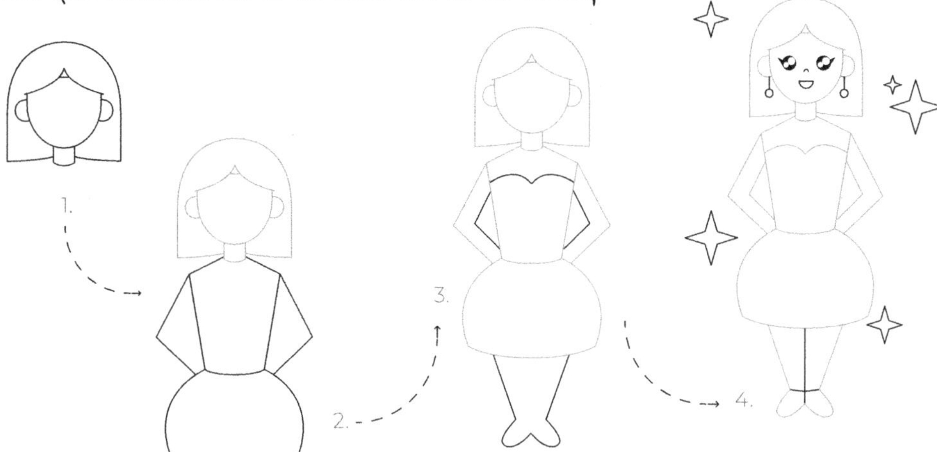

Your turn

FILM DIRECTOR

Begin with a round head and messy hair. Add a body and one raised arm.
Tip: Include a camera and director's chair to show movie action!

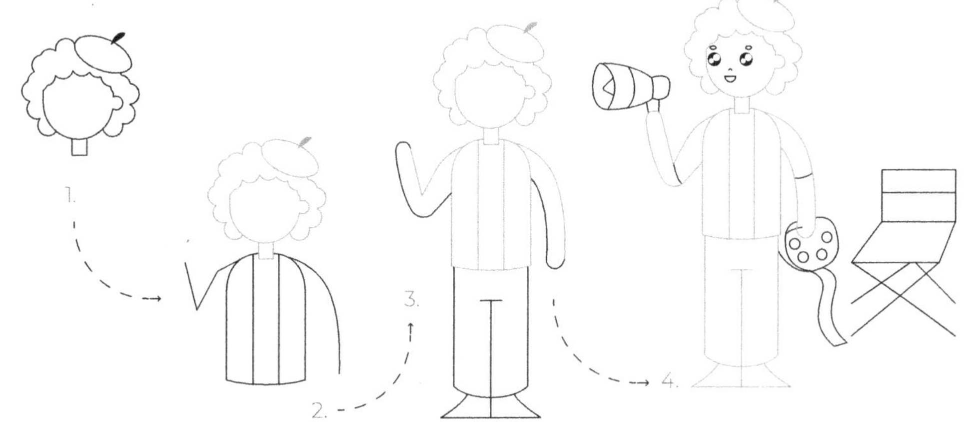

Your turn

MECHANIC

Put a construction hat on top of a round head. Give the body a
uniform with arms and pockets.
Tip: A wrench or toolbox in hand makes the mechanic look ready to work!

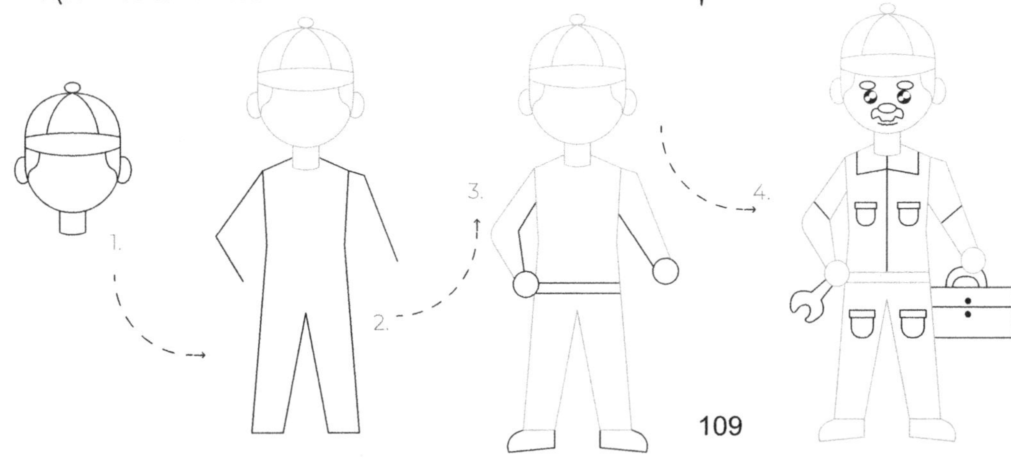

Your turn

RIDE DESIGNER

Start with a helmet on a round head. Add a body in a suit with strong boots.

Tip: Big goggles make the ride designer look super ready for action!

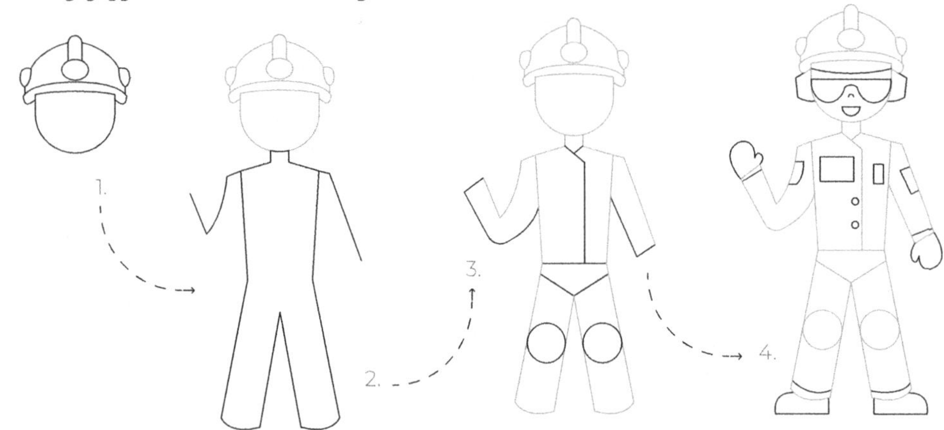

BUBBLE SCIENTIST

Begin with a round head and fluffy hair. Add a long coat with arms and pockets.

Tip: A big test tube in hand makes the bubbles look like a science experiment.

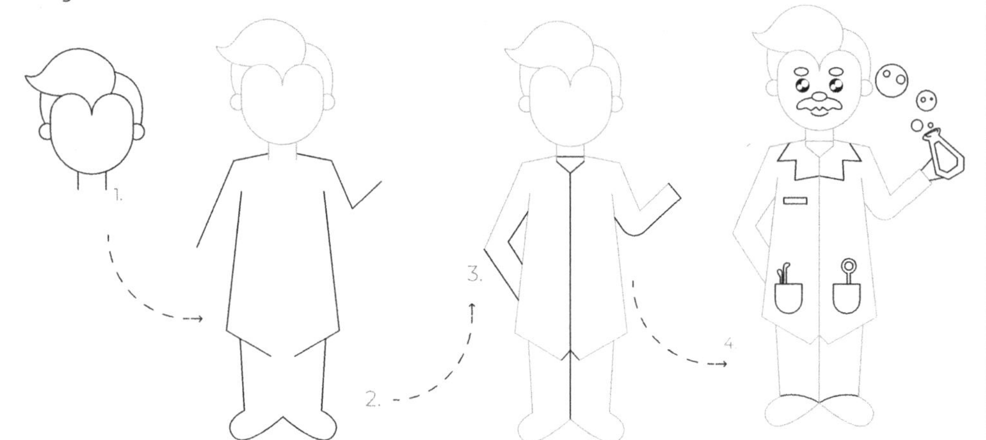

LABYRINTH DESIGNER

Make a round face with long wavy hair. Add a tall body holding a book or plan.

Tip: A maze drawing in the book shows what she's designing!

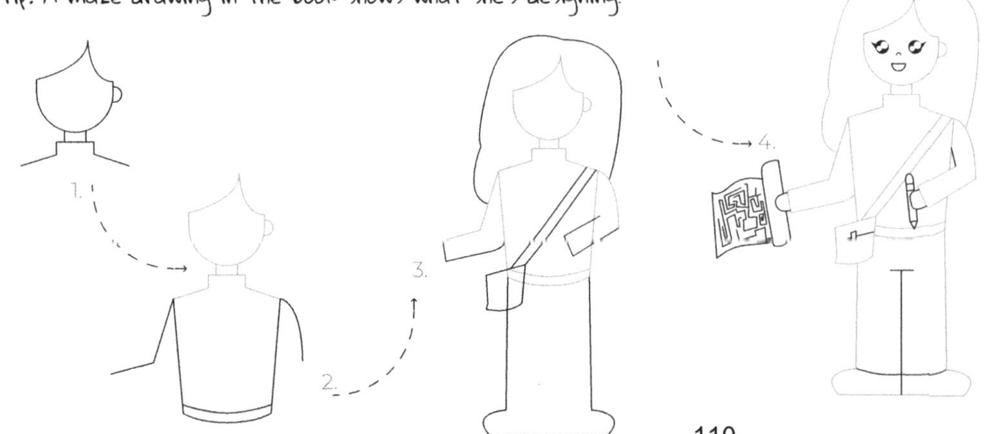

TREASURE HUNTER

Make a round head with spiky hair. Add a body holding a treasure map.
Tip: Add an X on the map so it looks like he's ready to find treasure!

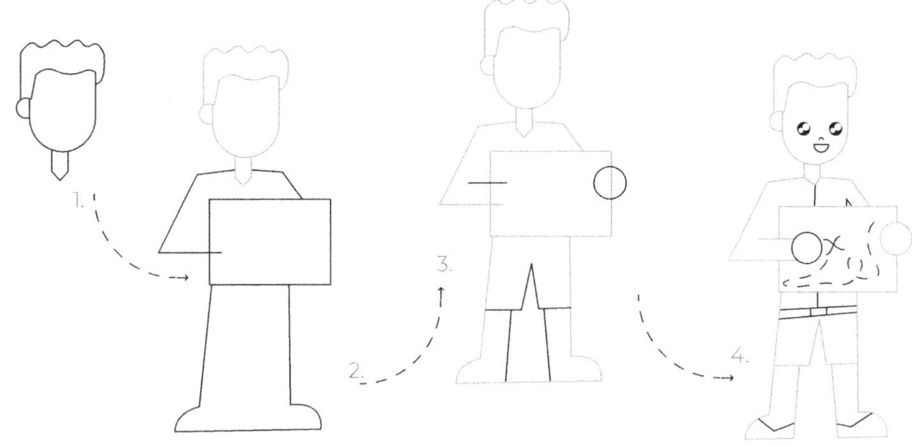

FASHION DESIGNER

Start with a round head and simple hairstyle.
Tip: Don't forget the tape measure around her neck—it's the perfect sign she's a real designer!

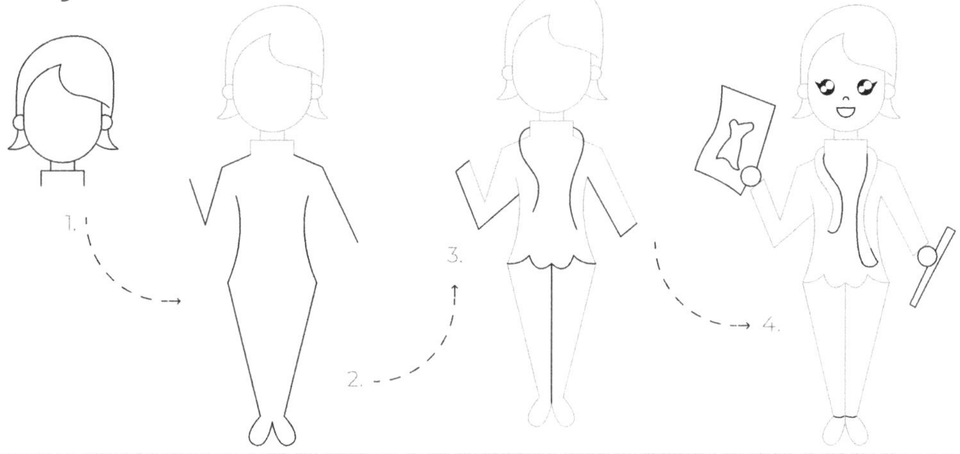

ACTRESS

Begin with a round head and wavy hair. Add a tall body with one leg forward.
Tip: A theater mask in her hand shows she's stepping into character

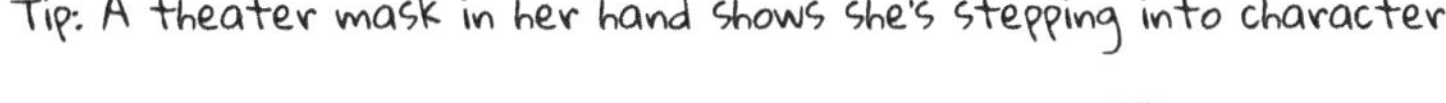
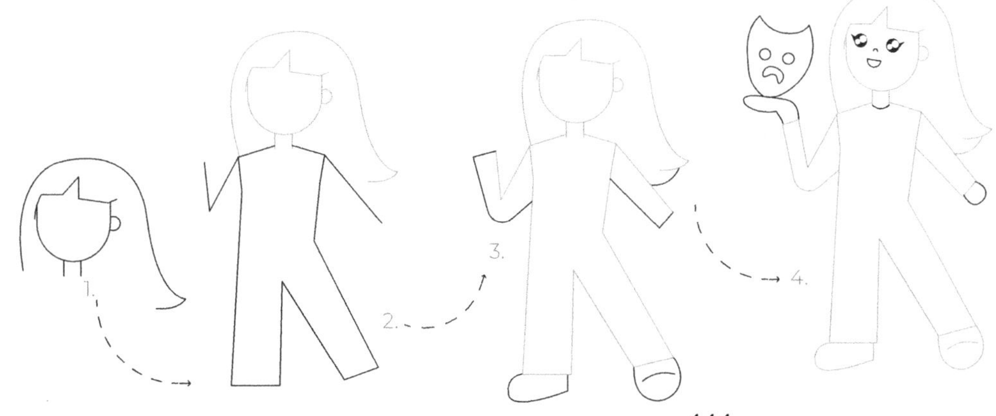

ENGINEER

Start with a round head and a helmet on top. Add a straight body with arms and legs.
Tip: Engineers wear helmets to stay safe while building big projects!

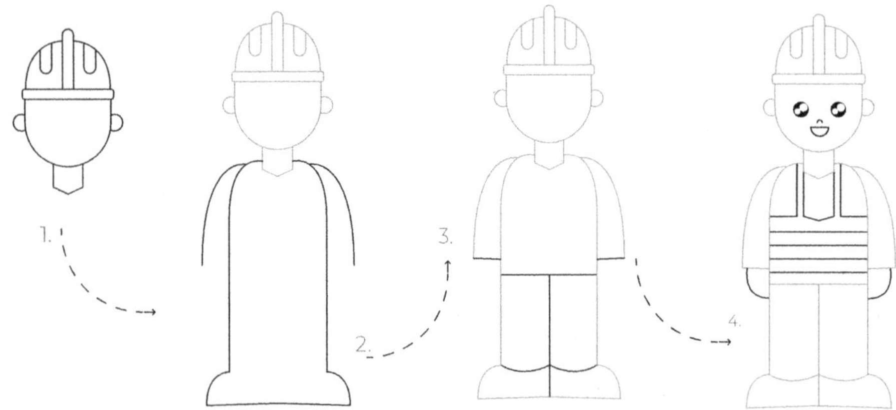

RACE CAR DRIVER

Make a round helmet with a big visor. Add a racing suit body with arms on the hips.
Tip: A bold stance and wide visor make the driver look super fast!

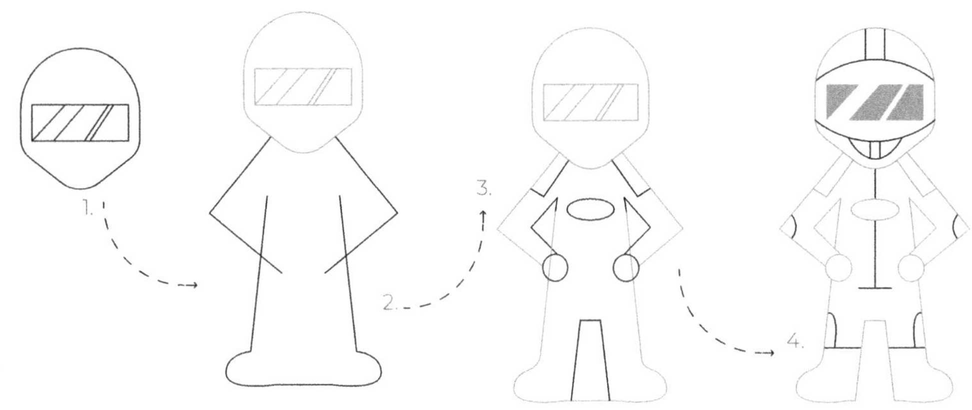

ANIMATOR

Begin with a round head and hair in two buns.
Tip: Draw the screen wide—animators create the coolest cartoons, maybe even for Disney or Pixar!

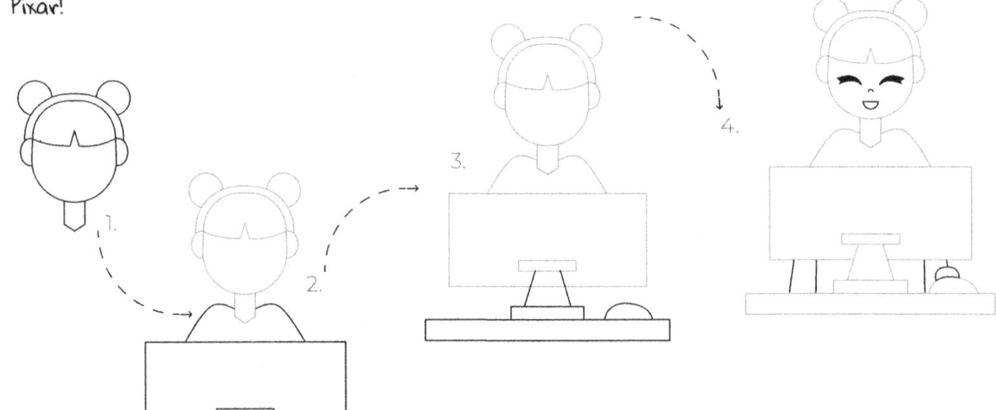

PLANETARIUM GUIDE

Start with a fluffy round hairstyle and a V-shaped upper body.
Tip: Add a curved arm holding the flashlight so it points upward like a beam!

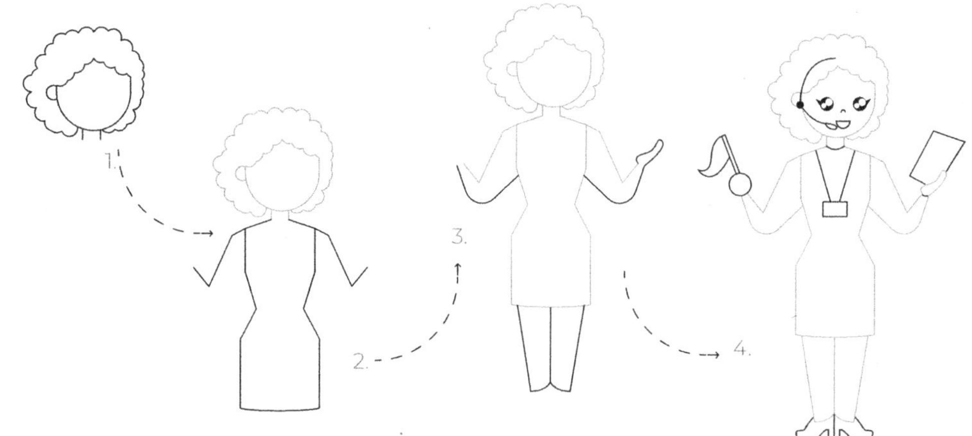

RINGMASTER

Draw a neat round head and a tall rectangle for the jacket.

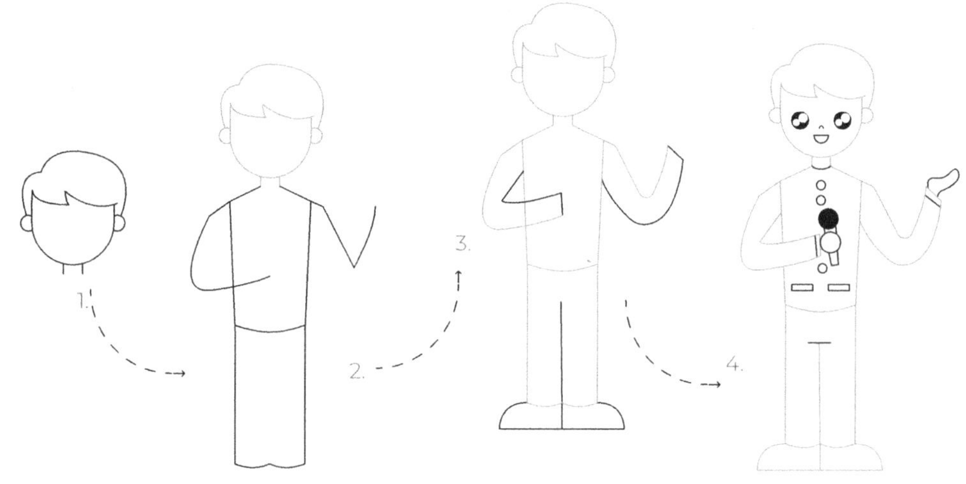

LIGHTHOUSE KEEPER

Begin with a round head under a helmet and a long coat with arms
and boots.
Tip: The lantern shows the way-just like a lighthouse keeping ships safe at night!

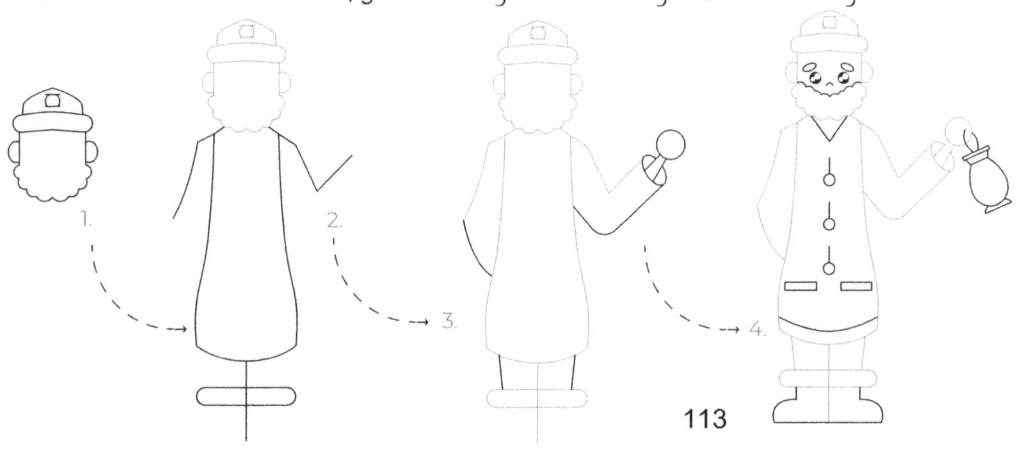

PIRATE

Draw a wavy pirate hat, round head, and triangle body with arms raised.
Tip: Add an eyepatch or a hook so the pirate looks ready for adventure on the seas!

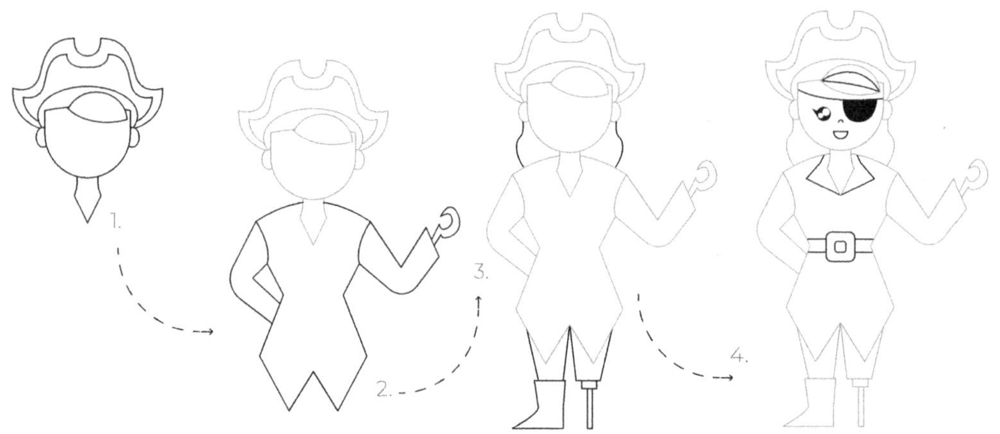

Your turn

PAINTER

Make a round head and apron-shaped body, then add arms holding a brush and palette.
Tip: Use bright colors on the palette painters bring the world to life with art!

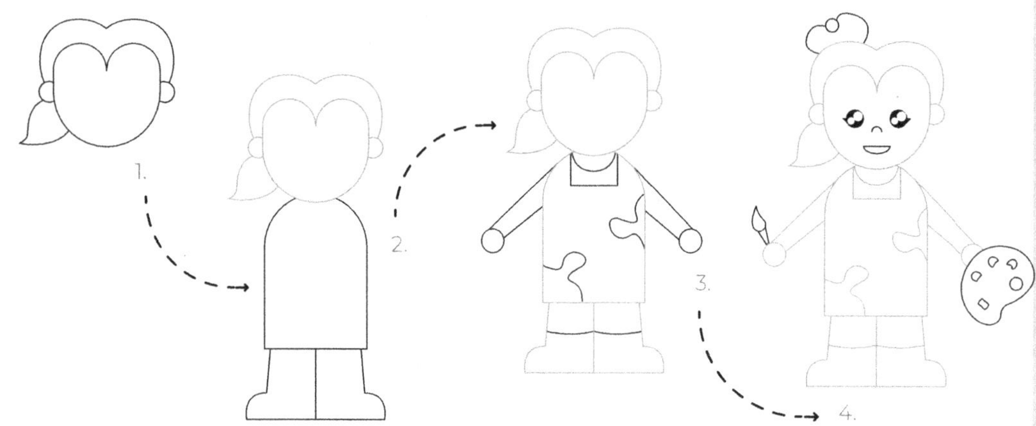

Your turn

STUNT DOUBLE

Begin with a helmet on a round head and a tall suit body with arms and legs.
Tip: Sunglasses and bold stripes make the stunt double look ready for action scenes!

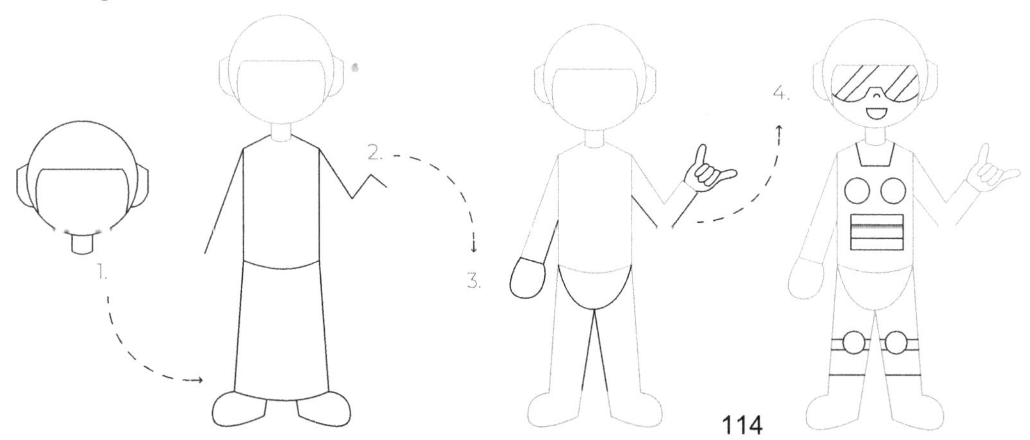

Your turn

SURFER

Draw a tilted head with flowing hair and a leaning body on the surfboard.
Tip: Keep the arms stretched out-it makes the surfer look balanced on the board!

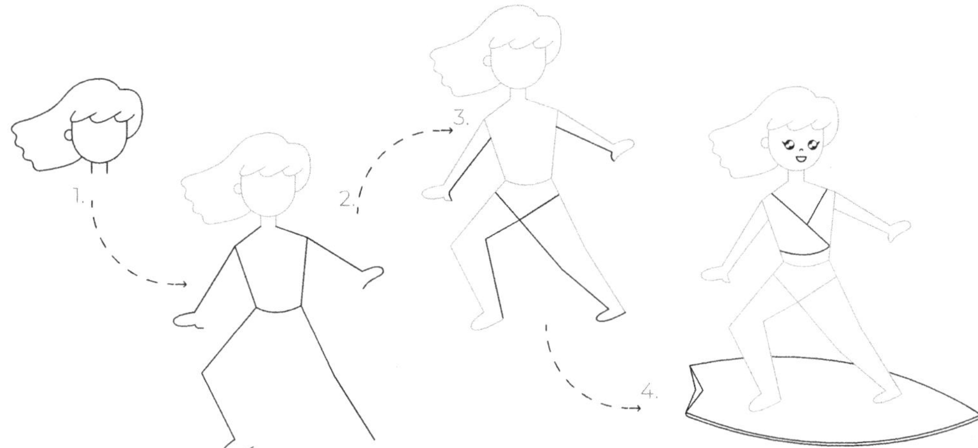

PHOTOGRAPHER

Make a round head and add a big camera rectangle in front with arms holding it.
Tip: A raised hand or a "click!" sign makes it look like the perfect photo moment!

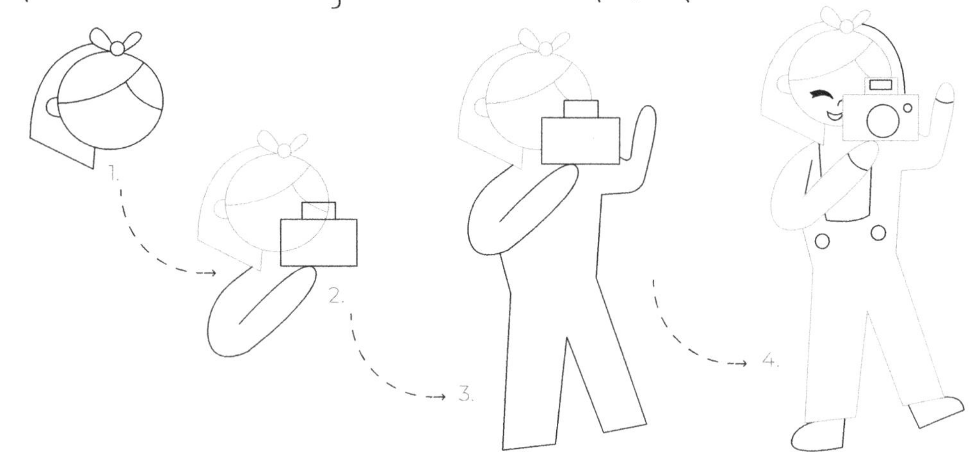

SAILOR

Draw a round head with a wide sailor hat and a tall body in uniform.
Tip: Add an anchor badge on the hat it shows the sailor is ready for the sea!

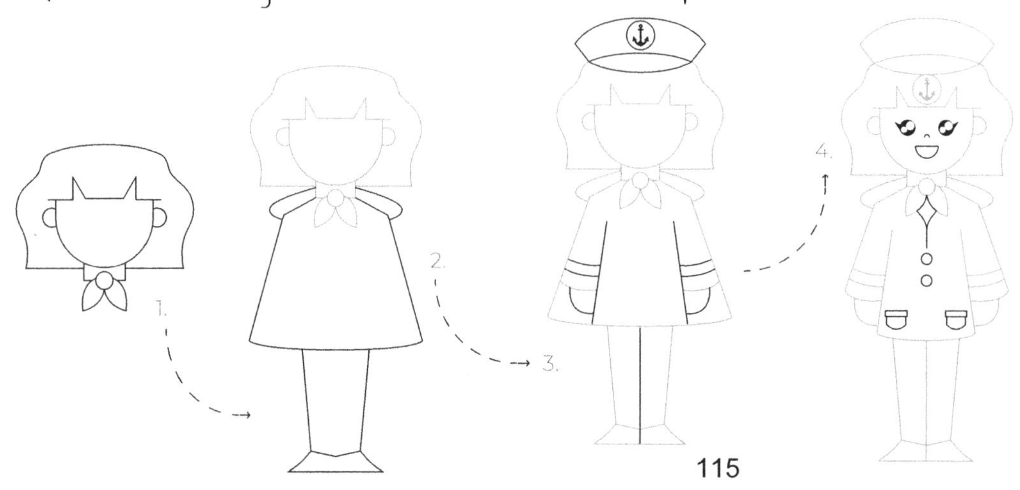

MAGICIAN

Add a round head and arms stretched high, then give him a cape and suit.
Tip: A tall hat and magic wand make the tricks look real!

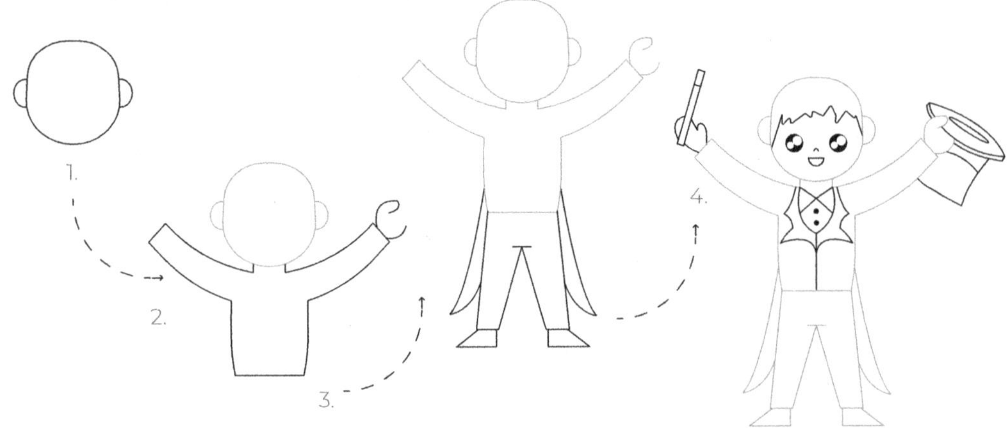

SCUBA DIVER

Shape a wide helmet for the head, then add a curved body with arms and legs.
Tip: Tiny bubbles near the mask show the diver exploring deep underwater!

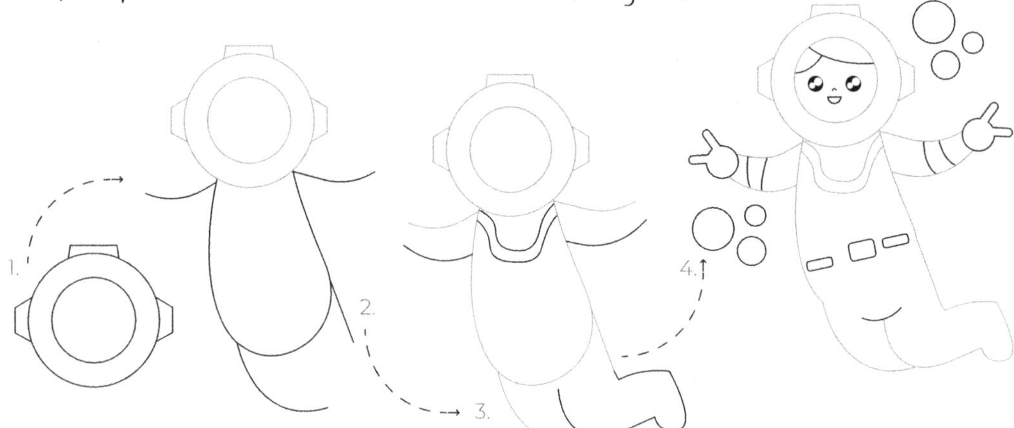

ZOOLOGIST

Give the character a round head and short uniform with open arms.
Tip: A parrot on the arm makes it clear he studies animals up close!

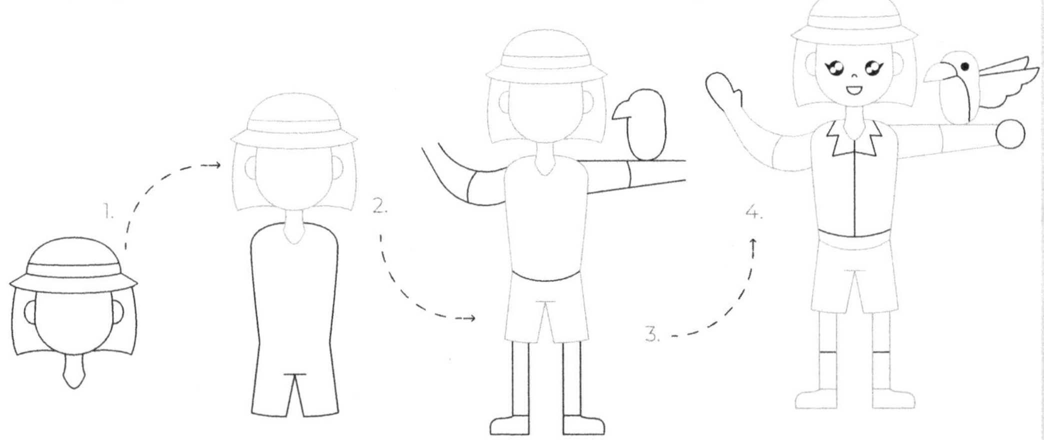

FOSSIL HUNTER

Add a round head with a hat on top, then sketch a body with arms holding tools.

Tip: A shovel or bone in hand makes the fossil hunter look ready for discovery!

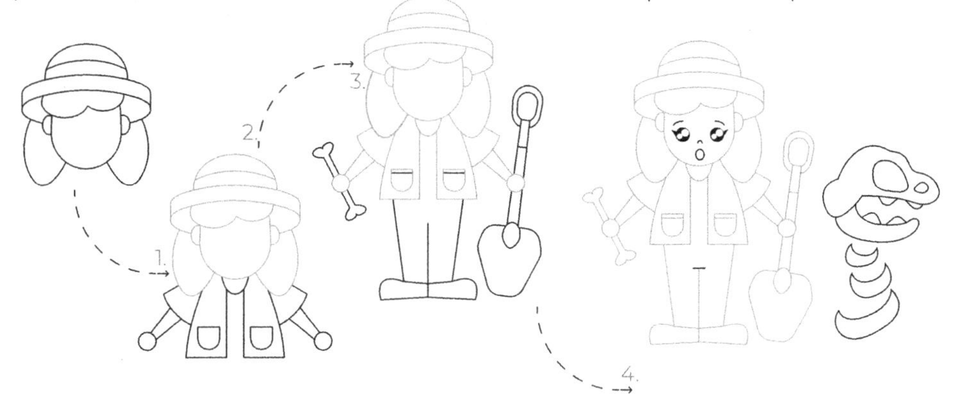

NINJA

Shape a round head with a mask, then set sharp arms and legs in a strong stance.

Tip: Keep the lines straight the ninja looks powerful when ready to strike.

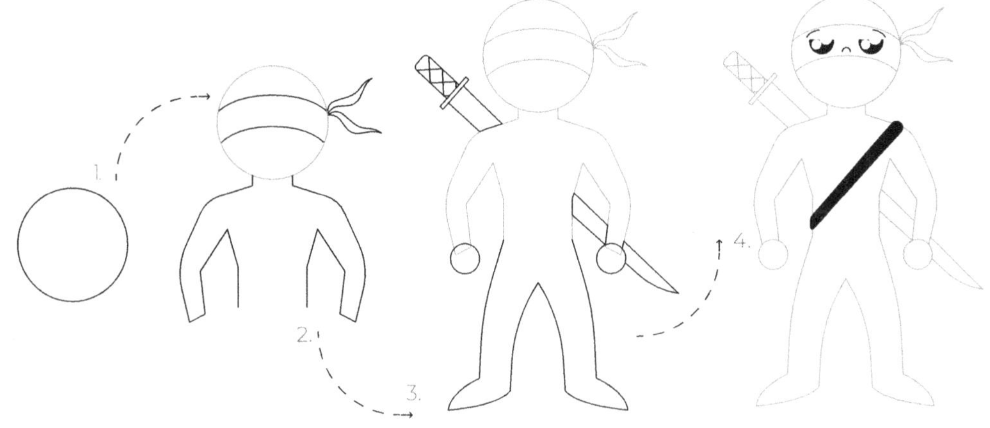

SAMURAI

Build a tall body with broad shoulders, then place a wide helmet on the head.

Tip: Strong armor plates show the samurai is ready for battle!

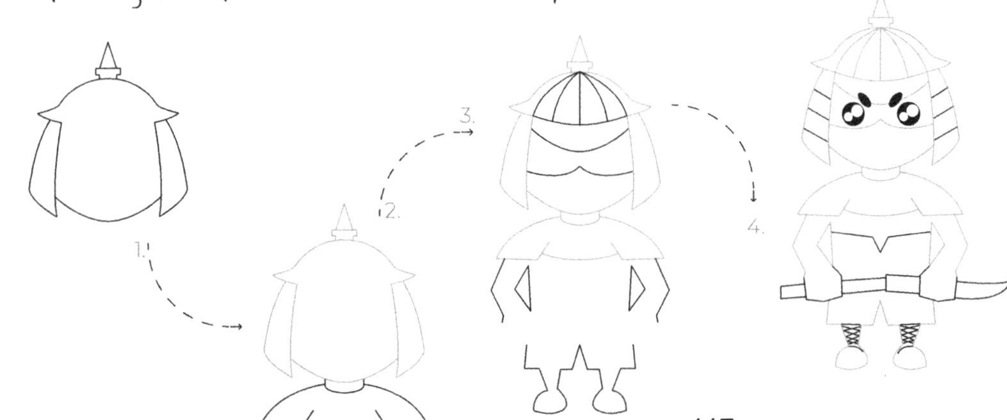

MUSICIAN

Shape a tall body with curly hair, then place a guitar across the arms.
Tip: Big strings on the guitar make it look ready to play real music!

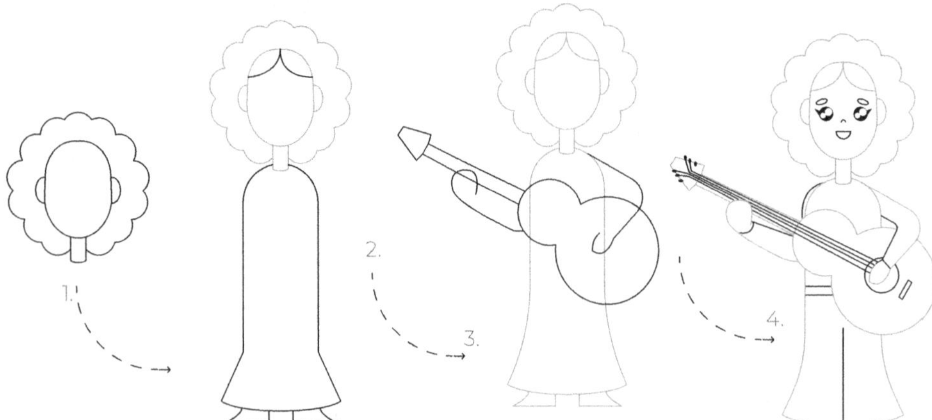

SOCCER PLAYER

Add a round head on a tall body, then set the legs wide in a kicking pose.
Tip: A soccer ball at the feet shows the player is ready to score a goal!

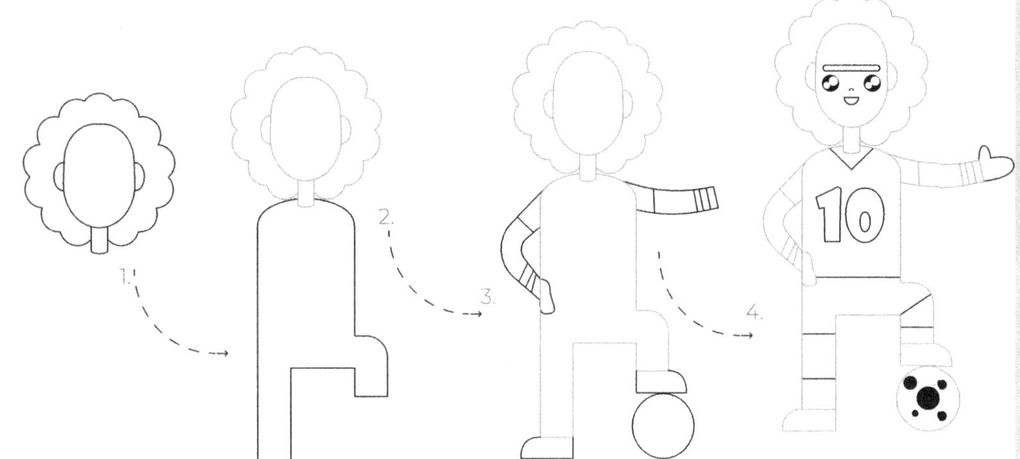

MINER

Put a helmet on a round head, then sketch a tall body holding a
pickaxe.
Tip: A lamp on the helmet makes the miner look ready to explore dark caves!

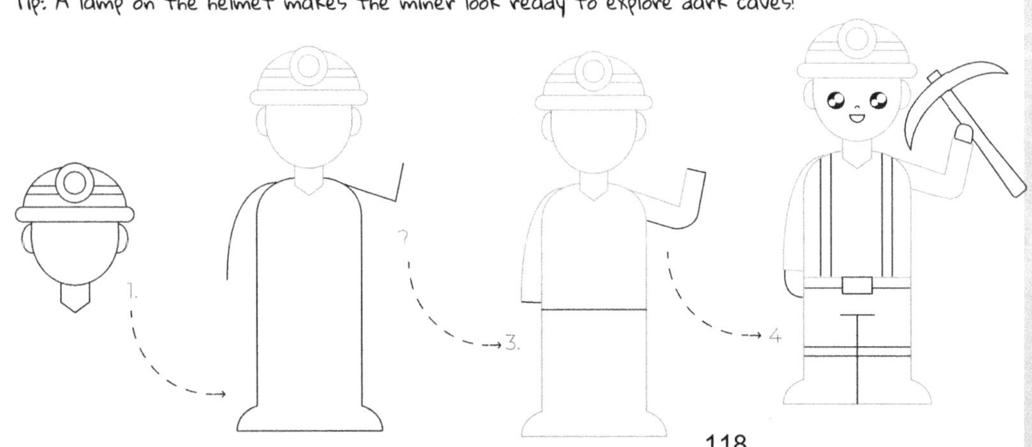

GARDENER

Give the character a round head, small hat, and tall body with arms ready to hold tools.
Tip: A watering can in hand makes the gardener look busy caring for plants!

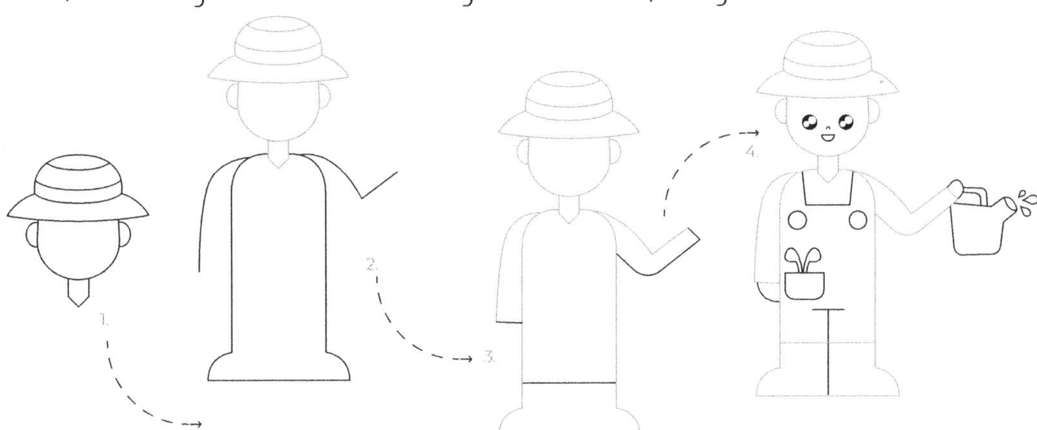

PUPPETEER

Sketch a round head with simple hair, then add a small body with arms stretched wide.
Tip: Hand puppets on each arm make the show fun-like magic toys that come alive!

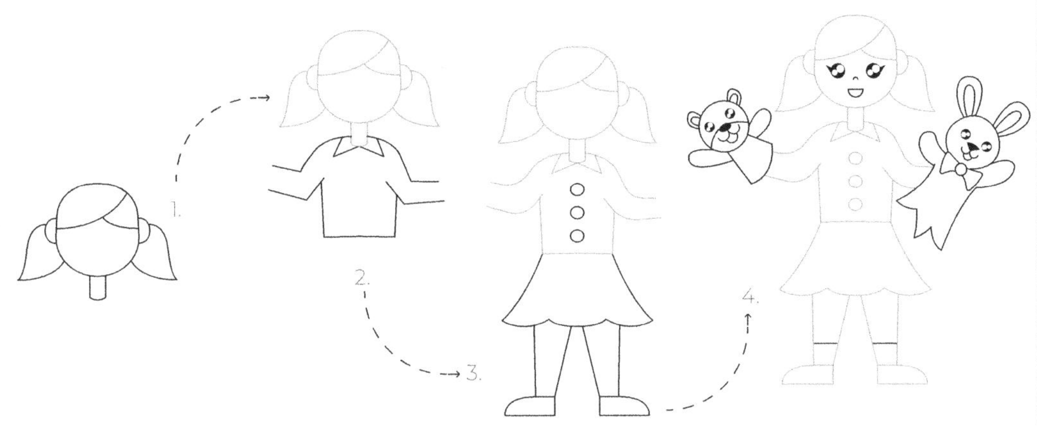

CIRCUS PERFORMER

Add a tall hat above a round head and a curved jacket body with open arms.
Tip: A juggling ball or cane makes the circus act look extra fun!

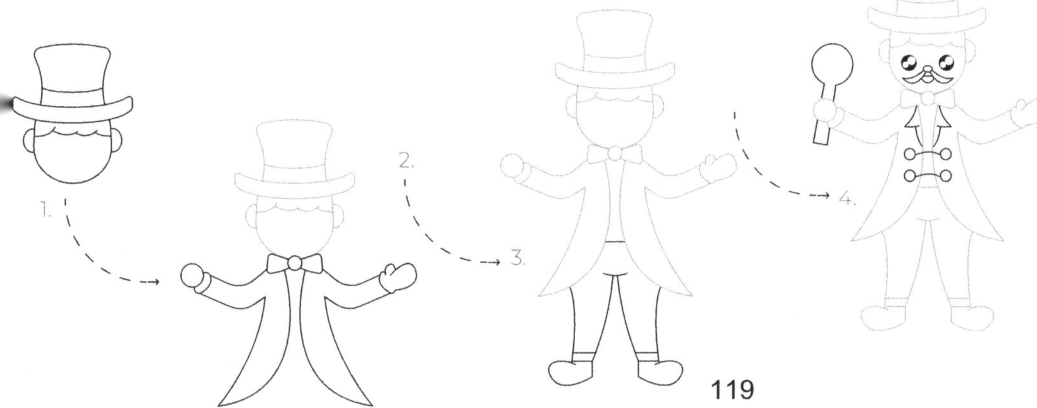

PILOT

Add a round head with a flat pilot hat, then sketch a tall uniform body with arms and legs.
Tip: A suitcase in hand makes the pilot look ready to fly around the world!

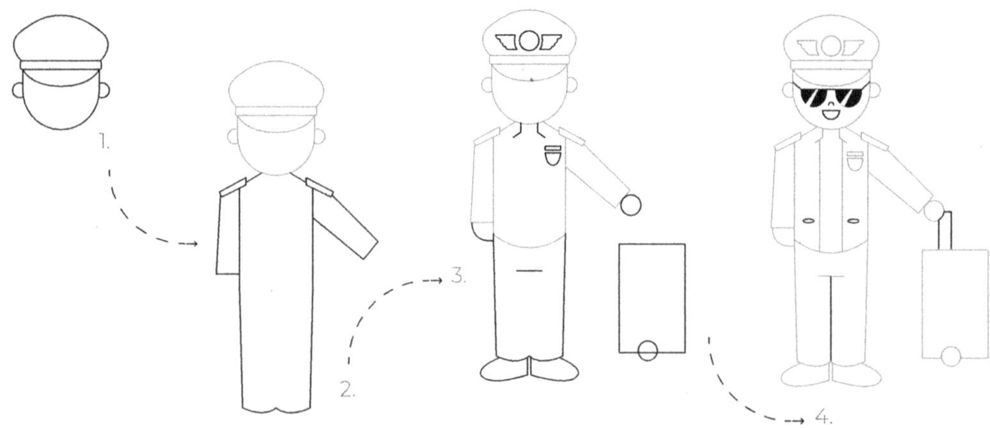

WEIGHTLIFTER

Shape a round head and strong arms holding a barbell above the body.
Tip: Wide arms and a big smile show the lifter's powerful victory pose.

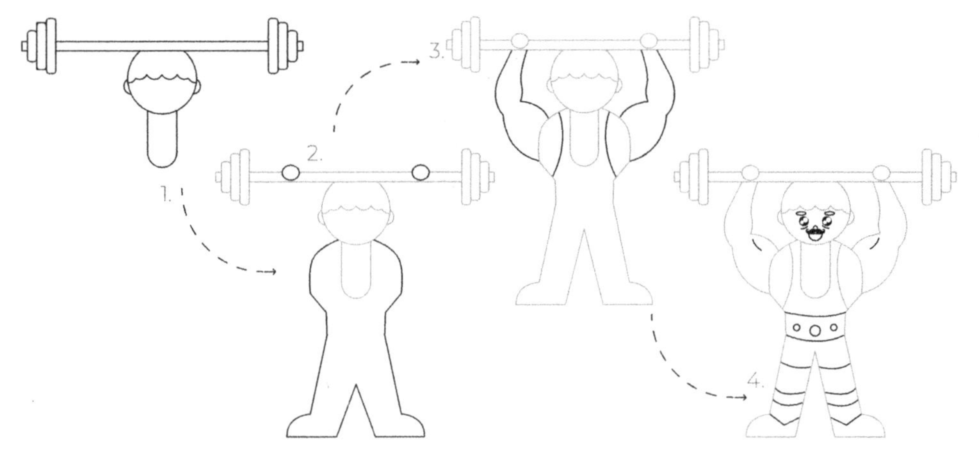

PLUMBER

Place a round head on a simple body, then set bent arms holding tools.
Tip: A wrench and toolbox make the plumber ready to fix pipes.

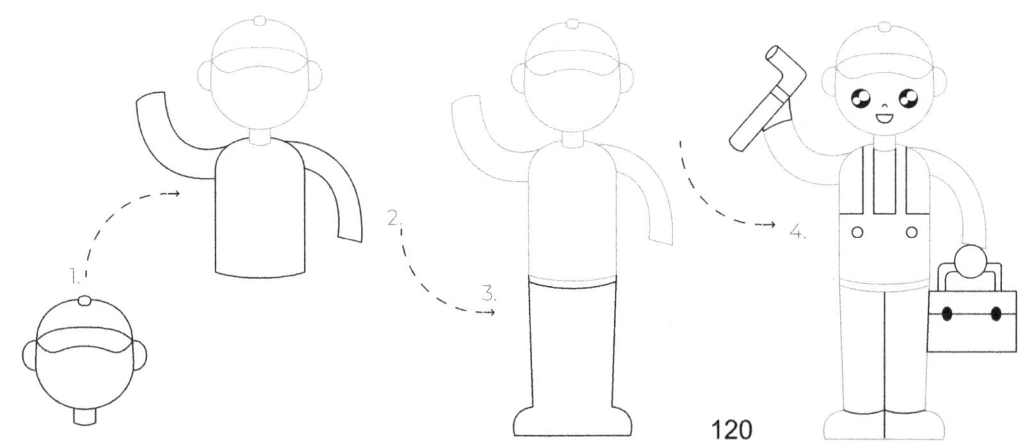

FARMER

Put a wide hat on a round head, then add a tall body with arms holding the harvest.
Tip: The backpack full of veggies and the carrot in hand show the farmer's fresh harvest.

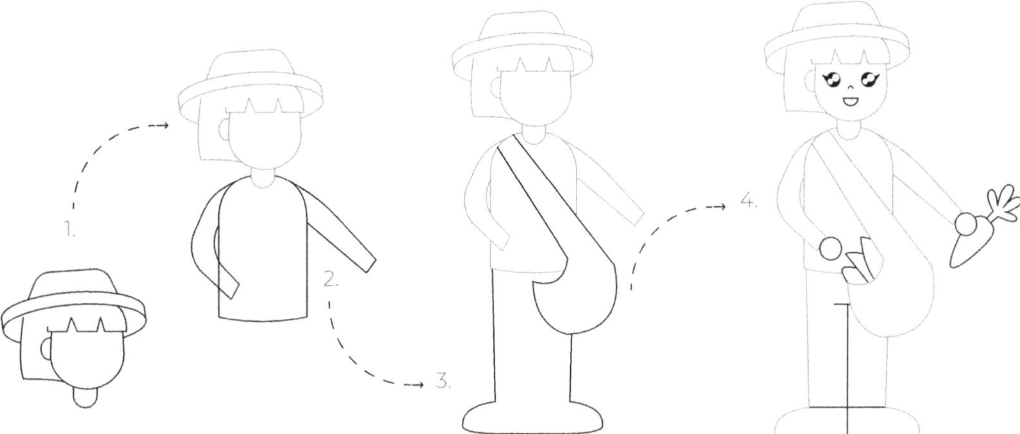

ROLLER SKATER

Sketch a tilted head with hair flying back, then shape the body leaning forward with bent legs.
Tip: Arms stretched out make the skater look fast and full of movement!

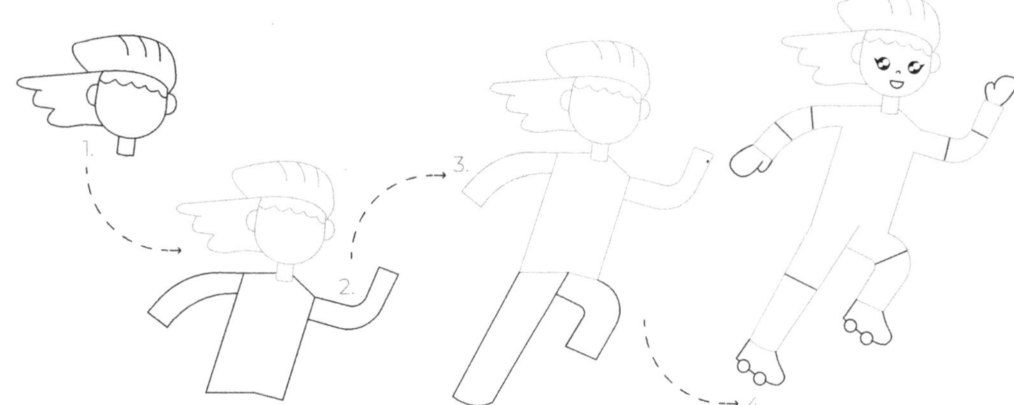

BOXER

Give the character a round head with fluffy hair, then add a body wearing gloves.

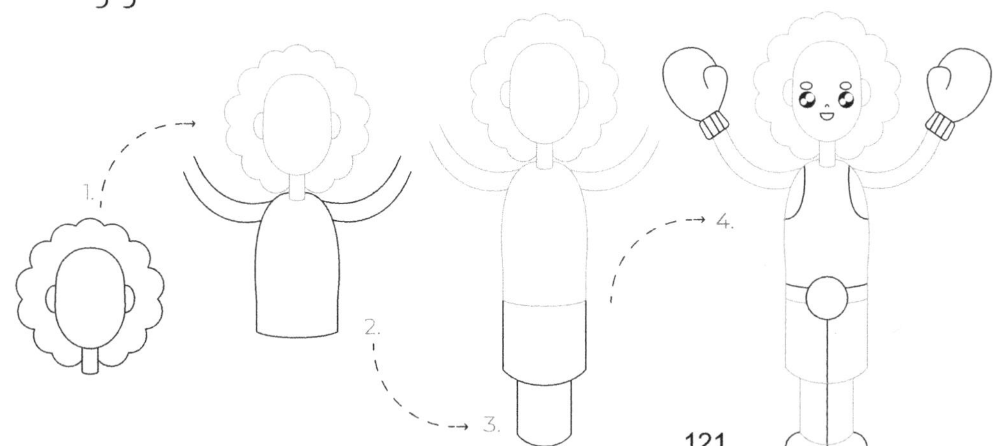

VETERINARIAN

Give the character long side hair and a simple body with arms holding a puppy.
Tip: Don't forget the stethoscope in her pocket-it shows she's a real vet!

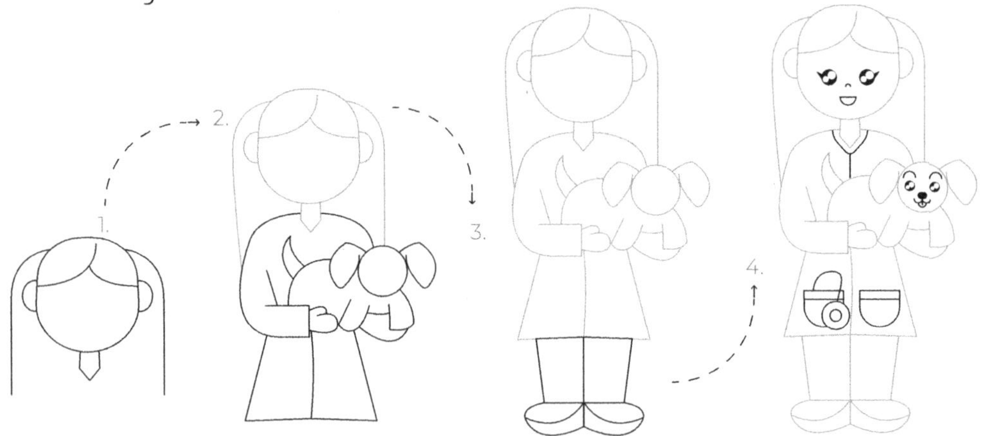

TIME TRAVELER

Shape a round time pod with a seat inside, then add the traveler at the controls.
Tip: A wide portal behind makes it look like she's zooming through time!

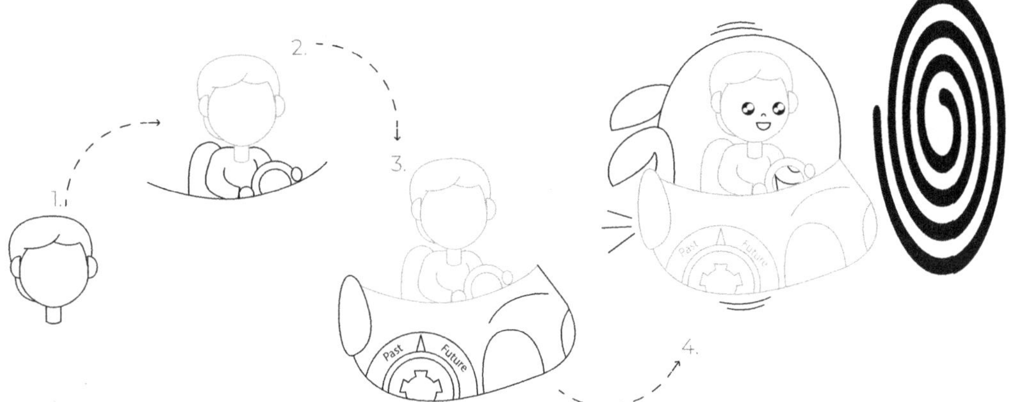

EXPLORER

Add a round head with a wide hat and a body holding a magnifying glass.

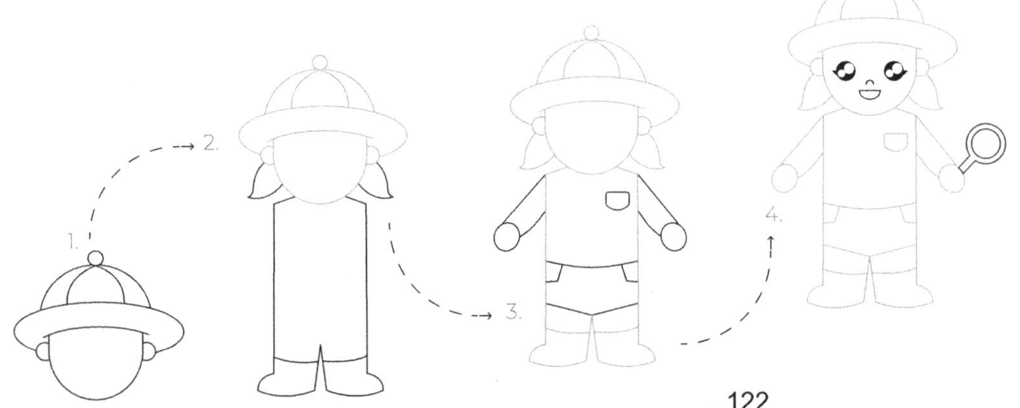

UNICYCLIST

Sketch a standing body with arms out and one leg down on the big wheel.
Tip: Keep the arms wide—the unicyclist needs balance to stay on one wheel!

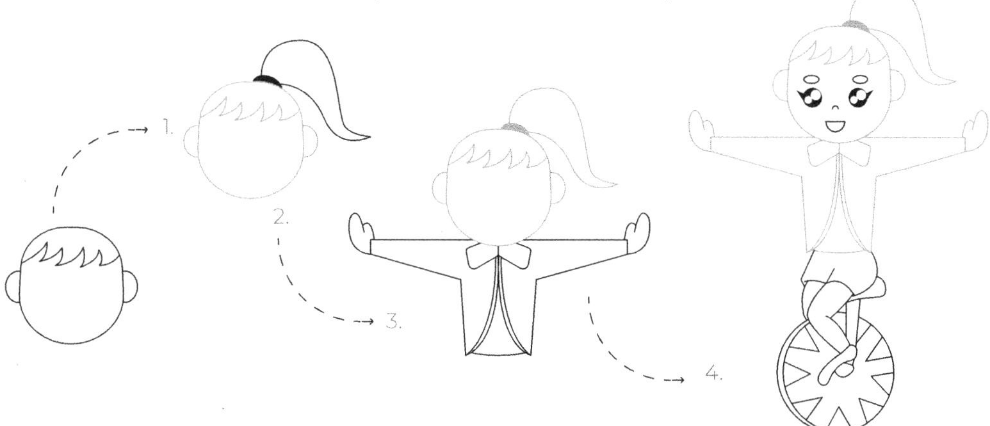

CHOCOLATE MAKER

Add a chef hat on a round head and a tall body holding a chocolate bar and spoon.

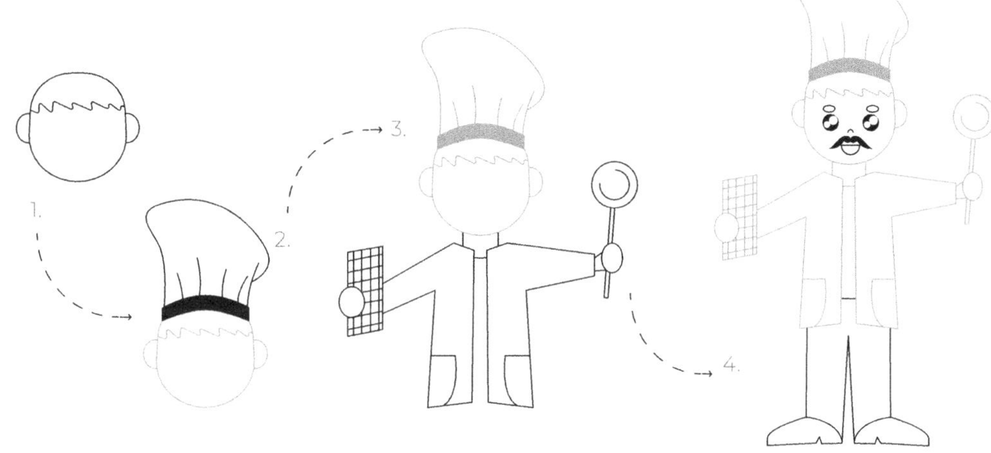

ECONOMIST

Shape a figure in front of a wide board filled with symbols and graphs.
Tip: Add the Bitcoin sign—economists explore new ideas, just like Max Keiser talking about the future!

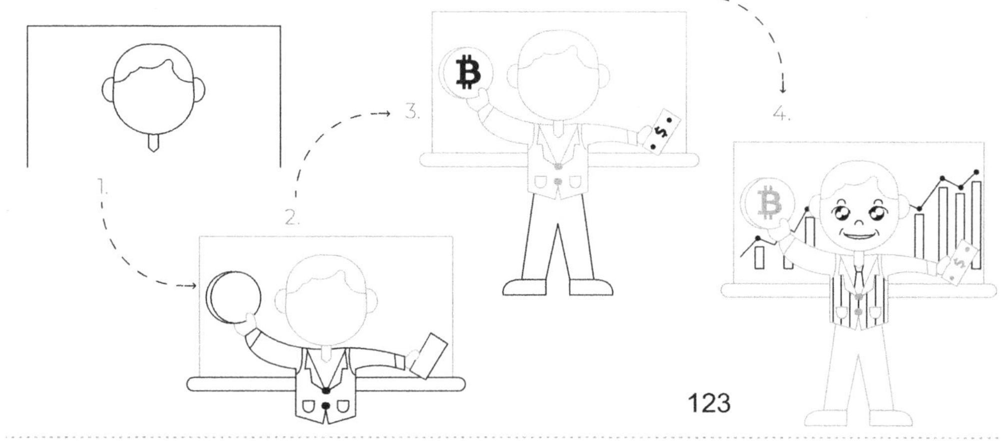

123

Invent Your Own Dream Job!

Use this page to create your own job — it can be real, magical, or a mix of both! Draw what you would wear, what you would do, and any cool tools or powers you'd use at work.

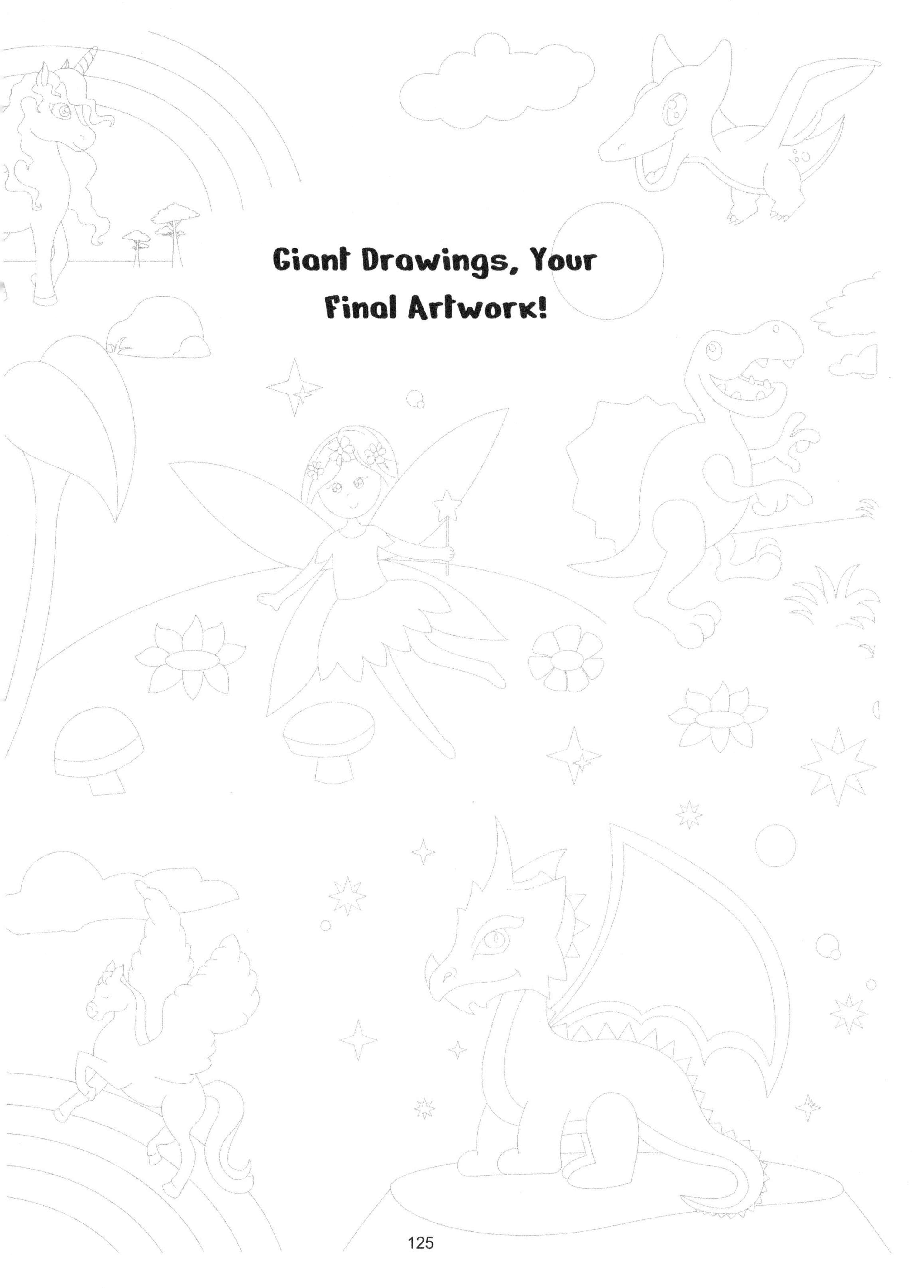

Giant Drawings, Your Final Artwork!

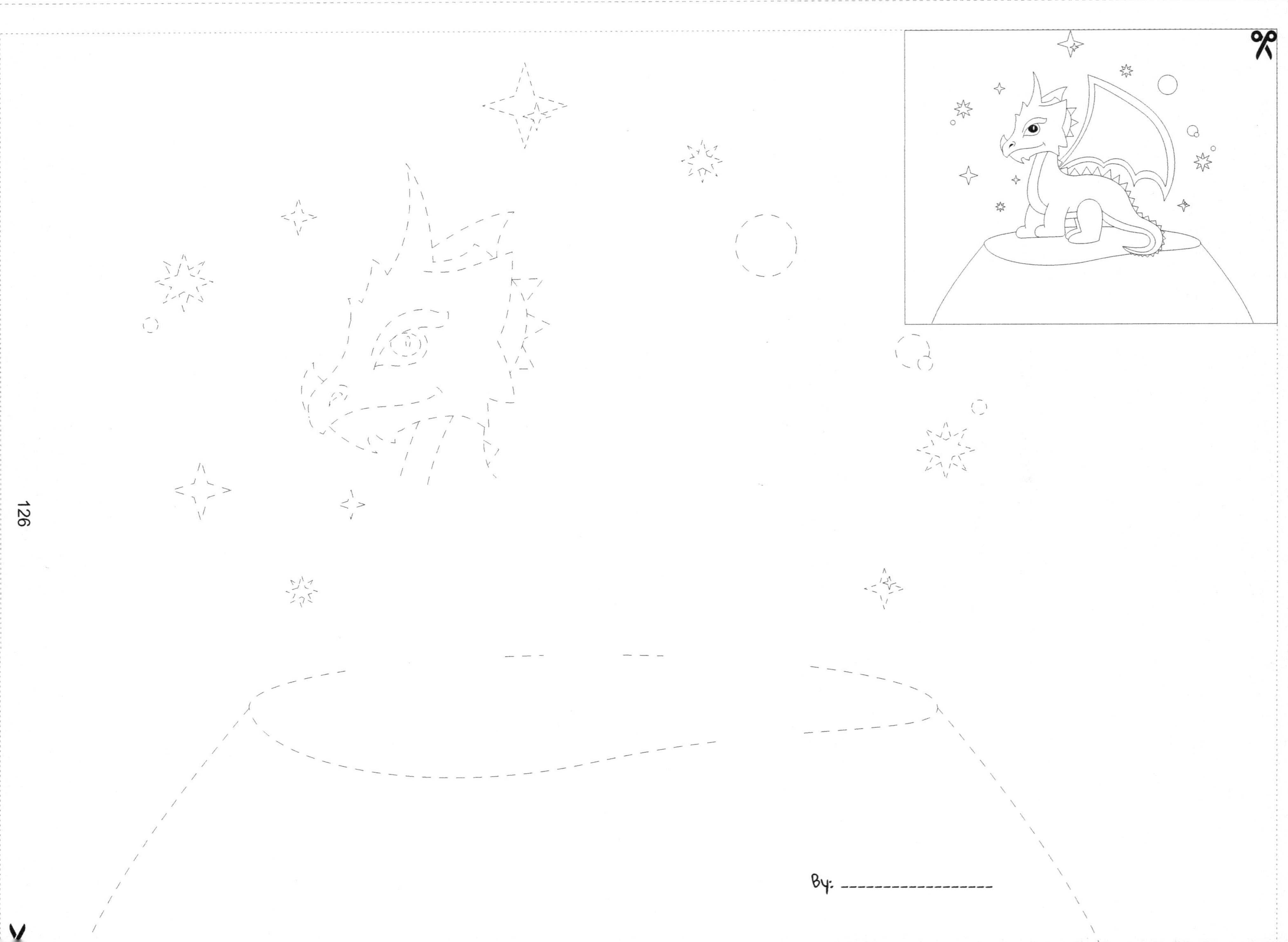

By: ________________

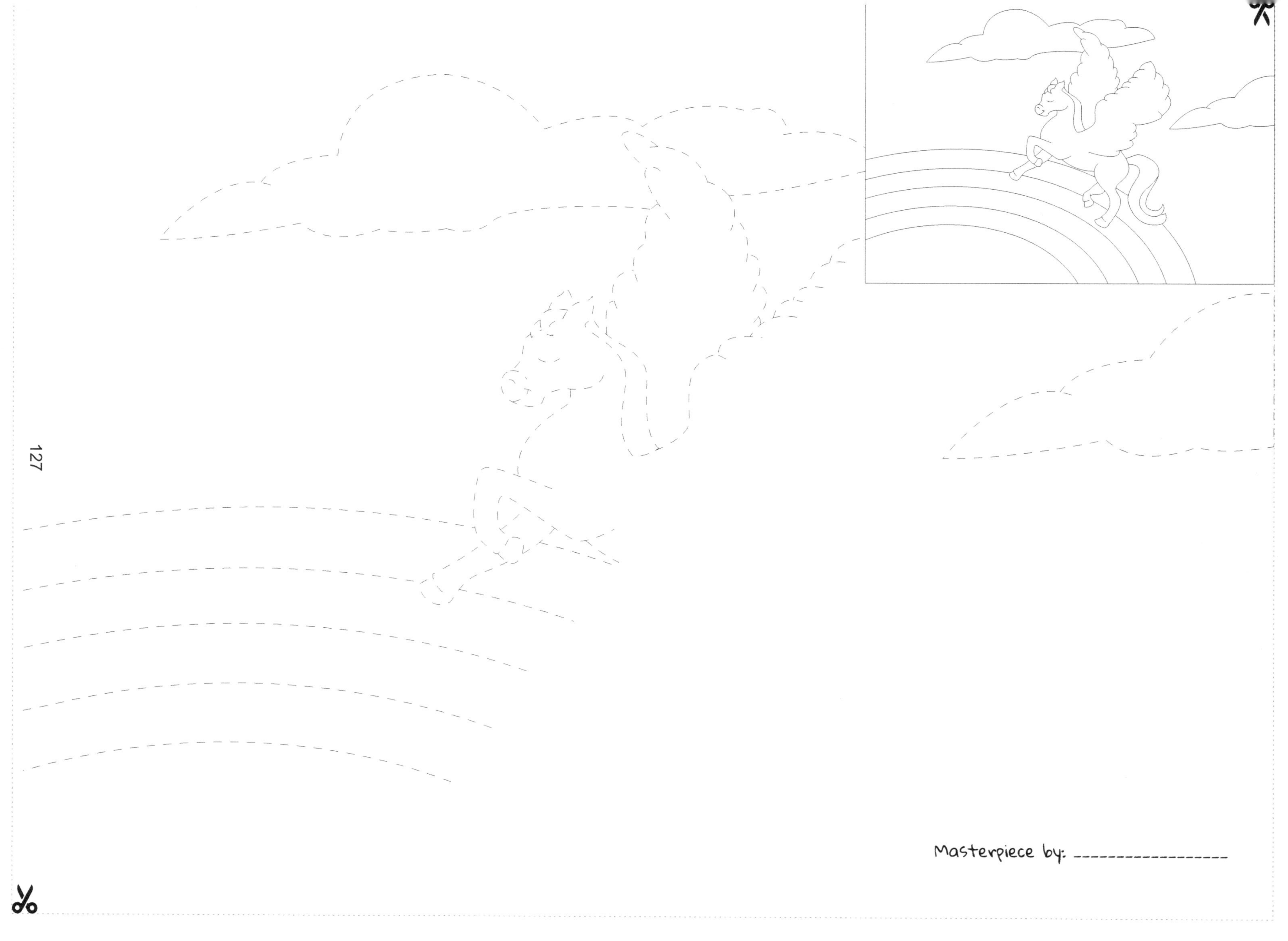

Masterpiece by: ---------------------

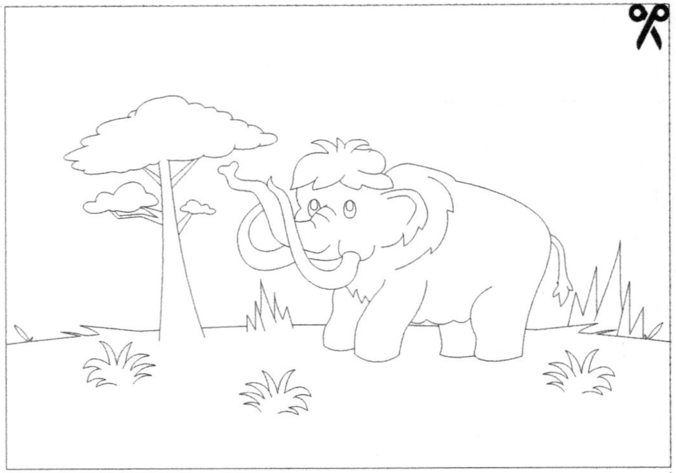

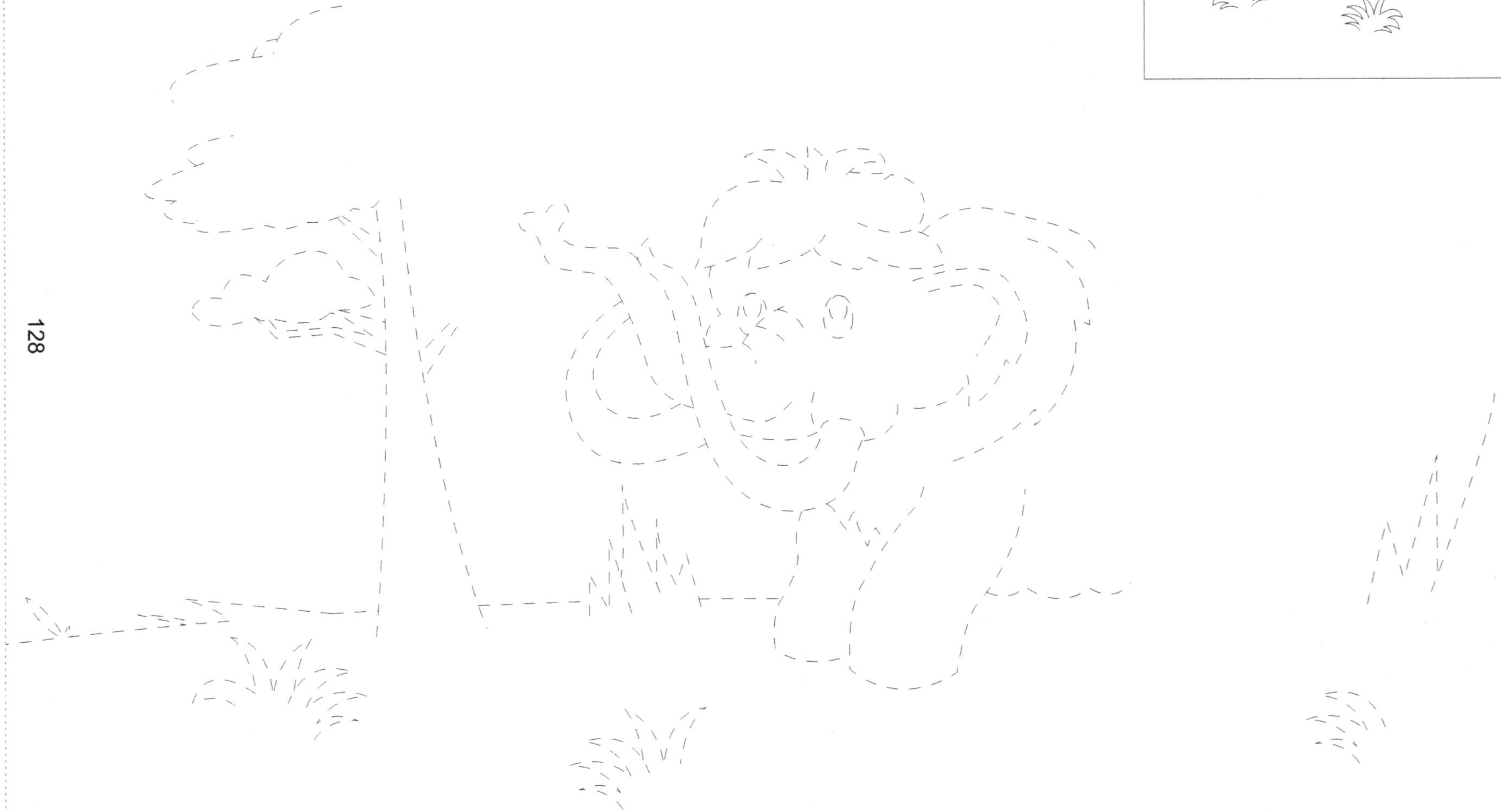

Signed with love by: ----------

Dear Young Artist,

I'm so glad this book found its way to you and could be part of your drawing time.

If you've enjoyed this book, I'd be very grateful if you could ask your parents to help you leave an honest review, along with any ideas you might have for future books. Your thoughts will help others and inspire new drawing adventures.

Thank you for sharing your imagination with me and with the world.

AMAZON US

AMAZON UK

Not in one of these countries? Use your local Amazon store.

AMAZON AU

AMAZON CA

Your Special Gift

Congratulations, you made it all the way to the end—and here is the surprise I promised you!

Just scan the QR code below to unlock your special gift, made just for you.

This little gift is to remind you how creative and amazing you are. Keep shining, keep imagining, and never stop drawing!

With gratitude,
AMELIA J. BLOOM

Don't forget to check our other top sellers!

Made in the USA
Monee, IL
07 July 2026

56685303R00077